Suing Alma Mater

SUING ALMA MATER
Higher Education and the Courts

Michael A. Olivas

The Johns Hopkins University Press
Baltimore

© 2013 The Johns Hopkins University Press
All rights reserved. Published 2013
Printed in the United States of America on acid-free paper
9 8 7 6 5 4 3 2 1

The Johns Hopkins University Press
2715 North Charles Street
Baltimore, Maryland 21218-4363
www.press.jhu.edu

Library of Congress Cataloging-in-Publication Data

Olivas, Michael A.
    Suing alma mater : higher education and the courts / Michael A. Olivas.
        p. cm.
    Includes bibliographical references and index.
        ISBN 978-1-4214-0922-1 (hardcover : alk. paper) — ISBN 978-1-4214-0923-8
(pbk. : alk. paper) — ISBN 978-1-4214-0924-5 (electronic) — ISBN 1-4214-0922-4
(hardcover : alk. paper) — ISBN 1-4214-0923-2 (pbk. : alk. paper) —
ISBN 1-4214-0924-0 (electronic)
    1. Universities and colleges—Law and legislation—United States.
    2. College teachers—Legal status, laws, etc.—United States.
    3. College students—Legal status, laws, etc.—United States.   I.   Title.
    KF4225.O44 2013
    344.73'074—dc23   2012036894

A catalog record for this book is available from the British Library.

The author adapted several earlier works in part and has substantially revised them for
this book. He either holds the copyright or has permission to use the excerpts from:
    "The Legal Environment," in *American Higher Education in the Twenty-First
Century: Social, Political, and Economic Challenges,* 3rd ed., ed. Philip G. Altbach,
Patricia J. Gumport, and Robert O. Berdahl (Baltimore: Johns Hopkins University
Press, 2011), 174–94 (with Benjamin Baez).
    "Constitutional Criteria: The Social Science and Common Law of College
Admissions," *University of Colorado Law Review* 68 (1997): 1065–1121.
    "*Brown* and the Desegregative Ideal: Higher Education, Location, and Racial
College Identity," *Cornell Law Review* 90 (2005): 101–127.
    "Reflections on Academic Merit Badges and Becoming an Eagle Scout," *Houston
Law Review* 43 (2006): 81–124.
    "An Essay on Friends, Special Programs, and Pipelines," *Journal of College and
University Law* 35 (2009): 463–473.
    "Governing Badly: Theory and Practice of Bad Ideas in College Decision
Making," *Indiana Law Journal* 87 (2012): 951–977.

*Special discounts are available for bulk purchases of this book. For more information,
please contact Special Sales at 410-516-6936 or specialsales@press.jhu.edu.*

The Johns Hopkins University Press uses environmentally friendly book materials,
including recycled text paper that is composed of at least 30 percent post-consumer
waste, whenever possible.

CONTENTS

Originally, this book was a project titled "Untroubled Immunity," based on a paper that had had a profound influence upon me at the start of my career as a professor. It was published in 1974 by Stephen K. Bailey, and I began teaching at the University of Houston in 1982, the year he died—far too early at age sixty-five. In Washington, D.C., I heard him give several lectures and workshops on legal issues and their important role in higher education policy. I was a law student at Georgetown University Law Center for much of that time, and he was unfailingly helpful and encouraging to me. (He once kidded me about the topic of my Ph.D. dissertation, on the establishment of the Ohio Board of Regents, saying, "Well, everyone needs a dissertation topic." He was correct.) I have worked on portions of this virtual project since then, not always consciously and certainly not consistently. I had become afraid that it might become my *Key to All Mythologies* or my *Smile*, the great unfinished work ridiculed by George Eliot in *Middlemarch* and the 1966 rock-and-roll album project left unfinished by Brian Wilson until 2004, when he recovered from the mental illness that had interfered with the execution of that towering work.

In the serendipity that has largely defined my professional life plans, Ashleigh Elliott McKown, an assistant editor at the Johns Hopkins University Press, then approached me with encouragement to move this project from its vague "forthcoming" vapors to the real thing. For this, I will always be grateful. She also pried loose two supportive and useful reviews, both anonymous, that provided both support and guidance. Although this is my fifteenth book, I still am paralyzed at the outset of each one, daunted by the time and effort each takes, even when I have thought about them for many years, as was the case here. The experience over several decades on my higher education law casebook, *The Law and*

Higher Education: Cases and Materials on Colleges in Court, in its third edition (2006), with supplements, a teacher's manual, and now a coauthor (Amy Gajda), helped more than was obvious, as I am forced to think about not only the cases and the need for legal reasoning but also the pedagogical value for instructional purposes. I have taught each of the cases highlighted here many times and still learn anew each time, in part because I am simply better at my craft of teaching but also because seeing them fresh with a new cohort of students who help dissect them helps me to look deeply each time. For those who think of teaching and producing scholarship as antithetical to each other, I am Exhibit A for the opposite proposition.

I was not new to the Johns Hopkins University Press, as I withdrew from a contract with them more than a decade ago, for a book on student financial aid policy issues, in part because I grew frustrated with the pace of congressional action on Title IV and related legislation, and because other events overtook my research agenda. I felt remorse for having withdrawn and felt special regret that I had let down Jacqueline Wehmueller, who had shown great faith and encouragement in the project. Jacqueline is now an executive editor at the Press, so I am glad to be back in her good graces. (The truth is, she was always very gracious and did not show me any disfavor or exasperation.)

I feel more than the usual debt of gratitude to the many people who helped on this project, especially since many of my collaborators had personal roles and stakes in the cases. In fact, several said that they had waited for someone to ask them about the case and were glad I had contacted them. Some were not as glad and succumbed to my charms (more likely, were worn down by my persistence) quite reluctantly. But I appreciated them all, and the book is much better for their elaborations or corrections of the record: Todd Ackerman, Judith Areen, Benjamin Baez, Vanessa Baird, Aaron Bruhl, Alvin O. Chambliss Jr., Matthew Finkin, Matthew L. M. Fletcher, Steven Friedman, Amy Gajda, Leslie C. Griffin, William A. Kaplin, Albert Kauffman, Barbara A. Lee, David T. Lopez, Marcee Lundeen, Stuart Nelkin, Michael S. Paulsen, Ellen Rabiner, Richard Spuler, Peggy Stone, Octavio Villalpando, and Leland Ware. Of course, all are absolved of any guilt by association.

I appreciated the technical research library assistance given me by Lauren E. Schroeder, Katy A. Stein, and Mon Yin Lung of the O'Quinn Law Library at the University of Houston Law Center, and by Heather N. Cook, UHLC Class of 2011, who assisted with analyzing the Supreme Court data. I also acknowledge with gratitude the assistance of Augustina H. Reyes and Deborah Jones in this and all such projects. In addition to the JHUP staff I singled out above, I thank

Gregory Britton, Martin Schneider, and Mary Lou Kenney. Lavina Fielding Anderson, copyeditor extraordinaire, saved me from my sorry self in so many instances that I will never undertake another book without her assistance.

The Cases Reviewed in This Book

This project was originally about a number of U.S. Supreme Court higher education cases and their backstories. The 120 cases in the fifty-year period that I counted for the study provided many well-known possible examples, but during the years that this project sat in my in-box, Foundation Press started its Law Stories series, and I wrote about immigration cases and civil rights cases in the Supreme Court for several of the readers, and with Ronna Greff Schneider, I coedited a series volume of our own, focusing on a dozen K–12 and higher education law cases (2008). This project confirmed that examining the backstory or litigation history was a genre that I enjoyed and even had a knack for. Having this background information invariably improves my understanding and my teaching of the cases in my higher education law seminar. It also scratched my Supreme Court itch, so when this project came along, I was ready to focus on important cases that had never made it to "SCOTUS," as insiders are wont to call the Supreme Court.

The truth is that this is a very big pond, and there are so many fascinating cases that never made it to the Court that I started out with dozens of favorite cases that I had tracked, been involved with, or studied, so that I had to winnow out dozens of potential candidates. I ended up choosing cases where not much had been written by other scholars. *Hopwood* is the exception, but I chose it because it might as well have been a Supreme Court holding in the Fifth Circuit, where I live and work. I also saw up close and personal how a case can transform practice, for good or ill, as my own law school struggled to implement *Hopwood*'s perverse holdings, even as we knew it was on the wrong side of history. My own professional involvement in ameliorating the effects of that case resulted both in my choosing to include it and in my being in a photo, now occupying my office shelf, in which Governor George W. Bush is signing the Texas Top Ten Percent Plan into law, surrounded by several of us who had assisted Rep. Irma Rangel in moving the bill through the Texas Legislature to his desk.

In addition, each case was about a different subject, with discrimination claims being a thread through all of them, in both state courts and federal courts. Even the civil procedure of the cases was mixed: two judgments notwithstanding the verdicts, a retrial after too many sick jurors ruined the first trial, a settlement after the appellate remand, complex class certification issues, a case where bad lawyering left subsequent appeals lawyers with bad facts wrongly stipulated to, and a frontal challenge to the Court which SCOTUS chose not to correct or rebuke. Here are the cases I chose, with their subject matter and the procedural notes on their disposition. While none made it all the way through the chute to the highest court in the land, they all could have, with either deeper pockets or slightly different facts or decisions or a different trajectory. They all stand on their own, representing difficult and deep issues.

Chapter 1 is "A Primer on Higher Education Law in the United States." Higher education law has developed over time from sometimes puzzling beginnings, but in essence, courts have been asked to resolve disputes over such basic questions as, What is a college? and Who is responsible for the governance of this entity? The simultaneous existence of both private and public institutions of higher education imposes different expectations and responsibilities for each. Another major wellspring of litigation is faculty, who justifiably feel that they have legal rights in their positions and control over how they teach. Both of these components are shifting and contested. The nature of collective bargaining has streamlined but also intensified such redefinitions. Students have an increased sense of ownership and legal entitlement. The most recent actors to undertake substantial litigation are nontraditional stakeholders in the many purposive organizations and external communities that assert standing and deeply held convictions.

Chapter 2 is another orientation essay. In it I describe how I constructed the database for this study, beginning with more than 300,000 items of potential interest and, through successive winnowings, reducing the figure to the 120 cases involving higher education that made their way to the U.S. Supreme Court in the last fifty years. I also produce a brisk statistical overview that profiles these cases by issue, plaintiff, defendant, and outcome. Perhaps the most interesting finding of the statistical exercise is that the odds are heavily weighted in favor of institutions. As an exemplar, I note the strikingly negative results of Native American litigation in the Court, supplying a stark example of such lopsided odds.

Chapter 3 provides the final orientation for nonspecialist readers: how cases make it to the U.S. Supreme Court. The simple appeals process, known even to elementary schoolchildren, provides a mighty river of potential cases that slows to a trickle that can be heard and ruled on—in some fashion—in a single term. I explain the role of certiorari in designating the winners and losers and describe the complex role that the Court itself plays in communicating what kinds of cases it would receive hospitably as well as the specialized role of policy entrepreneurs, also known as purposive organizations. In addition to the time-honored and effective ACLU, MALDEF, and the NAACP Legal Defense Fund are their newer conservative counterparts, many of them religiously affiliated, who have adopted similar techniques and parallel goals. One of them, the Alliance Defense Fund, renamed itself the Alliance Defending Freedom in July 2012, after this book went to press.

In Chapter 4, I illustrate some of these principles with a discussion of *U.S. v. Fordice,* a long and drawn-out case that was an alternative model for higher education litigation, one not brought by directed organizational interests. I conclude that such a case will not likely be seen again, revealing the changed landscape of how these cases arise.

Chapter 5 is about *Hopwood v. Texas,* which produced the interesting judgment, "A university may properly favor one applicant over another because of his ability to play the cello, make a downfield tackle, or understand chaos theory." This complex federal case was tried at the district court, with a 1994 decision. It was affirmed by the circuit, with later proceedings the same year. After it was re-considered at the district court, it was reversed and remanded by the circuit in 1996, at which time the appeal was dismissed. A request for a rehearing by the entire circuit was denied in 1996. Certain motions to add another party were granted by the U.S. Supreme Court in 1996, and this writ of certiorari was then denied. Additionally, the Court denied cert to hear the case. There was a final remand to the original district court in 1998, the judgment for which was affirmed in part and reversed in part by the circuit in 2000. The key decision that led to dismantling affirmative action in the circuit was *Hopwood v. State of Texas.* In 2003, another admissions case, *Grutter v. Bollinger,* overturned *Hopwood,* and in 2012, the issue is in play with *Fisher v. UT.*

Chapter 6 addresses *Lawrence M. Abrams v. Baylor College of Medicine,* a bench trial before a federal judge, with a verdict for the faculty member. The verdict was upheld by the court of appeals, and no cert appeal to the U.S. Supreme Court was sought by the medical school defendant.

Chapter 7 covers *Christina Axson-Flynn v. Johnson,* a federal case where the defendant university won at the trial level but which, on appeal, was overturned and remanded by the circuit back to the trial court. The parties then settled the matter.

In Chapter 8, I use *Richards v. League of United Latin American Citizens* to discuss the state district court's certification of the classes and the court of appeals' affirmation of this certification. At the end of the trial in October 1991, the district court entered its judgment for the plaintiffs three months later in January 1992 on undisputed facts (a directed verdict) and jury findings and then overruled adverse jury findings (JNOV). The judgment was directly appealed by the state to the Texas Supreme Court. Pending a ruling on the merits of the case, in June 1993the court issued a stay of all injunctive relief granted by the trial court. The court overturned the lower court on the merits, after the state legislature enacted substantial resources in the interim.

Chapter 9 examines *Reginald Clark v. Claremont University Center,* a suspenseful case where justice ground exceedingly slow and fine. The original jury trial was postponed almost a year due to jury illnesses, but the faculty plaintiff won his jury trial. The decision was upheld by the state appeals court, and the state supreme court then upheld the verdict on appeal. While I do not treat it as a full-blown case study, in Chapter 10 I treat the *Garcetti v. Ceballos* case for what it is, an important SCOTUS decision that further weakened *Pickering* and further solidified *Connick,* one that undermines faculty autonomy and public-employee speech jurisprudence—and ultimately academic freedom. Any new book on this topic in the future will have to reckon with the growing and insidious application of this case in higher education decisionmaking, at the individual faculty level, and in terms of the overarching governance system.

Together with the analysis of Supreme Court cases, I have followed the leads set out by George R. LaNoue and Barbara A. Lee in their pioneering book, *Academics in Court* (1987, p. 146). In this careful and interesting study, they used a dual method approach to study hundreds of federal cases involving college faculty and employee discrimination claims and then to fashion five chapter-length ethnographic litigation history case studies. I have adopted this approach; by broadening the large-scale database to fifty years of all the Supreme Court cases involving colleges, I shamelessly bogarted their approach to the case studies. I have even attempted to emulate the smart-assed humor they employed, although I know I fell short in this dimension. For one tongue-in-cheek chapter title, they label *Lieberman v. Gant,* a case about how to determine what a plaintiff's comparator is or should be, as being about "A Faculty Wife Who Was not a Gentleman." In another reference, this one in the chapter about an equal pay case, *Mecklenberg v. Montana State University,* they refer to the site of the case as "Marlboro country" (p. 146) and to the happenstance of the actual publication of the judge's opinion: "Indeed, if Greg Morgan had not responded to the invitation of the Commerce Clearing House to have the decision published in the *Employment Practices Decisions,* the *Mecklenberg* opinion might have been the legal equivalent to the Zen riddle of whether a tree makes a noise when it falls deep in the forest where no one can hear it" (p. v). For LaNoue and Lee, there were many trees crashing, and not in silence.

Most importantly, I have adopted their overarching purpose in my study that follows theirs by twenty-five years: "We are concerned with what happens to the particular people and institutions that get caught up in the litigation process. In 1983 there were about 13 million civil lawsuits in the United States. For the participants, these cases involved an enormous amount of time, money, expense, and often anxiety. Litigation in our society has assumed an unusual role in conflict resolution, and it is important to describe and, eventually, to measure the consequences of this process. This requires a new social science lens, which this book develops and applies" (p. 173). As they did, I inhabited Marlboro country with the various actors in these dramas, and I have sought to add details and nuance that round out the cases. All cases resemble life less the farther they move through various appeals processes toward whatever "resolution" there is in the arc of that case's life. I would be satisfied to be viewed as someone as successful as they were in their book.

PART I

CHAPTER ONE

A Primer on Higher Education Law in the United States

The year 1970 was in the middle of the civil rights era, the height of the anti–Vietnam War period, the tail end of the best rock-and-roll years (in this year Van Morrison wrote *Moondance,* Jimi Hendrix and Janis Joplin died, and the Beatles disbanded),[1] and the time of the Kent State and Jackson State University shootings. During this momentous year, John S. Brubacher wrote in *The Courts and Higher Education*:

> The occasion for judicial prying into discretionary matters has grown out of an accentuated public interest in civil liberties. As never before, courts are applying the principles of the First, Fifth, and Fourteenth Amendments to the transaction of academic affairs. Take the due process clause of the First and Fourteenth Amendments as an illustration. Dismissing a student used to be a simple matter within the autonomous discretion of the dean or faculty disciplinary committee. But now the courts may review this discretion both procedurally and substantively. Procedurally they inquire whether the student had a fair hearing, and substantively they examine whether college rules on discipline are reasonable. This review amounts to an important reduction in the traditional autonomy of the college or university. How much further is this encroachment likely to go?[2]

The "encroachment" he lamented has gone much further than he even had dared fear. However, not all observers of this period were as mortified as he was. Political scientist Stephen K. Bailey, looking out at the same landscape, saw a more balanced review of the relationship between the state and higher education that had given rise to Brubacher's concerns over the legalization of the academy:

Today, as we perceive this elemental paradox in the tensions between the academy and the state, it is useful to keep in mind its generic quality. For at heart we are dealing, I submit, with a dilemma we cannot rationally wish to resolve. The public interest would not . . . be served if the academy were to enjoy an untroubled immunity. Nor could the public interest be served by the academy's being subjected to an intimate surveillance. . . . Whatever our current discomforts, because of a sense that the state is crowding us a bit, the underlying tension is benign. . . . The academy is for the state a benign antibody and the state is the academy's legitimator, benefactor, and protector. Both perspectives are valid. May they remain in tension.[3]

I graduated from college seminary in 1972. When I first began doctoral work and legal studies hoping to carve out a niche in the growing field of higher education law, I leaned toward the Stephen Bailey view; after nearly forty years of observation, I have come to appreciate how prescient he was, writing in 1974. But even the most observant and astute scholar of higher education politics would be surprised at today's developments. In modern higher education, few major decisions are made without considering the legal consequences; although the core functions of higher education—instruction and scholarship—are remarkably and relatively free from external legal influences, no one would plausibly deny the increase of legalization on campus. We know surprisingly little about the law's effect upon higher education, but virtually no one in the enterprise is untouched by statutes, regulations, case law, or institutional rules promulgated to implement legal regimes. It is rather like the persistent heat and humidity in Houston: You need not measure them, but you know they are there, even if you do not consult a meteorologist.

Lewis Thomas, among our most thoughtful commentators on medicine and science in society, ascribed organic qualities to the university, and his view of a college as a "community of scholars" is grounded in an appreciation of the history of education. Paul Goodman's *The Community of Scholars* and John Millett's *The Academic Community*, both published in 1962, also exemplify this perspective.[4] Like a prism refracting light differently depending upon how you hold it up for viewing, higher education can appear differently. For Herbert Stroup and many other sociologists, colleges are essentially bureaucracies, a view from which no student confronting course registration today is likely to be dissuaded.[5] To Victor Baldridge, universities are indisputably political organizations, as they have also appeared to Clark Kerr, Burton Clark, and Cary Nelson.[6] To thirty years' worth of critics, higher education is stratified by class, resistant to legal change, too easily given to political correctness, too easily given to conservative politics, and in need of fundamental restructuring.[7] As many observers would insist, all are equally close to the truth or truths, depending upon which truth is being refracted. The cases to be examined in this book reveal many truths and, often frustratingly, few answers. To paraphrase the astute Stephen Bailey: All these perspectives are valid. May they remain in tension.

Legal Governance

As many cases reveal, legal considerations can pare governance issues down to essentials, chief among them the question: What is a college? Despite the seeming obviousness of this question, a variety of cases probe this fundamental definitional issue. In *Coffee v. Rice University,* the issues were whether the 1891 trust charter founding Rice University (then Rice Institute), which restricted admissions to "white inhabitants" of Houston and required that no tuition be charged, could be maintained in 1966.[8] The court held that an "institute" was a postsecondary institution by any other name, and its postcompulsory collegiate nature rendered it a "college." On the issue of whether the trust could be maintained with its racial restrictions and tuition prohibition, the court applied the doctrine of *cy pres,* which theory allowed the trustees to reformulate the provisions and admit minorities and charge tuition, for to continue the practices would have been impracticable; if the trust provisions can no longer be realistically carried out, a court can reconstitute the trust to make it conform to the changed circumstances.

A court is not always so disposed as the *Coffee* court. In *Shapiro v. Columbia University National Bank and Trust Co.,* a 1979 case, the court allowed a trust reserved only for male students to remain male-only, refusing to apply *cy pres.*[9] My personal favorite is *U.S. on Behalf of U.S. Coast Guard v. Cerio,* a 1993 case in which a judge allowed the Coast Guard Academy to reformulate a major student prize when the endowment's annual interest had grown to over $100,000.[10] The judge begins, "This is essentially a case of looking a gift horse in the mouth and finding it too good to accept as is." He then allowed the academy to reconstitute the gift and to use some of the prize interest for other support services.

Sometimes it is a zoning ordinance that raises the issue of what constitutes a college. In 1983's *Fountain Gate Ministries v. City of Plano,* a city wished to restrict colleges from being located in residentially zoned housing areas.[11] The Fountain Gate Ministries argued that its activities were those of a church, rather than those of a college. However, the court took notice of the educational instruction, faculty, degree activities, and other college-like activities and determined that these constituted a college, protestations to the contrary notwithstanding. In the opposite direction, a court held that a consultant firm's use of the term "Quality College" to describe its activities did not make it a "college" or subject it to state regulation.[12] In wry fashion, the court noted that to make use of "college" in an organization's title would make a college bookstore or the Catholic College of Cardinals into postsecondary institutions.

Sometimes the definition drives a divorce decree. In *Hacker v. Hacker*,[13] a father who had agreed to pay for his daughter's college tuition did so while she was a theater major at the University of California, Los Angeles, but refused to do so when she moved to Manhattan and enrolled in the Neighborhood Playhouse, a renowned acting school; that it was not degree-granting persuaded the judge that the Neighborhood Playhouse failed to meet the definition of a college. Occasionally the definition turns on accreditation language (*Beth Rochel Seminary v. Bennett*),[14] while other times it turns on taxation issues (*City of Morgantown v. West Virginia Board of Regents*).[15]

The Establishment of Public and Private Colleges

Due to the different constitutional considerations, such as free speech and due process not applying to private colleges, issues that vexed Brubacher when he wrote in 1970, it is important to distinguish between the two forms in order to understand the full panoply of rights and duties owed to institutional community members. Consider the public/private distinction as a continuum, with the 1819 case of *Trustees of Dartmouth College v. Woodward*[16] at the purely private end and, 165 years later, the purely public colleges, such as the University of Texas, Ohio State University, and other flagship institutions at the other. In *Dartmouth*, the first higher education case ever considered by the U.S. Supreme Court, the State of New Hampshire had attempted to rescind the private charter of Dartmouth College, which had been incorporated in the state nearly fifty years earlier, and to make it a public college with legislatively appointed trustees to replace the college's private trustees. The Court held that the college, once chartered, was private and not subject to the legislature's actions, unless the trustees wished to reconstitute it as a public institution.

Of course, if there are pure archetypes such as Dartmouth and the University of Pittsburgh, there must be intermediate life forms, such as Alfred University, where, in the 1968 case, *Powe v. Miles*,[17] several students were arrested; the court held that the regular students were entitled to no elaborate due process, as the institution was private. However, the ceramics engineering students were entitled to hearings before dismissal, as the Ceramics College in which they were enrolled was a state-supported entity; New York contracted with the private college to provide this program rather than establish such a program in a state school. Other such hybrid examples of a state-contracted unit within a private school include Cornell University's statutory agricultural sciences program and Baylor's College of Medicine, both of which operate as if they were state institutions. Also in the mix would be colleges such as Temple and Pitt: *Krynicky* held that Temple University and the University of Pittsburgh were public colleges, due to the amount of money given them by the state, the reconstitution of their boards to have publicly appointed trustees (including ex officio elected officials), state reporting requirements, and other characteristics that injected state action into the act of incorporating the institutions into the state system of higher education.[18] Even in the smallest institutions, such as those operated by Indian tribes, complex governance issues arise, as in *Clark v. Dine College*,[19] in which the Navajo Nation court had to sort out conflicts over who was responsible for the institution.

Complex issues also arise that are unique to public institutions, such as the reach of sovereign immunity.[20] A state's sovereign immunity is often referred to as its Eleventh Amendment immunity, although this nomenclature is somewhat of a misnomer. The Eleventh Amendment provides: "The Judicial power of the United States shall not be construed to extend to any suit in law or equity, commenced or prosecuted against one of the United States by Citizens of another State, or by Citizens or Subjects of any Foreign State." While the Eleventh Amendment grants a state immunity from suit in federal court by its citizens and citizens of other States, sovereign immunity is much more.

When the United States was formed, the Constitution created a system of government consisting of two sovereigns—one national and one state. Although the states have conceded some of their sovereign powers to the national government over the years, the states retained substantial sovereign powers within the constitutional scheme. Of this relationship, the Supreme Court has observed:

> The sovereign immunity of the States neither derives from, nor is limited by, the terms of the Eleventh Amendment. Rather, as the Constitution's structure, its history, and the authoritative interpretations by this Court make clear, the States' immunity from suit is a fundamental aspect of the sovereignty which the States enjoyed before the ratification of the Constitution, and which they retain today . . . except as altered by the plan of the Convention or certain constitutional Amendments.[21]

Although a state's sovereign immunity is significant, it is not absolute. Three exceptions have been created by the Supreme Court to limit a state's sovereign immunity: waiver, abrogation, and the *Ex Parte Young* exceptions.

The first exception to the doctrine of sovereign immunity occurs when a state waives its immunity. A state's waiver of sovereign immunity may subject it to suit in state court but it is not enough, absent some other indicator of intent, to subject the state to suit in federal court. A state can also abrogate its Eleventh Amendment immunity against suits in federal court by other clearly stated means such as successfully moving a federal case to state court. Brian Snow and William E. Thro have summarized the *Ex Parte Young* exemption as follows: "This doctrine holds that sovereign immunity does not bar federal court actions against individual state officer . . . seeking (1) declaratory judgment that the state officer is currently violating federal law; and (2) an injunction forcing the state officer to conform his current conduct to federal law."[22] This exception does not apply to violations that occurred in the past; rather, it "applies only where there is an ongoing violation of federal law, which can be cured by declaratory or injunctive relief."[23] The court has imposed two significant limitations on this doctrine. First, the Court found the *Young* doctrine inapplicable in those situations where Congress had enacted a comprehensive remedial scheme; and second, the Court has ruled "that the *Young* doctrine was inapplicable when there were 'special sovereignty interests' involved."[24]

Other important foundational issues have also resulted in litigation, resulting in a complex governing definitional process. For example, in *Cahn and Cahn v. Antioch University*,[25] trustees of the institution were sued by co-deans of the law school to determine who had authority for governance decisions; the court ruled that trustees have the ultimate authority and fiduciary duty. In contrast to *Dartmouth*, where there was a "hostile takeover" of the institution by the state, private trustees can close a college or surrender its assets, such as its accreditation (*Fenn College v. Nance* [1965][26] and *Nasson College v. New England Association of Schools and Colleges* [1988][27]) or insurance coverage, as happened with the defunct College of Santa Fe, in New Mexico, where the complex litigation continued years after the death of the institution and its rise as a reconstituted proprietary arts college (*Radian Asset Assurance, Inc. v. College of the Christian Bros. of New Mexico* [2010]).[28] Another important issue involving the definition and legal governance of colleges turns on consortial or collective behavior of institutions: Does their mutual recognition in athletics accreditation and information-sharing subject them to state action? In the 1984 decision *NCAA v. University of Oklahoma*,[29] the U.S. Supreme Court held that the NCAA was a "classic cartel" engaged in restraint of trade by its negotiated television contract; another court held that the activities of the Overlap Group—a group of elite institutions that share information on financial aid offers with other colleges that had also admitted the same students, so as to "coordinate" the awards—had similarly violated antitrust law (*U.S. v. Brown University,* 1993).[30] However, in accreditation activities, the mutual-recognition agreements have been allowed by courts as not constituting a restraint of trade, as in *Marjorie Webster Junior College v. Middle States Association* (1970)[31] and *Beth Rochel Seminary v. Bennett,*[32] where an institution that was not yet accredited failed to negotiate the complex exceptions to the accreditation requirement for financial aid eligibility.

In sum, despite the seeming simplicity of legally defining a "college," it is not always an easy task. Cases were cited where entities not labeled as colleges were indeed found to be colleges, while some institutions that very much resemble colleges were held not to be, including a commercial program ("Quality College") that was held not to be an institution of higher education. For some technical, eligibility-driven issues—such as child support or taxation—the definition was extremely important. From these cases, the bottom line appears to be that a college is an entity with instructional programs and degree-granting authority. In addition, the definitional issue is raised in the context of who is responsible for governance of the institution. The answer is ultimately the trustees, although the *Yeshiva* case, to be discussed in the next section, appears to hold the opposite. With this foundational layer in place, this chapter turns to the two major campus actors: the faculty and students.

Faculty and the Law

A growing number of studies examining litigation patterns in postsecondary law will be examined throughout. Several show that faculty bring many of the suits in higher education: A 1987 study of Iowa case law showed that, the litigation against colleges brought by students totaled 11 percent, faculty 31 percent;[33] a 1988 study of one hundred years of Texas litigation showed that faculty brought 35 percent of all college cases in that state.[34] These numbers are surprising, for two reasons. First, higher education has traditionally been a "Victorian gentlemen's club," to use William Kaplin's term.[35] This meant that if faculty members did not receive tenure or were forced to move for some other reason, they would simply find another position or fall upon their sword. To do otherwise would brand them as troublemakers or contentious colleagues. Second, there were no civil rights laws or widespread collective bargaining until the 1960s and 1970s, so faculty had fewer statutory or regulatory opportunities to bring suit or engage in collective protection, such as that afforded by security provisions in collective bargaining agreements.

Tenure and Employment Law

The two leading Supreme Court tenure cases were decided on the same day in 1972, and both *Perry v. Sinderman*[36] and *Board of Regents v. Roth*[37] turn on what process is due to faculty, should institutions wish to remove them. In *Perry,* a community college instructor who had been a thorn in the side of college administrators was fired for "insubordination," without a hearing or an official declaration of the reasons. The college's full tenure policy consisted of the following sentence: "The Administration of the College wishes the faculty member to feel that he has permanent tenure as long as his teaching services are satisfactory and as long as he displays a cooperative attitude toward his coworkers and his supervisors, and as long he is happy in his work." The court, holding that he thus had a property interest in his continued employment, ordered the lower court to determine whether he had been fired for his protected speech or for cause. In short, they were required to give him notice of the reasons for his firing and an opportunity to explain his side of the matter. This is what tenure grants: a presumption of continued employment, absent certain circumstances (financial exigency and so on). In *Roth,* the Court held that an untenured professor had no constitutional right to continued employment beyond the contractual period for which he was hired.

These two cases, taken together with several others fleshing out the terms of faculty employment, delineate the contours of tenure. For example, in *Wellner v. Minnesota State Junior College Board* (1973), an untenured teacher was removed from his position for allegedly making racist remarks; he was sanctioned without a hearing or an opportunity to explain his behavior. The appeals court ordered that he be accorded a hearing, as his liberty interest had been infringed; that is, his record was stigmatized and his reputation was at stake. The court ordered a hearing to allow him to clear his name. In addition to contract and liberty interests, faculty may have property interests as well, as in *State ex rel. McLendon v. Morton* (1978),[38] where the court held that Professor McLendon had a property interest in being considered for tenure when she had ostensibly qualified by being in rank for the requisite period of time. Although many cases, including *Roth,* have held that no reasons need be given for denying tenure, she had, on the surface, appeared to earn tenure by default, and a hearing was required to show why she was not entitled to tenure. Such cases as these will be very fact-grounded and case-specific, due to the terms of the individual institutional policy and the development of contract law or employment law in each state.

A surprising number of cases have arisen exploring the ambiguities of tenure rights, as in whether or not American Association of University Professors (AAUP) guidelines apply (*Hill v. Talladega College*, 1987), exactly when the tenure clock applies (*Honore v. Douglas*, 1987), if financial reasons can apply without a declaration of financial exigency once a candidate has been evaluated in the tenure review process (*Spuler v. Pickar*, 1992), and whether institutional error can be sufficient grounds for overturning a tenure denial (*Lewis v. Loyola University of Chicago*, 1986).[39] As for discrimination in the tenure process, hundreds of cases have been reported, most of which defer to institutional judgments about the candidates.[40] Most of the cases find that the plaintiffs, whether a person of color or Anglo woman, do not carry their burden of proof that the institution acted in an unfair or discriminatory fashion. In those cases, like *Scott v. University of Delaware* (1978), the court held, "While some of this evidence is indicative of racial prejudice on the University campus, it does not suggest to me that [Professor] Scott was a victim of racial discrimination by the University in its renewal process, or that he was treated differently than [were] non-black faculty by the University."[41] That this is so is particularly due to the extraordinary deference accorded academic judgments, as in *Faro v. NYU*: "Of all fields, which the federal courts should hesitate to invade and take over, education and faculty appointments at a University level are probably the least suited for federal court supervision."[42]

Even so, occasionally an institution goes too far and gets caught, as occurred in the 1992 case of *Clark v. Claremont University Center*, examined more carefully in chapter 9. In this extremely interesting case, a black professor chanced upon the meeting where his departmental tenure consideration was being reviewed. From the adjacent room, where the door was apparently left ajar, he overheard the committee making racist remarks, such as "us white folks have rights, too" and "I couldn't work on a permanent basis with a black man." When the court and jury reviewed his entire record, compared it with others at the institution who had recently been considered for (and received) tenure, and noted that no other minority professor had ever received tenure at Claremont, it was determined that Professor Clark had been discriminated against due to his race, and he was awarded $1 million in compensatory damages as well as punitive damages and lawyers' fees.[43]

While few minority men have won discrimination claims, women, particularly white women, have won several cases where it was held that they were treated discriminatorily, as in *Sweeney v. Board of Trustees of Keene State College* (1978), *Kunda v. Muhlenberg College* (1978), *Mecklenberg v. Montana State Board of Regents* (1976), *Kemp v. Ervin* (1986), and *Jew v. University of Iowa* (1990), among others, where courts or juries found for women faculty plaintiffs.[44] Professor Jan Kemp particularly prevailed, winning six years on the tenure clock and over $2.5 million in compensatory and punitive damages from the University of Georgia.[45] She left the university at a later date without having earned tenure.

Collateral developments in employment law have made it more difficult for faculty to prevail in state and federal court, particularly by extending cases outside higher education to the college enterprise. Thus, *Hazelwood School District v. Kuhlmeier,* a 1988 U.S. Supreme Court decision about the right of school boards to control editorial content in a public K–12 school setting, has been cited in college faculty cases such as *Bishop v. Aronov* (1991) and *Scallet v. Rosenblum* (1997),[46] while *Connick v. Myers* (1983), a New Orleans District Attorney's office employment matter, affected dozens of college law cases, and *Waters v. Churchill* (1994), a public hospital case that held that public employees whose speech was "disruptive" could be removed for cause, reached into a 1995 faculty case, *Jeffries v. Harleston.*[47] Professor Leonard Jeffries, removed from his department chair position for his offensive and anti-Semitic speech, had won at trial and upon appeal, but the Supreme Court remanded and ordered the appeals court to review his case in light of *Waters.* After this review, the appeals court overturned and vacated its earlier opinion.[48] And the 2006 *Garcetti v. Ceballos* case involving the Los Angeles District Attorney's staff lawyers has begun to show up in public college employment decisions, as I note in chapter 10.[49] As the theme of this chapter and book indicate, higher education is highly contextual, and cases from a variety of other subject matter often will have bearing upon college law.

Collective Bargaining

Since the first college faculties were unionized in the 1960s and 1970s, collective bargaining has become widespread in higher education. In a 1988 article, Joel Douglas compiled union data indicating that more than 800 of the 3,284 institutions in the United States (25%) were covered by faculty collective bargaining agreements; the figures for nonfaculty college employees were even higher. By 1984, nearly 200,000 faculty (27% of all faculty) were unionized. Of these, 83 percent were in public colleges, while 17 percent were in private institutions.

Unionized public senior colleges total 220, private four-year colleges total 69, public two-year colleges total 524, and private two-year colleges include 13. He also reported that, in the last two decades, there had been 138 full-time college faculty strikes (or work stoppages), averaging almost 15 days each; the longest was 150 days at St. John's University in 1966.[50]

Collective bargaining is governed by federal and state laws, although several states also authorize local boards of junior colleges (hence local laws) to govern labor. More than half the states and the District of Columbia have such authorizing legislation. While state or local laws, if they exist, govern the respective state or local institutions, the National Labor Relations Act (NLRA) governs faculty collective bargaining in private institutions. In 1951, the National Labor Relations Board (NLRB) decided that colleges would not fall under NLRB jurisdiction if their mission was "noncommercial in nature and intimately connected with the charitable purposes and education activities" (*Trustees of Columbia University*).[51] This refusal to assert jurisdiction remained in force until 1970, when the NLRB reversed itself in the *Cornell University* case, in which Syracuse University was also included. After reviewing the development of labor law trends in the twenty years that had passed, the NLRB noted, "We [now] are convinced that assertion of jurisdiction is required over those private colleges and universities whose operations have a substantial effect on commerce to insure the orderly, effective and uniform application of the national labor policy."[52] The board set a $1 million gross revenue test for its standard, a figure that would today cover even the smallest colleges.

The NLRB decision to extend collective bargaining rights to Yeshiva University faculty, however, was overruled by the U.S. Supreme Court, which held that faculty members are, in effect, supervisory personnel and therefore not covered by the NLRA.[53] This important decision, of course, reversed a decade of organizing activity and struck a heavy blow to faculty unionizing efforts. Since the decision not to entitle Yeshiva faculty to organize collectively, over one hundred private colleges have sought to decertify existing faculty unions or refused to bargain with faculty on *Yeshiva* grounds. Dozens of faculty unions have been decertified, and an untold number of organizing efforts have been thwarted because of the decision or because of the absence of state enabling legislation.[54]

The decision, which affected only private colleges, has come to be applied even to public institutions, such as the University of Pittsburgh. The state of Pennsylvania has a labor law (Public Employment Relations Act, PERA) that was construed in 1987 by a Pennsylvania Labor Relations Board hearing examiner to exclude faculty: "As the faculty of the University of Pittsburgh participate with regularity in the essential process which results in a policy proposal and the decision to [hold a union election] and have a responsible role in giving practical effect to insuring the actual fulfillment of policy by concrete measures, the faculty of the university are management level employees within the meaning of PERA and thereby are excluded from PERA's coverage."[55]

In some instances, a court has found that *Yeshiva* criteria were not met, and the faculty really did not govern the institution, as in *NLRB v. Cooper Union* (1985) and *NLRB v. Florida Memorial College* (1982).[56] Scholars and courts will continue to sort out the consequences of *Yeshiva* and its successors; unless legislation is enacted at the federal level (to amend the NLRA, for instance) or in the states (to repeal "right to work" legislation), this issue will remain a major bone of contention between faculty and their institutions, both public and private. In addition, since the late 1990s, graduate students, adjunct faculty, and academic staff have successfully negotiated labor contracts, although these remain a small part of the organized higher education enterprise. By 2011, approximately a quarter of the full-time faculty members and one-fifth of the part-time faculty are represented by collective-bargaining units, according to National Center for the Study of Collective Bargaining in Higher Education and the Professions data.[57]

Students and the Law

There are many ways to approach the topic of students and the law, but the most interesting and historically based approach is to note how the common law has changed to define the legal relationship between colleges and college students. This is a useful and stimulating review, as the history of the legal status of students has resembled that of faculty—namely, from relatively few rights to a more balanced contemporary state of common law and statutory protections. However, as is the case with faculty, private institutions afford students fewer rights than their public college counterparts have, and most constitutional rights extend only to students in public institutions. Moreover, nowhere is there evident the statutory development to improve their status comparable to the rise of Title VII in employment, or the Equal Pay Act, or other safeguards afforded faculty employees. Since *Bakke,*[58] applicants have used Title VI to gain legal standing, while student athletes, especially women, have used Title IX to litigate for parity in intercollegiate athletic programs. Nonetheless, the status of students is largely the province of more inchoate constitutional protections.

The traditional status of students relative to their colleges was that of child to parent or ward to trustee: *in loco parentis,* literally, "in the place of the parent."

This plenary power gave institutions virtually unfettered authority over students' lives and affairs. Thus, the hapless Miss Anthony of *Anthony v. Syracuse University* (1928) could be expelled from school for the simple offense of "not being a typical Syracuse girl."[59] An even earlier case, *Gott v. Berea College* (1913),[60] had held that colleges could regulate off-campus behavior, while more recent cases, up until the 1970s, still held that students were substantially under institutional control. The weakening of this doctrine began with *Dixon v. Alabama State Board of Education*,[61] a 1961 case involving black students dismissed from a public black college for engaging in civil disobedience at an off-campus lunch counter. When the court held that they were entitled to a due process hearing before expulsion, it was the first time such rights had been recognized.

The age of majority changed from twenty-one to eighteen years in 1971; since that time, student rights have either been grounded in tort law (*Tarasoff v. Regents of University of California*, 1976, or *Mullins v. Pine Manor College*, 1983)[62] or in contract theories (*Johnson v. Lincoln Christian College*, 1986, or *Ross v. Creighton University*, 1992).[63] An area that has developed recently to accord rights to students has been "consumer fraud" or "deceptive trade practices" legislation.[64] While it has been used primarily for tuition refunds or assorted proprietary-school (for-profit) issues, such cases have picked up momentum and, in some states, can provide for damage awards.[65] For example, courts used the theory of fraudulent misrepresentations against a college in *Gonzalez v. North American College of Louisiana* (1988) and consumer statutes in *American Commercial Colleges, Inc. v. Davis* (1991).[66]

The case studies that follow in this book are excellent proxies for the many cases in admissions, affirmative action, and other student issues; they involve subjects that are litigated often and represent important societal developments outside the academy. I have tried to situate the case studies in their proper legal and societal context and to suggest alternative ways in which they could have been decided. In law, as in life, it is not always the end result that is important but, often, the reasoning itself.

Admissions and Race

In June 2003, the Supreme Court decided two admissions cases involving the University of Michigan, the undergraduate program (*Gratz v. Bollinger*)[67] and the law school (*Grutter v. Bollinger*).[68] In *Gratz*, the Court struck down UM's use of a racial point system in undergraduate admissions by a 6–3 majority. The Court found that the use of a points system was not "narrowly tailored" sufficiently to survive strict scrutiny. UM had awarded 20 points (on a 100-point scale) to all minority applicants, and the Court ended this particular practice. However, by a 5–4 decision, the Court upheld the full-file review practice of the UM Law School, which took racial criteria into account for reasons of diversity (upholding the original rationale of *Bakke*) and to obtain a "critical mass" of minority students. This opinion has become the key decision, as many schools follow the full-file review of the *Gratz* case and now have the imprimatur of the Supreme Court to use race as *Bakke* had allowed twenty-five years earlier. Race is a fugue that plays throughout U.S. society, including higher education. Since the 1980s, there has been a strong societal backlash against affirmative action, as evidenced by a major political party's platform plank against the principles, the California and Michigan voters' ballot initiative to outlaw affirmative action in state services and employment, the University of California regents' action to overturn years of admissions affirmative action (later rescinded), and congressional action to dismantle a number of federal education programs.[69]

In addition, there is a new and resurgent nativism evident, as seen in the 1994 California Ballot Initiative 187, which sought to deny public education to undocumented children (struck down by the courts) and which resurfaced nearly two decades later in Alabama and Arizona initiatives to deny school attendance to undocumented children and to exclude college students.[70] Some of these prejudicial measures have even taken deep root in areas of the country where the number of Latinos and other recent arrivals has been very small and where employers actively seek workers from the same segment of society, especially in agricultural and other dangerous and low-paying employment sectors.[71] As the polity has become more conservative on affirmative action, immigration, and other social issues, so too have the courts and legislatures. The *Grutter* decision will likely lead to other state ballot initiatives in the thermodynamics of college admissions politics.

Faculty Rights versus Student Rights

In several important legal cases, faculty and student rights have come into direct conflict. One involved prayer in the public college classroom, in which the court precluded the practice, finding that the Establishment Clause mandated that the college teacher discontinue the practice (*Lynch v. Indiana State University*).[72] Another religion case, *Bishop v. Aronov*, pitted a public university, the University of Alabama, against an exercise physiology professor who invited students in his class to judge him by Christian standards and to admonish him if he deviated from these tenets. The appeals court held that colleges exercised broad authority over pedagogical issues, and that "a teacher's speech can be taken as directly and deliberately representative of the school."[73] This troubling logic, which reaches the correct decision to admonish the professor, does so for the wrong reasons and rests upon the erroneous ground that faculty views are those of the institution. The court could have more parsimoniously and persuasively reached the same result by analyzing the peculiar role of religion injected into secular fields of study, especially when the teacher invites a particular religious scrutiny.

In another course, a studio art teacher was dismissed for his habit of not attending his studio classes or supervising his students; he argued that this technique taught students to act more independently (*Carley v. Arizona Board of Regents*).[74] The court disagreed that his behavior was a protected form of professorial speech, as did a court that considered another professor's extensive use of profanity in the classroom (*Martin v. Parrish*).[75] A professor also lost his position for making derogatory references during class to one of his students as "Monica Lewinsky" in an attempt to humiliate her (*Hayut v. SUNY*).[76]

These and other cases made it clear that students are not without rights in a classroom, while well-known cases such as *Levin v. Harleston*[77] and *Silva v. University of New Hampshire*[78] have made it clear that courts will still go a long way in protecting professors' ideas—however controversial (*Levin*)—and teaching styles—however offensive (*Silva*). A proper configuration of professorial academic freedom is one that is normative and resilient enough to resist extremes from without or within, to fend off the New Hampshire legislative inquiry of *Sweezy* and the proselytizing of *Bishop*. In this view, professors have wide-ranging discretion to undertake their research and to formulate teaching methods in their classroom and laboratories. However, this autonomy is, within broad limits, highly contingent upon traditional norms of peer review, codes of ethical behavior, and institutional standards. In the most favorable circumstances, these norms will be faculty-driven, subject to administrative guidelines for ensuring requisite due process and fairness. Even the highly optimistic and altruistic 1915 AAUP Declaration of Principles holds that "individual teachers should [not] be exempt from all restraints as to the matter or manner of their utterances, either within or without the university."[79] In short, academic freedom does not give and never has given *carte blanche* to professors but rather vests faculty with establishing and enforcing standards of behavior to be reasonably and appropriately applied in evaluations. Although I have attempted to persuade that the academic common law is highly normative, contextual, and faculty-driven, I have not lost sight of the range of acceptable practices and extraordinary heterogeneity found in classroom styles.

Additionally, persuasive research has emerged to show that persons trained in different academic disciplines view pedagogy differently. John Braxton and his colleagues summarize how these norms operate across disciplines: "Personal controls that induce individual conformity to teaching norms are internalized to varying degrees though the graduate school socialization process. Graduate school attendance in general and doctoral study in particular are regarded as a powerful socialization experience. The potency of this process lies not only in the development of knowledge, skills, and competencies, but also in the inculcation of norms, attitudes, and values. This socialization process entails the total learning situation. . . . [T]hrough these interpersonal relationships with faculty, values, knowledge, and skills are inculcated."[80] Moreover, to paraphrase Tolstoy, they are all inculcated differently. To grab a student and put my hands on his chest would be extraordinarily wrong in my immigration law class, but it could happen regularly and appropriately in a voice class, a physical education course, or an acting workshop. Discussing one's religious views in an exercise physiology class may be inappropriate, but certainly it is appropriate in a comparative religion course. Discussions of sexuality, salacious in a legal ethics course, could be appropriately central to a seminar in human sexuality. Each academic field has evolved its own norms and conventions.

However, courts are not in the business of contextualizing pedagogical disputes, as was evident in *Mincone v. Nassau County Community College*,[81] a case that wended its awkward way through the judicial system. Although *Mincone* had forebears in other decisions, it is sufficient to make my points: If colleges do not police themselves, others will; disputes between teachers and pupils are on the rise; and poor fact patterns and sloppy practices will lead to substantial external control over the classroom. One other thread is that it arose in a two-year community college, making it likely that the results will be taken by subsequent judges as directly pertinent for higher education in a way that K–12 cases have not been held to be controlling. Given the overlap with the mission of senior institutions and their usual transfer function, two-year colleges will not be easily distinguished. If a K–12 case is not in my favor, I can always try and convince a judge to limit it to the elementary/secondary sector; I will not be able to muster such a finely graded distinction in a postcompulsory world, even though two-year colleges are, on the average, more authoritarian and administrator-driven than four-year colleges. The widespread use of part-time and non-tenure-track faculty makes academic freedom more problematic at community colleges, where faculty do not always have the security or autonomy to develop the traditional protections of tenure and academic freedom.

The second round of this case began as a request for public records or, in this instance, course materials for Physical Education 251 (PER 251), "Family Life and Human Sexuality." The course is taught in several sections to nearly three thousand students each year, and in *Mincone,* a senior citizen auditor (enrolled under terms of a free, noncredit program for adults over sixty-five years of age) who reviewed the course materials before he took the class to be offered in summer 1995 sued to enjoin the course from using the materials or from using federal funds to "counsel abortion in the PER 251 course materials." Mincone, the representative of a co-plaintiff party, the Organization of Senior Citizens and Retailers (OSCAR), filed in May 1995 a lawsuit with eight causes of action: PER 251, under these theories, violates the strict religious neutrality required of public institutions by the New York State Constitution; burdens and violates state law concerning the free exercise clause of the New York State Constitution by "disparagement" of Judeo-Christian faiths and by promotion of the religious teaching of Eastern religions with regard to sexuality; violates the federal First Amendment; violates the plaintiffs' civil rights guaranteed under Sec. 1983; teaches behavior that violates Sec. 130.00 of the New York State Penal Law (sodomy statutes); violates federal law concerning religious neutrality by singling out one "correct view of human sexuality"; disregards the duty to warn students of course content so that they can decide whether or not to enroll in the course; endangers minors who may be enrolled in the course; and violates federal law enjoining abortion counseling.

This broad frontal attack on the course was virtually without precedent, as the plaintiff was not even enrolled in the course for credit and enjoined the course even before the term had begun and before he had taken the course as an auditor. But the wide-ranging claims, particularly those that allege religious bias, were so vague and poorly formulated that it was difficult to believe they would survive. But as in *Axson-Flynn,* examined in detail in chapter 5, religious challenges continue to flummox courts and present special circumstances.

We begin with the premise that faculty members have the absolute right, within the limits of germaneness and institutional practice, to assign whatever text they wish, subject only to the text being appropriate for the course and to academic custom. Sometimes this means a compromise, as in using a central text supplemented by all the extra materials you wish were in the basic text, because not everyone can or is inclined to write his or her own book. As AAUP General Counsel, I would have no qualms in defending the physical education course materials: They were picked by professionals with considerable expertise in this field; the course is required for the major, widely accepted, and regularly fully enrolled; it does what it sets out to do, expose students to wide-ranging issues of sexuality; and the materials clearly put students on notice about what the course covers. Except for the personal and moral objections of the plaintiffs concerning the materials, this course is generically like any course. Context counts, as does the professional authority to determine how it will be taught.[82]

Cases like this are fraught with implications for higher education practice, especially for teacher behavior. In *Cohen v. San Bernardino Community College*, the District Court could have gone in the opposite direction[83] as courts had done for Professors Silva and Levin, primarily by stressing academic freedom rather than by balancing the competing interests. However, by characterizing the issues as those of classroom control and students' learning environment, Professor Cohen's interests are trumped, at least with the admonishment. (His orders were to do essentially as Professor Silva was ordered by the University of New Hampshire to do: take counseling, alter his class style, and so forth.) He had been admonished to stop teaching from *Hustler* and other "pornographic" materials in his remedial English class. And the court did suggest that the admonishment was mild: "A case in which a professor is terminated or directly censored presents a far different balancing question." But does it? Can there be any doubt that Cohen considers himself "directly censored" by the formal complaint of one student? Was Levin censored by City University of New York's "shadow section"? Is reading *Hustler* letters a good idea for a remedial English class?

Additionally, there is the issue of a solution to the conundrum of faculty autonomy and sexual harassment jurisprudence. The difficulty is in acknowledging that a classroom can be a hostile environment in some instances. The AAUP hammered out a compromise attempt to preserve faculty autonomy yet to acknowledge and deal with an environment so hostile that it can stifle learning opportunities. The 1995 AAUP Statement of Policy for Sexual Harassment, suggested for institutional adoption, reads as follows:

> It is the policy of this institution that no member of the academic community may sexually harass another. Sexual advances, requests for sexual favors, and other speech or conduct of a sexual nature constitute sexual harassment when:
>
> 1. Such advances or requests are made under circumstances implying that one's response might affect academic or personnel decisions that are subject to the influence of the person making the proposal; or
>
> 2. Such speech or conduct is directed against another and is either abusive or severely humiliating, or persists despite the objection of the person targeted by the speech or conduct; or

3. Such speech or conduct is reasonably regarded as offensive and substantially impairs the academic or work opportunity of students, colleagues, or co-workers. If it takes place in the teaching context, it must also be persistent, pervasive, and not germane to the subject matter. The academic setting is distinct from the workplace in that wide latitude is required for professional judgment in determining the appropriate content and presentation of academic material.[84]

In our search for the perfect, clarifying epiphany—one that will illuminate once and for all examples that can guide behavior—this proposed policy falls short: what is "severely humiliating"? How much more "humiliating" is it than just "humiliating"? How long does harassment have to persist in order to be found "persistent"? Most important, isn't the classroom a "workplace" for faculty?

Even so, to me, in interpreting academic standards, what's surprising isn't that things work so badly but rather that they work so well. My own experiences as a student and professor lead me to believe that any comprehensive theory of professorial authority to determine "how it shall be taught" must incorporate a feedback mechanism for students to take issue, voice complaints, and point out remarks or attitudes that may be insensitive or disparaging. At a minimum, faculty should encourage students to speak privately with them to identify uncomfortable situations. Professor Bishop asked his students to point out inconsistencies between his Christian perspectives and his lifestyle. This is excessive and could itself provoke anxiety on the part of both Christian and non-Christian students. But a modest attempt to avoid stigmatizing words and examples is certainly in order for teachers, and schools should have in place some mechanism to address these issues and resolve problems. I cringe when I see exam questions that consign "Jose," "Maria," or "Rufus" to criminal questions, or when in-class hypotheticals use "illegal aliens" or sexist examples and stereotypes to illustrate legal points. Such misuse may be especially prevalent in difficult fact patterns involving criminal activities, such as rape and consent. Given the asymmetrical relationships between faculty and students in a classroom, students have a right to expect more thoughtful pedagogical practices, and such carelessness and insensitivity is evidence of faculty corner-cutting or worse. But increasingly emboldened by the availability of counsel and a larger agenda about the place of religion in the curriculum and secular public college settings, students will bring these cases, which will likely increase.[85]

Finally, there is the issue of grading. For years, I have told my students that no properly awarded grade has ever been overturned by a court, so they should not try and overturn mine. (For the record, several have done so, unsuccessfully, over the years.) However, that was before *Sylvester v. Texas Southern University*.[86] *Sylvester* is, arguably, the first federal case where a grade was overturned. But the circumstances are so bizarre that no one can really insist that the grade was "properly awarded." Therein lies a very odd tale, one that should make everyone aware of just how obstinate a faculty member can be and how badly a mistake can compound without proper faculty or administrative leadership.

Karen Sylvester, a Two L at Thurgood Marshall Law School, of Texas Southern University in Houston, was at the top of her class, having received almost all As. In the spring of 1994, she completed her wills and trusts class and was awarded a D. This had the effect of dropping her from first in her class, whereas a C or a "Pass" would have kept her in first place. First, she protested orally to the associate dean, who did not respond. The next semester, she protested in writing several times without receiving any response from the professor or the administration of the law school. The professor was later asked to produce her exam book. He said it had been lost. After a more thorough search, it was discovered. She had appealed to the law school's committee that had review powers over such disputes, a standing committee that included faculty and student members. Nearly a year later, when she was scheduled to graduate, Sylvester sought to enjoin the graduation ceremony until her grade and its effect upon her rank in class could be resolved. TSU promised the judge that if he allowed the ceremony to go forward, it would review the case and adjust her standing accordingly.

What follows is not pretty. The judge found that "[Professor] Bullock was defiant." The court ordered him to meet with the student to review the grade. As she now lived in Dallas, she had to return to Houston, where it developed that the professor either had no answer key or had not used one, so he could not review the exam properly. Angered, the judge ordered him to pay her travel expenses and to attach all subsequent meetings scheduled on this issue. The record tersely records, "He did neither." At the next court session, the judge sent marshals to fetch the missing professor, who admitted that he had received proper notice.

The issue was punted back to the law school committee, which decided—contrary to its published regulations—that students could not serve on the committee, as there were issues of privacy. The committee, without its student members, decided that the review had been adequate and that "no inconsistencies were found." Yet one member told the court that the committee had been informed by the professor that the correct answer to the essay question was "Yes." The judge, incredulous that this defiance had been ratified by the committee, threw the book at them. He wrote in a remarkable and sweeping voice, "Governmental actions cannot be arbitrary. Having no basis for comparison is arbitrary.

Changing the committee on the chairman's malicious whim is arbitrary. Once the committee had been changed from the official, university-constituted form it was nothing but a mob." He then ordered that she be given a "Pass" for the course and that she be listed as co-valedictorian, extraordinary actions needed to provide an "equitable adjustment."

This may be the only federal case overturning a grade, but its extraordinary facts reveal poor faculty and law school judgment and decisionmaking. Therefore it is likely that such judicial action will be limited to similarly egregious situations. Rather than expanding grade challenges, this decision will rein in excesses in institutional behavior and extend a modicum of due process to aggrieved students harmed by faculty carelessness or fecklessness.

Policy Implications

If events continue as in the past, there can be no doubt that higher education will become increasingly legalized, by the traditional means of legislation, regulation, and litigation as well as the growing areas of informal lawmaking, such as ballot initiatives, insurance carrier policies, and commercial or contract law in research.[87] This cascade will shower down upon institutions, each leaving its residue in the form of administrative responsibility for acknowledging and implementing the responsibilities.

Understanding better how legal initiatives become policy, particularly complex regulatory or legislative initiatives, should contribute greatly to improving administrative implementation of legal change on campus. Even with this modest review, it is clear that some legal policies will be more readily adopted than others. It is also clear that academic policymakers have substantial opportunities and resources to shape legal policy and smooth the way for legal changes on campus. Of course, no one can be expected to endorse all legal initiatives with equal enthusiasm or to administer them as if they were all high institutional priorities. Not all will be. Some will be implemented only grudgingly. However, understanding the implementation of legal change will influence the amount of policy output produced, the distribution of policy outputs, and the overall extent of compliance achieved.

The considerable autonomy and deference accorded higher education often translate into institutions designing their own compliance regimes for legislative and litigative change, and increased understanding of this complex legal phenomenon should increase this independence. As no small matter, higher education officials could begin to convince legislators that mandated legal change has a better chance of achieving the desired effects if institutions are allowed to design their own compliance and implementation strategies. This role could ease the sting so many campuses feel when another regulatory program is thrust upon them, or when they lose an important case in court, as happened at the University of Texas in *Hopwood v. State of Texas*. But it would require complete and full compliance, with the particularized regime and administrative details necessary to effectuate the statutes. It could also lead higher education officials to seek reasonable compliance rather than exemption, as occurs often in practice. As higher education continues to be reliant upon government support, and as colleges offer themselves for hire as willing participants in commercial ventures and as social change agents, additional regulatory legal restrictions are sure to follow.

Apprehending the consequences of legalization is an essential first step toward controlling our own fate. This review and the other chapters in this book show how interdependent the higher education system is and reveal why we need to adapt to the times but also to secure our timeless values, such as academic freedom, tenure, institutional autonomy, and due process. These safeguards are in danger of being legislated or litigated away should we fail to remain vigilant and alert, and if we do not self-police. If we do not, there are many police outside the academy all too willing to do so.

A Brief History of Higher Education Litigation in the United States Supreme Court

Although it is, for a variety of reasons, more difficult to get a case before the U.S. Supreme Court today than it has been in the past, many cases involving colleges have been heard by the Justices, beginning with the first college case to be tried, *Trustees of Dartmouth College v. Woodward*,[1] an 1819 governance dispute brought by the Dartmouth College board. The case resolved whether the state of New Hampshire, which had issued the corporate charter to establish Dartmouth, could amend the charter and reconstitute the independent, private institution as a public entity, rather than start its own college. It was the first hostile takeover of a private college ever attempted by a state. The Court, persuaded by lawyer and Dartmouth graduate (class of 1801) Daniel Webster, reversed the lower court decision and held that the New Hampshire State Legislature could not unilaterally rescind the college charter and violate the terms of the original simply by appropriating the institution, stripping the self-perpetuating trustees of their authority, and substituting its own appointed trustees. Frederick Rudolph, among the leading college historians of this period, calculated the effect of the *Dartmouth College* decision in these terms: "The decision discouraged the friends of strong state-supported and state-controlled institution . . . [and] by encouraging [private] college-founding and by discouraging public support for higher education, probably helped to check the development of state universities for half a century."[2] I am not persuaded that Rudolph gets this account right: He might have—as easily and equally—calculated the effect of allowing states to take over other private corporate entities, which would have helped to check the development of corporations. It is not clear how states were thwarted from establishing public colleges, simply because they could not disestablish private ones.

Since this 1819 case, higher education matters have regularly come before the Court, as have other subject matter cases that have had some bearing upon colleges. Elementary and secondary school issues, for example, have bled over into higher education, such as the 1968 *Pickering v. Board of Education*,[3] an important decision holding that public school employees had free speech rights. In 1982, *Connick v. Myers* (like the 2006 *Garcetti* case)[4] originated in an employment dispute within a public district attorney's office but had an immediate impact on the speech rights of public employees generally, if their speech were deemed not to be a matter of public concern. While it is evident that all cases have some bearing upon others, where the vectors align and the Court is convinced of the precedential value of an earlier decision due to the underlying facts or reasoning, cases across the spectrum may be analogized to one another. The quintessential act of lawyering and advocating for one's client is to select the cases that present the best and most advantageous reasoning so as to argue the case in the best light. Choosing the correct precedents and advancing the most persuasive legal theory is what litigators do—in every courtroom, at every level, every day.

U.S. Supreme Court Higher Education Cases

That said, the common law of higher education rests largely on authoritative cases involving higher education participants, and it is clear that such disputes have a perennial and regularly set place at the table. In the fifty years after 1959–60, the U.S. Supreme Court has decided approximately 120 cases with college participants. Arriving at this number is not as straightforward as one would think. The Court is the recipient of many documents, such as requests for permission to file amicus briefs, and many official contacts from many cases and other matters, some of which become consolidated on the way to Damascus. For one recent example, in the 2010 term, there were over 7,800 petitions to SCOTUS, including requests to file amicus briefs or other procedural motions.[5]

In order to examine this cohort of cases, I constructed a database of reported cases, drawing from approximately 300,349 total entries, employing several considerations: I grouped the results by case citation. If, for example, the Court consolidated two cases—each with a different docket number—under the same "U.S." citation, I used only the first or "lead" case in any analyses. This process resulted in a total number of 6,781 cases heard from December 31, 1958, to January 1, 2010.

Next, I searched all these cases, using the key terms (COLLEGE! UNIVERSITY "HIGHER EDUCATION" POSTSECONDARY REGENTS "BOARD OF TRUSTEES!"). This

TABLE 2.1. The Arithmetic of College Law Cases

Reported cases: 300,349
"Higher Education" cited: 1,904
Actual cases (unduplicated, not remanded, etc): 1,405
Cases without postsecondary marker: 27
Cases briefed and argued: 122

produced 1,904 cases. I reviewed, but did not count, another group that included COLLEGE or one of the other words as a marker but did not deal with higher education; for example, one case involved College Park, Maryland. Removing the wheat from the technical chaff resulted in 1,405 cases, of which 122 were actually briefed and argued by the parties before the Court. The remaining cases, including petitions for rehearing, were disposed of by withdrawals or included technical issues such as requests for extra filing time, denials of the cert petitions, or other actions, such as petitions proceeding *in forma pauperis,* and so on. The 122 cases constituted 8.5 percent of the total with which I began. The arithmetic of this winnowing process is summarized in table 2.1.

Conversely, because not all college cases would be evident from the names or titles of the parties, I made additional efforts to identify more cases. These were also counterintuitively difficult to ascertain. As examples, *Grutter v. Bollinger* and *Gratz v. Bollinger,* the important 2003 admissions companion cases brought by different aggrieved white plaintiffs against the University of Michigan, were suits against university president Lee Bollinger; without additional review, neither case would have surfaced using the standard postsecondary search markers. Fortunately, there have been several useful published series of annual reviews and thorough analyses of college law cases at all levels—federal and state—which I consulted for the Supreme Court decisions (appendix A). This extensive review yielded 27 additional cases for the relevant period, making a total of 122 of the 1,405 (8.5%). The stark math is 300,349 items to 6,781 cases to 1,904 cases to 1,405 cases down to 95 cases, up to 122 total cases. Thus, by my math, in the last fifty years, the Court has decided an average of between two and three higher education cases per year.

As a style exemplar for this book, I was guided by the useful and comprehensive 1987 study by George R. LaNoue and Barbara A. Lee, *Academics in Court: The Consequences of Faculty Discrimination.*[6] They examined over three hundred federal cases at the district and appeals court levels between 1970 and 1984, involving a range of faculty employment issues governed by federal employment and antidiscrimination statutes. (Several of these cases made it to the Supreme

TABLE 2.2. Higher Education Cases in the U.S. Supreme Court, 1959–2009

University of Notre Dame v. Laskowski, 551 U.S. 1160 (2007)
Central Virginia Community College v. Katz, 546 U.S. 356 (2006)
*Rumsfeld v. Forum for Academic and Inst. Rights, Inc., 547 U.S. 47, 126 S.Ct. 1297, 164 L.Ed.2d 156, 74 U.S.L.W. 4159, 19 Fla. L. Weekly Fed. S 125 (2006).
*Lockhart v. United States, 546 U.S. 142, 126 S.Ct. 699, 163 L.Ed.2d 557, 74 U.S.L.W. 4037, 19 Fla. L. Weekly Fed. S 23, 108 Soc. Sec. Rep. Service 1 (2005)
*Gratz v. Bollinger 539 U.S. 244 (2003)
*Grutter v. Bollinger 539 U.S. 306 (2003)
Parr v. Middle Tennessee State University, 541 U.S. 1059 (2004)
Oden v. Northern Marianas College, 539 U.S. 924 (2003)
Gonzaga University v. Doe, 536 U.S. 273 (2002)
Lapides v. Board of Regents of University System of Georgia, 535 U.S. 613 (2002)
Edelman v. Lynchburg College, 535 U.S. 106 (2002)
Raygor v. Regents of University of Minnesota, 534 U.S. 533 (2002)
Board of Trustees of University of Alabama v. Garrett, 531 U.S. 356 (2001)
Board of Regents of University of Wisconsin System v. Southworth, 529 U.S. 217 (2000)
Tennessee Bd. of Regents v. Coger, 528 U.S. 1110 (2000)
Illinois State University v. Varner, 528 U.S. 1110 (2000)
Bd. of Regents of University of New Mexico v. Migneault, 528 U.S. 1110 (2000)
Board of Trustees of University of Connecticut v. Davis, 528 U.S. 1110 (2000)
State University of New York, College at New Paltz v. Anderson, 528 U.S. 1111 (2000)
Board of Trustees of Southern Illinois University v. Wichmann, 528 U.S. 1111 (2000)
Kimel v. Florida Bd. of Regents, 528 U.S. 62 (2000)
Regents of University of California v. Genentech, Inc., 527 U.S. 1031 (1999)
Board of Regents of New Mexico State University v. Cockrell, 527 U.S. 1032 (1999)
College Sav. Bank v. Florida Prepaid Postsecondary Educ. Expense Bd., 527 U.S. 666 (1999)
Florida Prepaid Postsecondary Educ. Expense Bd. v. College Sav. Bank, 527 U.S. 627 (1999)
Board of Trustees of University of Illinois v. Doe, 526 U.S. 1142 (1999)
Central State University v. American Ass'n of University Professors, Cent. State University Chapter, 526 U.S. 124 (1999)
*Roberts v. Galen of Virginia, Inc., 525 U.S. 249 (1999)
City of Chicago v. International College of Surgeons, 522 U.S. 156 (1997)
*Gilbert v. Homar, 520 U.S. 924 (1997)
Regents of the University of California v. Doe, 519 U.S. 425 (1997)
University of Houston v. Chavez, 517 U.S. 1184 (1996)
*United States v. Virginia, 518 U.S. 515, 116 S.Ct. 2264, 135 L.Ed.2d 735, 1996 U.S. LEXIS 4259, 64 U.S.L.W. 4638, 10 Fla. L. Weekly Fed. S 93, 96 Cal. Daily Op. Service 4694, 96 D.A.R. 7573 (1996).
Rosenberger v. Rector and Visitors of University of Virginia, 515 U.S. 819 (1995)
*Harleston v. Jeffries, 513 U.S. 996 (1994)
Shalala v. Ohio State University, 512 U.S. 1231 (1994)
Thomas Jefferson University v. Shalala, 512 U.S. 504 (1994)
Milligan-Jensen v. Michigan Technological University, 509 U.S. 903 (1993)
*United States v. Fordice, 505 U.S. 717, 112 S.Ct. 2727, 120 L.Ed.2d 575, 60 U.S.L.W. 4769, 6 Fla. L. Weekly Fed. S 518, 92 Cal. Daily Op. Service 5577, 92 D.A.R. 8885 (1992).
Salve Regina College v. Russell, 499 U.S. 225 (1991)
*Lehnert v. Ferris Faculty Ass'n, 500 U.S. 507, 111 S.Ct. 1950, 114 L.Ed.2d 572, 59 U.S.L.W. 4544, 91 Cal. Daily Op. Service 3972, 91 D.A.R. 6313, 137 L.R.R.M. (BNA) 2321 (1991), reh'g denied by, in part, 501 U.S. 1244, 111 S.Ct. 2878, 115 L.Ed.2d 1044, 59 U.S.L.W. 3850 (1991).
West Virginia University Hospitals, Inc. v. Casey, 499 U.S. 83 (1991)
University of Pennsylvania v. E.E.O.C., 493 U.S. 182 (1990)
Board of Trustees of State University of New York v. Fox, 492 U.S. 469 (1989)
Volt Information Sciences, Inc. v. Board of Trustees of Leland Stanford Junior University, 489 U.S. 468 (1989)
Bowen v. Georgetown University Hosp., 488 U.S. 204 (1988)
Board of Governors of State Colleges and Universities v. Akins, 488 U.S. 920 (1988)

TABLE 2.2. (continued)

*National Collegiate Athletic Ass'n v. Tarkanian, 488 U.S. 179, 109 S.Ct. 454, 102 L.Ed.2d 469, 57 U.S.L.W. 4050 (1988)

University of Cincinnati v. Bowen, 485 U.S. 1018 (1988)

Regents of University of California v. Public Employment Relations Bd., 485 U.S. 589 (1988)

Carnegie-Mellon University v. Cohill, 484 U.S. 343 (1988)

Saint Francis College v. Al-Khazraji, 481 U.S. 604 (1987)

*Bazemore v. Friday, 478 U.S. 385, 106 S.Ct. 3000, 92 L.Ed.2d 315, 1986 U.S. LEXIS 131, 54 U.S.L.W. 4972, 40 Empl. Prac. Dec. (CCH) P36199, 41 Fair Empl. Prac. Cas. (BNA) 92, 4 Fed. R. Serv. 3d (Callaghan) 1259 (1986).

University of Tennessee v. Elliott, 478 U.S. 788 (1986)

*Witters v. Washington Dep't of Services for Blind, 474 U.S. 481, 106 S.Ct. 748, 88 L.Ed.2d 846, 1986 U.S. LEXIS 49, 54 U.S.L.W. 4135 (1986).

Regents of University of Michigan v. Ewing, 474 U.S. 214 (1985)

National Collegiate Athletic Ass'n v. Board of Regents of University of Oklahoma, 468 U.S. 85 (1984)

Hillsdale College v. Department of Education, 466 U.S. 901 (1984)

Grove City College v. Bell, 465 U.S. 555 (1984)

Minnesota State Bd. for Community Colleges v. Knight, 465 U.S. 271 (1984)

N.L.R.B. v. New York University Medical Center, 464 U.S. 805 (1983)

Long Island University v. Spirt, 463 U.S. 1223 (1983)

Peters v. Wayne State University, 463 U.S. 1223 (1983)

Bob Jones University v. U.S., 461 U.S. 574 (1983)

Block v. North Dakota ex rel. Bd. of University and School Lands, 461 U.S. 273 (1983)

Brigham Young University v. U.S., 459 U.S. 1095 (1983)

University of Houston v. Wilkins, 459 U.S. 809 (1982)

Mississippi University for Women v. Hogan, 458 U.S. 718 (1982)

*North Haven Bd. of Educ. v. Bell, 456 U.S. 512, 102 S.Ct. 1912, 72 L.Ed.2d 299, 1982 U.S. LEXIS 105, 50 U.S.L.W. 4501, 28 Empl. Prac. Dec. (CCH) P25120, 28 Empl. Prac. Dec. (CCH) P32675, 28 Fair Empl. Prac. Cas. (BNA) 1393 (1982).

*Toll v. Moreno, 458 U.S. 1 (1982)

Patsy v. Board of Regents of State of Fla., 457 U.S. 496 (1982)

U.S. Dept. of Educ. v. Seattle University, 456 U.S. 986 (1982)

Valley Forge Christian College v. Americans United for Separation of Church and State, Inc., 454 U.S. 464 (1982)

*Washington v. Chrisman, 455 U.S. 1, 102 S.Ct. 812, 70 L.Ed.2d 778, 1982 U.S. LEXIS 63, 50 U.S.L.W. 4133 (1982).

University of Texas v. Camenisch, 451 U.S. 390 (1981)

Universities Research Ass'n, Inc. v. Coutu, 450 U.S. 754 (1981)

*Widmar v. Vincent, 454 U.S. 263, 102 S.Ct. 269, 70 L.Ed.2d 440, 1981 U.S. LEXIS 134, 50 U.S.L.W. 4062 (1981).

Delaware State College v. Ricks, 449 U.S. 250 (1980)

Board of Regents of University of State of N.Y. v. Tomanio, 446 U.S. 478 (1980)

Trustees of Boston University v. N.L.R.B., 445 U.S. 912 (1980)

N.L.R.B. v. Yeshiva University, 444 U.S. 672 (1980)

Southeastern Community College v. Davis, 442 U.S. 397 (1979)

Cannon v. University of Chicago, 441 U.S. 677 (1979)

*Nevada v. Hall, 440 U.S. 410, 99 S.Ct. 1182, 59 L.Ed.2d 416, 1979 U.S. LEXIS 69 (1979), reh'g denied, 441 U.S. 917, 99 S. Ct. 2018, 60 L.Ed.2d 389 (1979).

Board of Trustees of Keene State College v. Sweeney, 439 U.S. 24 (1978)

N.L.R.B. v. Baylor University Medical Center, 439 U.S. 9 (1978)

*Friday v. Uzzell, 438 U.S. 912 (1978)

Regents of University of California v. Bakke, 438 U.S. 265 (1978)

University of Texas System v. Assaf, 435 U.S. 992 (1978)

Cleland v. National College of Business, 435 U.S. 213 (1978)

Board of Curators of University of Missouri v. Horowitz, 435 U.S. 78 (1978)

*Nyquist v. Mauclet, 432 U.S. 1, 97 S.Ct. 2120, 53 L.Ed.2d 63, 1977 U.S. LEXIS 110 (1977).

TABLE 2.2. (continued)

Smith v. Board of Governors of University of North Carolina, 434 U.S. 803 (1977)
*Roemer v. Board of Public Works, 426 U.S. 736, 96 S.Ct. 2337, 49 L.Ed.2d 179, 1976 U.S. LEXIS 70 (1976).
University of Chicago v. McDaniel, 423 U.S. 810 (1975)
Skehan v. Board of Trustees of Bloomsburg State College, 421 U.S. 983 (1975)
Bob Jones University v. Simon, 416 U.S. 725 (1974)
DeFunis v. Odegaard, 416 U.S. 312 (1974)
*Koscherak v. Schmeller, 415 U.S. 943 (1974)
Kister v. Ohio Board of Regents, 414 U.S. 1117 (1974)
*Scheuer v. Rhodes, 416 U.S. 232, 94 S.Ct. 1683, 40 L.Ed.2d 90, 1974 U.S. LEXIS 126, 71 Ohio Op. 2d 474 (1974)
Board of Regents of the University of Texas System v. New Left Education Project, 414 U.S. 807 (1973)
Glusman v. Board of Trustees of University of North Carolina, 412 U.S. 947 (1973)
*In re Griffiths, 413 U.S. 717, 93 S.Ct. 2851, 37 L.Ed.2d 910, 1973 U.S. LEXIS 35, 6 Empl. Prac. Dec. (CCH) P8683 (1973).
*Vlandis v. Kline, 412 U.S. 441 (1973)
Papish v. Board of Curators of University of Missouri, 410 U.S. 667 (1973)
Board of Regents of State Colleges v. Roth, 408 U.S. 564 (1972)
*Healy v. James, 408 U.S. 169, 92 S.Ct. 2338, 33 L.Ed.2d 266, 1972 U.S. LEXIS 160 (1972).
*Perry v. Sindermann, 408 U.S. 593 (1972)
Board of Visitors of the College of William and Mary in Virginia v. Norris, 404 U.S. 907 (1971)
Adams v. Board of Regents of State of Florida, 403 U.S. 915 (1971)
Blonder-Tongue Laboratories, Inc. v. University of Illinois Foundation, 402 U.S. 313 (1971)
*Tilton v. Richardson, 403 U.S. 672, 91 S.Ct. 2091, 29 L.Ed.2d 790, 1971 U.S. LEXIS 20 (1971), reh'g denied, Tilton v. Richardson, 404 U.S. 874, 92 S.Ct. 25, 30 L.Ed.2d 120 (1971).
*Williams v. McNair, 401 U.S. 951, 91 S.Ct. 976, 28 L.Ed.2d 235, 1971 U.S. LEXIS 2794 (1971).
Hadley v. Junior College Dist. of Metropolitan Kansas City, Mo., 397 U.S. 50 (1970)
Alabama State Teachers Association v. Alabama Public School and College Authority, 393 U.S. 400 (1969)
Knight v. Board of Regents of University of New York, 390 U.S. 36 (1968)
*Whitehill v. Elkins, 389 U.S. 54 (1967)
Keyishian v. Board of Regents of University of State of N.Y., 385 U.S. 589 (1967)
Trans-Lux Distributing Corp. v. Board of Regents of University of New York, 380 U.S. 259 (1965)
Kingsley Intern. Pictures Corp. v. Regents of University of State of N.Y., 360 U.S. 684 (1959)

* Higher education case without postsecondary title

Court.) Their book also included five wonderful case studies, with additional details gained from public information, interviews, and ethnographic research. Their approach and format informed my own project. I found illuminating their mixed-method study with richly detailed case information and interview materials, as well as extensive summary data from their case count.

Additionally, I examined several studies of noncollegiate legal issues for their stylistic and format insights. As one example, a 2009 study of denials of cert by Native American plaintiffs added a nuanced understanding of how the formal practices and mainstream assumptions about tribal sovereignty work to the detriment of Native parties. Legal scholar Matthew L. M. Fletcher showed that in the 136 petitions filed between 1986 and 1993, the Court granted only one cert petition of the ninety-two submitted to tribal interests bringing the claim, while it granted fourteen of thirty-seven to consider claims brought by state and local governments against tribal interests.[7] He attributes part of this pattern to the manner in which cert petitions are assigned to a "cert pool," from which almost all the Justices, through their clerks—recent law graduates—draw the preliminary information about the many cases. These clerks may not appreciate the features of a given case or highlight the features of the cases in a way that the Justices will notice.[8] He noted:

> The modern certiorari process, with its dependence on law clerks applying the Court's Rule 10, virtually guarantees that the cert pool will denigrate petitions filed by tribal interests. Tribal petitions, often involving the interpretation of Indian treaties or complicated and narrow common law questions of federal Indian law, are readily deemed "factbound" and "splitless." Conversely, the cert pool values and perhaps better understands the interests of state and state agency petitions. The pool's audience (a majority of the Roberts Court . . .) also highly understands and values the states' interests. Thus, the pool's recommendations favor states and state agencies. The result, frankly, is that tribal petitions on a question will almost never be favored, whereas state petitions on the same question will often be favored.
>
> The solutions to this discrepancy are not simple to effectuate. The Court's commitment to the certiorari process and the cert pool is powerful and not subject to outside interference. This commitment likely is linked to the Court's interest in placing all cert petitions—with the notable exception of original jurisdiction petitions—into one category.
>
> As the occasional clerk and the occasional Justice recognize, however, federal Indian law resists categorization into the mainstream. The certiorari process simply does not work for federal Indian law. The cert pool, and its reflection of the political makeup of the Court, cements the prejudice that tribal interests face in the certiorari process.[9]

As a result, more recently, American Indian lawyers have chosen not to seek cert petitions, as they have lost all five of the cases brought by tribes before the Roberts Court. Although tribes had won in the lower courts on three of the cases during the same period, all three were overturned by the Supreme Court when the losing sides appealed.[10] Most notably, the fifteen cases in this narrow and specialized field in the seven-year period (one brought by tribes and fourteen against tribes) approximated the two to three annual higher education claims granted cert by the Court on average, over the fifty-year period of my study.

Finally, I conducted a thorough review of the large political science and legal literatures with a special focus on studies of certiorari denial and Supreme Court interest group theory, in order to situate the body of college cases relative to other domains.[11] These rich and detailed literatures, heavily inclined toward quantitative research, include work that draws upon extensive computer databases of cases, court filings, and statistical treatments of their characteristics.[12] Of particular value were studies that utilize the computerized United States Supreme Court Judicial Database,[13] thus allowing broad and deep research into these cases, coded for consistent statistical treatment. Unfortunately, none of the coding could be adopted for college cases, for the technical reasons noted earlier.

Characteristics of the Cases

My research assistants and I read all 122 U.S. Supreme Court college law cases and coded them to categorize them by subject matter and type of original claim, by plaintiff and defendant type, by prevailing party, and by other criteria. Over two-thirds (69 percent) of the higher education cases could be grouped into five large areas upon which they were decided: free speech/free exercise/freedom of association: eighteen cases (15%); equal protection: twenty-one (18%); sovereign immunity: sixteen (13%); Title IX/sexual harassment: ten (8%); and employment discrimination/disability: eighteen (15%). Three other areas produced nine cases each, or 8 percent each of the total: employee discipline/promotion, student discipline, and general religious issues. The remaining twenty-two cases (18%) fell across a number of other, miscellaneous subject matter areas.

As can be imagined, many more claims are made in the pleadings that are accepted than become the grounds of the actual Supreme Court decisions, for obvious reasons. The Court decides narrowly on the facts when it can and so will not always resolve neatly all the original claims. It can remand, leaving some claims unaddressed. It can pour out or exclude what it considers to be less salient claims. A comprehensive claim can swamp lesser claims, leaving the other claims unaddressed or mooted. A case that produces multiple opinions may leave the actual grounds unclear or unresolved. A statute or key issue may resolve itself or change during the pendency of the case life. And, of course, other outcomes can occur in the rough and tumble of Supreme Court decisionmaking.

In the cases that I categorized by the type of original claim, only three large areas included double-digit claims: Free speech/free exercise/freedom of association, Title IX/sexual harassment, and employment discrimination/disability.

TABLE 2.3. U.S. Supreme Court Higher Education Law Cases (Original Claim)

Original Claim Type(s)	Count	Percentage of Total Cases
Free Speech / Exercise / Association	23	19
First Amendment Academic Freedom	2	2
First Amendment Establishment	9	8
Equal Protection	21	18
Sovereign Immunity	16	13
Bankruptcy	1	1
Statute of Limitations	2	2
Statutory Construction	2	2
Jurisdiction	1	1
Student Discrimination / ADA / Rehab Act	2	2
Faculty Discrimination / Tenure Denial / Title VII	3	3
Title IX / Sexual Harassment / Student-on-Student Harassment	10	8
Employment Discrimination / Disability / Age / Sex (includes Equal Pay Act) / Title VII	18	15
Fair Labor Standards Act	1	1
FERPA / § 1983	1	1
Intellectual Property / Trademark / Patent / Copyright	4	3
Title VI / Discrimination Based on Race, Color, National Origin	3	3
Collective Bargaining	6	5
Fifth Amendment Due Process	2	2
Employee Discipline / Promotion / Due Process	10	8
Student Discipline / Due Process	9	8
Breach of Contract	5	4
Medicare / Medicaid	5	4
Internal Revenue Code	3	3
Supremacy Clause	1	1
Immigration and Nationality Act	1	1
Davis-Bacon Act / Prevailing Back Pay Wages	2	2
Other	23	19

Religion appeared separately nine times, as did student disciplinary claims, each accounting for 8 percent of the total. Considering the claims brought and the resolution of the cases reveals a shrinkage of sorts, with the Court narrowing its decisional focus and determining the essence of the cases—thus defining the quintessential nature of the grievances. And the actual grounds on which these are decided also can elide or guise similarities, as "free exercise" claims can and often do turn on religious issues, and vice versa; when the cases are combined and analyzed as a discrete group no matter the legal theory or claim, it is clear that not only are religious claims the largest set of issues but, increasingly, the most apparent and transformative as well.

A careful look at the parties who brought the 122 college cases and the parties they sued reveals interesting patterns. As is evident from table 2.4, which allows for multiple parties (so the totals exceed 100%), it appears that colleges

TABLE 2.4. U.S. Supreme Court Higher Education Law Cases (Plaintiff/Defendant)

	Count	Percentage of Total Cases
Plaintiff Type		
Student(s) or Student Organization(s)	34	28
Faculty or Faculty Association	25	21
Non-Faculty University Employees or Applicant	21	18
Taxpayer(s) / Private Citizens / Residents	9	8
College(s) / University(ies) and/or Officials	15	13
State Government / Entity and/or Officials	3	3
Federal Government and/or Official(s)	7	6
Corporation or Other Business Entity	11	9
Other	5	4
Defendant Type		
Student(s) or Student Organization(s)	1	1
Faculty or Faculty Association	2	2
College(s) / University(ies) and/or Officials	87	73
State Government / Entity and/or Officials	26	22
Federal Government and/or Official(s)	16	13
Corporation or Other Business Entity	10	8
Other	2	2

qua organizations (in their corporate or legal form) and individual institutional officials (employees and trustees) were defendants in 87 of the 120 cases (73% of the total); the various states and/or state officials were defendants in 26 cases (22%); the federal government and/or federal officials were defendants in 16 instances (13%); corporation or businesses were defendants in 10 cases (8%); and others, including faculty and students, made up 5 defendants, or 5 percent.

The parties who brought suits as plaintiffs were much more diverse: 34 were filed by students (28%); 25 by faculty (21%); 21 by other nonfaculty college employees (18%); 15 by colleges/college officials on behalf of colleges (13%); eleven by corporations or business interests (9%); seven in the form of private individual or taxpayer suits (8%); seven federal agencies/officials (8%); three state agencies/officials (1%); and five miscellaneous plaintiffs (4%).

While there are usually always winners and losers, the cases reveal that the final resolution is not always so clearly evident—and not always even "final." In one complex Maryland case involving nonimmigrant students seeking classification as in-state resident students, the U.S. Supreme Court heard the case several times, certified a single question of law to the Maryland State Supreme Court, and incrementally and eventually ruled for the students.[14] Indeed, 47 of the cases, well more than a third of the total, were remanded by the Court for one reason or another, prolonging the eventual resolution of the original dispute. For example, *Christian Legal Society v. Martinez,* which had begun as *Christian Legal Society v. Kane,* was decided in June 2010 and remanded on the narrow

TABLE 2.5. Prevailing Party

Prevailing Party	Count	Percentage of Total Cases
Student(s) or Student Organization(s)	18	15
Faculty or Faculty Association	11	9
Non-Faculty University Employees or Applicant	5	4
Taxpayer(s) / Private Citizens / Residents	3	3
College(s) / University(ies) and/or Officials	43	36
State Government / Entity and/or Officials	11	9
Federal Government and/or Official(s)	13	11
Corporation or Other Business Entity	5	4
Other	3	3
Agreed Dismissal Under U.S. Supreme Court Rule 46.1	1	1
Remanded	47	39

issue of pretext—whether the law school said one thing and then did another, to the detriment of the CLS—and whether the CLS could argue "that in practice Hastings selectively applies its policy against CLS because of its particular beliefs."[15] The case finally ended in November 2010 when the Ninth Circuit determined on remand that the CLS had not preserved the issue of selective enforcement; by this time, the matter had morphed again, to *Christian Legal Society v. Wu,* reflecting both the case's shelf life and the turnover in the U.C. Hastings law deans.[16] Federal and state governments (24 cases and 20% of the total) and colleges (43 instances, or 36%) together win more than half the time, while students (18, or 15%), faculty (11, or 9%), other college staff (5, or 4%), corporations (5, or 4%), and others (a total of 6, or 6%) prevailed in these actions. It is not only in Native American claims where governments prevail more often than not, a result that on its face is unsurprising. Finally, the dispositive issues often changed by the time the case was decided, so we also coded them for dispositive issue (see table 2.6).

LaNoue and Lee concentrated on faculty discrimination claims in federal court cases between 1971 and 1984 in an attempt to capture the dynamics of recently enacted federal legislation such as the Equal Pay Act, Title VII, the Rehabilitation Act, and the Age in Discrimination Act. (Not all of the statutes applied to colleges in their early existence, and several were subsequently amended to include colleges.) By limiting their analysis to published opinions (not all cases in state or federal courts are issued for publication by the deciding judges), they counted 316 federal cases decided in that period at the district court or circuit court levels, of which 160—slightly more than half—were decided on the merits, while the remaining 156 cases were decided on procedural and jurisdictional grounds.[17] Of course, to the parties, the reasons for winning or losing do

TABLE 2.6. Main Dispositive Issue Type(s)

Main Dispositive Issue Type(s)	Count	Percentage of Total
Standing / Mootness / Ripeness	8	7
Public Forum Analysis	5	4
Sovereign Immunity	20	17
First Amendment Free Speech / Exercise / Association	16	13
First Amendment Establishment / Lemon Test	6	5
First Amendment Academic Freedom	2	2
Statute of Limitations / Tolling	5	4
Statutory Construction Interpretation	12	10
Jurisdiction	4	3
FERPA / § 1983	1	1
Intellectual Property / Copyright / Patent / Trademark	1	1
Student Discrimination / ADA / Rehab Act	1	1
Faculty Discrimination / Tenure Denial / Title VII	3	3
Title IX / Sexual Harassment / Student-on-Student Harassment	9	8
Employment Discrimination / Disability / Age / Title VII	7	6
Rational Basis Equal Protection Review	6	5.
Heightened Scrutiny Equal Protection Analysis	1	1
Equal Protection / Strict Scrutiny Analysis	3	3
"Close Judicial Scrutiny" / Equal Protection	1	1
Equal Protection / De Jure Segregation	1	1
Collective Bargaining / Unions	7	6
Employee Discipline / Promotion / Due Process	6	5
Student Discipline / Due Process	4	3
Fifth Amendment Due Process	1	1
U.S. Supreme Court Rule 46.1 Agreed Dismissal	1	1
Internal Revenue Code	3	3
Class Certification	2	2
Supremacy Clause	1	1
Immigration and Nationality Act	1	1
Other	23	19

not always matter if they prevail, and it was not always entirely clear who prevailed.

But LaNoue and Lee found the deck very tilted towards defendant colleges: "Of the 156 procedural/jurisdictional decisions, 58 have been in favor of the plaintiff and 77 for the defendant and 21 have been split decisions in which both parties have won and lost on different issues. On the other hand, plaintiffs have won only 34 of the 160 decisions that reached the merits (6 were split)."[18] While discrimination cases were the only object of their study and only one subset of higher education litigation, it was clear that aggrieved faculty plaintiffs prevailed in very few of their federal court claims during that period when the statutes were fresh and civil rights enforcement was on the rise.

More recently, legal and business law scholars Pat Chew and Robert E. Kelley, in their important 2006 article "Unwrapping Racial Harassment Law," identified twenty-six years' worth of racial harassment claims brought in federal courts under federal statutes.[19] They found cases alleging over six hundred harassment claims in the workplace (not just college workplaces) in six federal judicial circuits. Their study spanned the 1976–2002 period, thus overlapping several of the years examined by LaNoue and Lee. They estimated that the entire universe of such claims brought in all federal courts would have been more than 1,250 cases, some of which were also accepted and then decided by the Supreme Court.[20] They found that there were many procedural hurdles and technical roadblocks for plaintiffs in successfully bringing statutory civil rights claims and that only 21.5 percent of all reported decisions—itself the result of a ruthless and complex winnowing process—were decided for the plaintiffs.[21] Their database revealed a number of features that were more detailed than this Supreme Court project, but particularly striking were the various informal means by which judges manage such cases and narrow their scope. Chew and Kelley noted:

> Every published case thus begins with an employee believing he or she was racially harassed. If an aggrieved employee decides to take some action, a likely next step is to explore grievance procedures within the organization. If the dispute is not resolved within the company, the employee may consider pursuing litigation on the basis of Title VII or other statutes. Before filing a private lawsuit based on Title VII, however, the employee must first go through administrative procedures administered by the EEOC. This includes strict time limits within which the individual must file charges with the EEOC. This charge triggers a number of EEOC procedures, including notice to the employer, an investigation of the facts, and efforts to settle the charge. After these administrative procedures, many employees do not proceed further even if the dispute has not been resolved. They may have exhausted their financial or emotional resources, reassessed their legal claim and determined it is not sufficiently viable, or simply wanted to move on to other priorities in their lives. Some do move ahead with private litigation.

As employees move through the various stages of the dispute resolution process, the number of cases declines. Ultimately, only a small percentage of the original incidents are litigated, and an even smaller number are then reported in opinions.[22]

The Chew and Kelley study found that plaintiffs in racial harassment cases won only 20.8 percent of federal district court cases and 24.5 percent of their appellate cases; in contrast, sexual harassment plaintiffs won nearly half the time—48.2 percent, with 51.2 percent at the district level and 39 percent at the circuit courts.[23] Although their database and definitions are different studies than both those of LaNoue and Lee and those presented in this Supreme Court of the United States (SCOTUS) study, which records the ultimate disposition of the disputes, it is evident that, in all these treatments, plaintiffs rarely prevail while institutions, broadly defined as colleges or governments, rarely lose.

Matthew 22:14 famously informs believers that "many are called, but few are chosen" to enter the parable's wedding feast. This logic also surely applies to college law litigants, when so few plaintiffs challenging higher education institutions prevail in the highest court in the land. Even with these daunting odds, however, many feel called to express their grievances in the courts. While only a surprisingly small number of these many cases make it to the Supreme Court and result in a decision, they do appear—and when they do, they bind our colleges or ratify a practice or policy.

As the several case studies in this book reveal, the many not chosen to the Supreme Court wedding feast still have strong reasons for being, particularly in discrimination litigation. I chose these cases for their pedagogical value, their intrinsic interest (who could have dreamed up such fact patterns?), their implications for good and bad policy and policymaking,[24] and their not being among the chosen—that is, none made its way to the Supreme Court. The one exception to this, my analysis of the *Fordice* case, stands as an exemplar of a different era, the most recent and perhaps the last comprehensive civil rights college case brought by minority litigants.

CHAPTER THREE

Making It to the Supreme Court and the Rise of Purposive Organizations

Before examining the many higher education cases that have arisen, it is useful to consider how cases move through the system. Cases make their way to the United States Supreme Court, as all schoolchildren learn in civics lessons. The most obvious route is that cases percolate or bubble up to the apex from below, being tried by lower courts, either in the federal system or through state courts, when federal questions are presented. The losers in these disputes then petition to have the case heard at the next level, on appeal. A small number of disputes have automatic, accelerated, or special pathways to the Court, as with some death penalty appeals or Voting Rights Act matters. In most instances where the Court has discretion to take a case, it denies the petition (termed a writ of certiorari—literally, "it shall be certified for hearing"—such as "seeking cert" or "cert denied"); these petitions will average over eight thousand in a given year's term, which run from the first Monday in October until approximately June, by which time all the cases will have been heard, decided, and announced.

In a small number, usually fewer than one hundred in a given year, the Court will grant a writ of certiorari and then hear and decide the case on the merits with full opinion (or opinions). These petitions include both "fee paid" applications, for which a filing fee is required, and those from petitioners who are allowed to proceed in *forma pauperis,* usually state and federal prisoners seeking hearings on habeas corpus claims or challenging their prison conditions. Only a very small number of these non–fee-paid petitions are ever granted.[1] Thus, several tributaries flow into the current of Supreme Court appellate jurisdiction, including appeals from various state courts presenting federal questions, certified questions from certain federal courts, appeals from three-judge district courts, other appeals from federal courts, cert petitions for federal courts or state courts, and stays of execution.[2]

Cases can be settled after they have been accepted and briefed for the Court, as happened in 1997 in *Piscataway Board of Education v. Taxman,* a racial discrimination case.[3] After encountering financial problems, the school board felt it had to reduce one teaching position from the high school. New Jersey law required that tenured teachers be laid off in reverse order of seniority. The most recently tenured teachers, Sharon Taxman (who was white) and Debra Williams (who was African American), had begun as teachers on the same day. In the interest of affirmative action (Williams was the only black teacher in the department, and 50 percent of the students were minorities), the board voted to lay off Taxman even though she had a master's degree and Williams had only a bachelor's degree. Taxman sued for her job. The Third Circuit ruled in her favor. The school board appealed to the U.S. Supreme Court, and a hearing was scheduled for January 1998; however, national civil rights groups, afraid that the case was a poor choice with "bad" facts that might compromise affirmative action, raised money to resolve the matter. The case was settled before it was heard, and Taxman was rehired. In 2012, both teachers were still teaching in Piscataway.

Since 1925, the Supreme Court has operated under Rule 10 ("Considerations Governing Review on Writ of Certiorari"), which it promulgated to sort out the many petitions for certiorari it receives each term. The rule reads:

> Review on a writ of certiorari is not a matter of right, but of judicial discretion. A petition for a writ of certiorari will be granted only for compelling reasons. The following, although neither controlling nor fully measuring the Court's discretion, indicate the character of the reasons the Court considers:
>
> (a) a United States court of appeals has entered a decision in conflict with the decision of another United States court of appeals on the same important matter; has decided an important federal question in a way that conflicts with a decision by a state court of last resort; or has so far departed from the accepted and usual course of judicial proceedings, or sanctioned such a departure by a lower court, as to call for an exercise of this Court's supervisory power;
>
> (b) a state court of last resort has decided an important federal question in a way that conflicts with the decision of another state court of last resort or of a United States court of appeals;
>
> (c) a state court or a United States court of appeals has decided an important question of federal law that has not been, but should be, settled by this Court, or

has decided an important federal question in a way that conflicts with relevant decisions of this Court.

A petition for a writ of certiorari is rarely granted when the asserted error consists of erroneous factual findings or the misapplication of a properly stated rule of law.[4]

The exercise of "judicial discretion" here is obvious, in determining what issues presented are "important," whether and how a "conflict" is presented, or what constitutes the "accepted and usual course" of the matter. For those cases that are brought to the conference, where all the Court members determine which cases they will hear, a "Rule of Four" requires that at least four of the nine Justices vote to hear a fully briefed and argued case. Thus, a drastic winnowing process assures that only the cases with the requisite support for full hearings will actually make it to the full Court each term: The nearly eight thousand cases shrink to the approximately eighty or ninety that live on to their day in court that term. Changing jurisdictional statutes, provisions for determining standing, administrative procedures, and, most importantly, the Justices themselves over time have made it harder to get questions before the Court. The shrinkage of obligatory jurisdiction makes clear the significance of writs of certiorari, as they have become virtually the only means by which the Court considers cases for review. Thus, it is the denial of certiorari ("cert denials") that is the most treacherous shoals a case must navigate to make it onto the Court's docket.[5]

It is the consideration of cert denials and the mechanisms by which case selection is accomplished that have been the preoccupation of generations of political scientists, historians, and legal scholars. Here, the complexities of the processes are well understood by the many players, including the Justices (especially the Chief Justice, who maintains the primary sorting mechanisms) and the many institutional players, such as the Supreme Court clerks who review the pooled cert petitions; the solicitor general, who represents the U.S. government when the United States is a party, and who signals preferences by briefs and alignment choices; Congress, which is able to command attention by passing statutes; and other lawyers and interest groups, many of whom are repeat players with broad ideological and political characteristics. All the players form a *dramatis personae*, with competing scripts and opportunities to convey their interests and preferences. More than thirty years ago, law professor Peter Linzer, in a thorough and painstaking review of the cert denial process, deserved:

[It is] time to stop pretending that denial of certiorari means nothing. Many times it gives us a glimpse, imperfect to be sure, into the Justices' preliminary attitudes on a given issue. Some may take a public stance in a dissent, others' views may be deducible from their current silence when compared to an earlier position. When six or more Justices vote to deny review in a case of apparent national importance or when there is a conflict among the courts below, especially if there is also a strong dissent on the merits, this denial cannot be explained away by a bland recital of the orthodox view. Their votes to deny certiorari do not prove that the silent Justices would have voted to affirm, but they do permit the lawyer or lower court to make an educated guess based on precedent, the "neutral" importance of the case, the stridency and number of dissents, and the silent Justices' past practices in similar cases.

The observer should always remember that not every Justice may have considered the merits and that those who did likely made only a tentative examination that may change with a different record and a different presentation on certiorari. A dissent may give a future petitioner an argument that can garner the fourth vote for certiorari and the fifth vote on the merits.

The dissents and other separate opinions also can provide starting points for reexamination of an issue in law reviews and by courts faced with similar questions. If the issue returns to the Supreme Court, the analyses spawned by the previous denial of certiorari may lead to a different approach by several Justices, possibly including the former dissenters.

The denial is a sort of litmus paper giving the observer a first reading of the Court. Used sensitively and cautiously, it can be a valuable tool. Because denials of certiorari are unclear, and often are only rough indicators, neither the Supreme Court nor the courts below need be embarrassed about ignoring them. Yet the analyses made by the Justices, whether express or implicit, are available, and may lead those deciding later cases to see new ways to deal with a problem. In this way, denials of certiorari may help the law grow far beyond the particular cases in which they first appear.[6]

Linzer noted that explanatory denials of cert had themselves become elaborate and detailed signaling devices. Such judicial explanations or elaborations had been rare but became much more commonplace by the 1970s. In 1978, there were more than four hundred notations of dissent, and virtually all the Justices had conveyed their reason for granting and/or denying certiorari, with individual dissents and notations, dissents that indicated positions on the merits, dissents that indicated reasons for granting certiorari but not discussing merits, dissents without opinions, and even notations other than dissents.[7] The number of such dissents has shrunk with changes on the Court, but when it does occur, such signaling or conveying has been taken as a sign of a politicized or contentious Court—and the phenomenon may be just such an indicator—but it also evidences the likely intent of the Justices to elaborate upon their reasoning, as a further means of discursive behavior or winnowing to interested parties, either inviting or disinviting the types of cases and controversies that they would like to hear or not hear.

As just one example of how nuanced and effective this discourse can be, consider how Justice Thurgood Marshall (who served on the Supreme Court bench from 1967 to 1991) was frustrated by the turn of death penalty jurisprudence and used the tactic as a colloquy with his colleagues on the bench to reconceptualize the unfairness of the entire regime of criminal law and its disproportionate effect upon minority defendants. In an article on the Justice for whom he had clerked at the Supreme Court, Professor Randall L. Kennedy described how the Justice had begun his campaign by dissenting in cert denials and eventually won others over to his view, both on the Court and in the lower Article III courts, where judges took him up on the invitation to fashion opinions that, over time, led to the requisite conflicts among the circuits.[8]

Legal scholar Omari Simmons has noted a similar common exchange mechanism in the form of amicus curiae ("friend of the court" or "amicus") briefs, the formal devices used by third parties to draw attention to a given point or to elucidate and urge a specific action in a case that is pending before the lower courts or the Supreme Court:

> Open door access to amici helps preserve the Court's institutional legitimacy among varied stakeholders without significantly undermining the Court's independence. Amicus participation dispels external criticism that the Court is detached and indifferent to the public. In the absence of a restrictive rule governing amicus participation, the Court has developed its own filtering mechanisms for analyzing amicus briefs and provided informal guidance to potential filers concerning the Court's preferences. Ultimately, criticisms of broad participation are outweighed by the resulting legitimacy gains. The Court's function as a quasi-representative institution is neither without tension nor imperfection. But, in the end, this function is unavoidable.[9]

Political scientists Tom S. Clark and Benjamin Lauderdale have suggested that another signaling device is the means by which Supreme Court opinions are located in what they term "doctrine space," or the Justices' citations to other precedents in their own writing. The authors noted,

We seek to estimate the legal position taken by a given opinion. One way that court opinions reveal their content is by which precedents they cite positively (affirming the argument of the older opinion) and which they cite negatively (disputing the argument of the previous opinion). We develop a scaling model which estimates the location of opinions by assuming that the probability of positively citing another opinion is a decreasing function of the policy distance between the two opinions. Using original data on which precedents are cited positively or negatively by each opinion, we estimate locations in a single-dimensional space for each search and seizure and freedom of religion opinion authored by the Warren, Burger, and Rehnquist Courts (1953–2004). These estimates allow fine-grained, systematic analysis of the doctrinal content of Supreme Court opinions. Our method can be used to study a variety of substantive problems, including, but not limited to, intracourt bargaining, the judicial hierarchy, the effect of separation-of-powers mechanisms on judicial policymaking, and the consequences of Supreme Court nominations.[10]

Their systematic measurement of judicial citation is highly technical and quantitative, but they do attempt to explain intracourt bargaining, an important feature in explaining why Justices cite precedents as they do, how they attempt to influence each other, how the centrist view often prevails, or how outliers alter their own opinion writing to negotiate this discursive doctrine space to win a majority or to influence a dissent.

Listing these many liminal spaces would likely understate the informal communication networks that exist and are used by all the parties. For example, I have attended law school and bar association events with Justices who simply made nice or who spoke in platitudes about cases and legal matters, and I have heard others engage in serious discussions in other public academic settings where they prepared formal papers or had their scholarly remarks published. The former is social networking, while the latter is substantive evidence in the discourse. In 2011, Justices Stephen G. Breyer and Antonin Scalia even testified before the U.S. Senate Judiciary Committee on conflicts of interest and other serious matters of Court administration.[11] Political scientist Vanessa A. Baird has carefully observed the various cues, noting that, although the Justices can decide only cases and controversies that ripen and make their way to them, they are acutely attuned to the many ways that they can convey their desires and preferences to parties and potential parties, especially the policy elites (what she dubs "policy entrepreneurs") who regularly practice in front of the Court and who offer up the cases that will advance their organizational interests: "The litigants pay attention to information about the justices' policy priorities, prompting them to 'find' appropriate cases for the justices in those desired policy areas. . . . Justices benefit from the litigants' perceptions that their reputations are important; they also depend on litigants' willingness to support cases to influence political or legal change."[12] Her research identified four- to five-year cycles, during which cases ripen—or, better, the right cases ripen—in accord with the Court's personnel, the timing of issues, the tactics of the litigants, and the calendaring of lower court issues that could move an issue forward.

The Rise of Purposive Organizations

Thus far, I have attempted to explain how cases move through the complex system to full consideration by the Supreme Court. This forward progress has observable criteria and features, all of which shape the arc of cases and the choices the Court makes. Having laid this introductory groundwork, I turn here to what Baird characterized as one such "policy entrepreneur" organization, the American Civil Liberties Union (ACLU), founded in 1920. It has a clear and definable policy focus and ideological identity, a large base of members who support its goals and who provide resources and expertise, and many hundreds of disputes that ripen on a regular basis to produce cases—those that can supply the disputes invited by the Court. In addition, the core values of the ACLU cross into many dimensions of national public life and discourse and across a broad ideological span of influence, such as progressive nondiscrimination issues of racial profiling and immigrant rights and more libertarian issues of privacy and free speech. They are repeat players in important legislative, public policy, and litigation events and are well established with geographic reach and membership. For example, ACLU lawyers successfully argued *Tinker v. Des Moines,* a landmark 1969 student speech issue (students do not "shed their constitutional rights to freedom of speech or expression at the schoolhouse gate")[13] and unsuccessfully defended the right of Professor Tariq Ramadan, a Swiss Muslim excluded from the United States for his views, to assume the faculty position for which he had been hired at the University of Notre Dame in 2009–2010.[14]

In his 1995 book *Political Organizations,* political scientist James Q. Wilson formulated the notion of a "purposive" organization: "The dramatic increase in the membership of civil rights, environmental, civil liberties, political reform, and feminist organizations that occurred in the 1970s could not be explained entirely or even largely by the ability of such groups to exert social pressure or supply selective benefits, although these inducements no doubt played a role. To some extent, members were appealing to purposive ideals," defined as a theory of focused incentives, salient appeals, perceived threats, and "solidarity, materials, and purposive incentives" communicated to members and potential members.[15] Omari Simmons has noted the role of these organizations in participating through litigation, but especially through the targeted use of amicus briefs: "In addition to robust participation by diverse amici, the content of the arguments raised by amici illustrates how amicus participation provides a deliberative and discursive forum. The perspectives of amici may enhance the prospect of better substantive decisions and the mere opportunity to participate in the lawmaking process enhances the Court's legitimacy even where a party disagrees with the ultimate outcome. Discursive debate and participation is particularly important for groups normally excluded from the legislative process."[16]

The quintessential "policy entrepreneur" or "purposive" educational organization is the NAACP Legal Defense Fund, the organization founded in 1940 and led for many years by lawyer Thurgood Marshall, which had as its clear focus to dismantle the apartheid system of Jim Crow America, leading to the towering 1954 *Brown v. Board of Education* case and other civil rights actions before and since.[17] Conservative groups have successfully adopted the LDF model to advance their causes, particularly in opposing racial affirmative action; their rise has coincided with the more conservative direction evident since the Burger, Rehnquist, and Roberts Courts. Not only have these groups employed the litigation tactics of LDF, the Mexican American Legal Defense and Educational Fund (MALDEF), and other progressive public interest racial organizations, but some of the more prominent have even appropriated the language and nomenclature of the earlier progressive and liberal groups, calling themselves "The Center for Equal Opportunity" (CEO), which touts itself as "the nation's only conservative think tank devoted to issues of race and ethnicity" and "The Center for Individual Rights" (CIR), "a nonprofit public interest law firm dedicated to the defense of individual liberties against the increasingly aggressive and unchecked authority of federal and state governments."[18] CIR, for example, litigated the 2003 *Gratz* and *Grutter* affirmative action cases against the University of Michigan and UM Law School, while CEO has filed several actions to thwart postsecondary affirmative action programs. One attorney who has litigated many anti-immigrant cases has indicated that he took his nativist inspiration from MALDEF, a provenance and attribution that must set the proimmigrant organization's lawyers' teeth on edge.[19]

In celebrating its twentieth anniversary in 2009, CIR acknowledged its debt to the earlier civil rights firms and their struggles for racial equality: "Nowhere did liberal public interest law firms enjoy greater moral authority than in the area of civil rights. The NAACP Legal Defense Fund's forty-year effort to end discrimination in public schools stands for many as the model of tenacious public interest law advocacy. Yet what began as a principled effort to enforce the Fourteenth Amendment's requirement that the state neither favor nor disfavor any individual because of his race turned into a systematic effort to favor particular racial groups in employment, government contracting, and college admission, often in blatant disregard of Supreme Court precedent in this area."[20] In claiming lineage to the Legal Defense Fund, CIR successfully undertook the *Hopwood* litigation, only to see the U.S. Supreme Court eventually overturn *Hopwood* in the 2003 *Gratz* and *Grutter* cases, reestablishing the 1978 precedent of *Bakke v. UC Regents* and upholding the use of affirmative action in college admissions.[21] Following this defeat, CIR took to the electorate, cosponsoring the Michigan "Civil Rights Initiative," by which the state's voters acted to abolish the use of affirmative action; this ballot initiative was invalidated in a July 2011 Sixth Circuit case.[22] This action is currently bogged down in the Michigan courts, but such a ballot measure tactic can be successful, depending on the state and the circumstances.

As another recent example, a new resident tuition law in 2011 in Maryland that would have enabled undocumented college students to gain in-state tuition eligibility was stalled when a state ballot measure to repeal the tuition law received enough signatures to move forward.[23] A third example was the earlier 1996 California Civil Rights Initiative (Proposition 209) that was brought under the auspices of the American Civil Rights Institute, a national purposive organization created to educate the public on what its adherents consider the harms of racial and gender affirmative action, which they term "racial and gender preferences." Following the enactment of CCRI/Prop. 209, California government agencies may not "discriminate" based on race, sex, color, ethnicity, and national origin in public employment, education, and contracting.[24]

Among the earliest of these conservative litigation groups were the Liberty Institute (née the Liberty Legal Institute) and the Washington Legal Foundation (WLF), founded in 1977, which does not focus specifically on higher education but is involved in college law disputes in a number of areas such as *Martinez v. University of California,* a challenge to the California statute that accords resident college tuition status, allowed by federal law, that worked its way through the state courts, until the California Supreme Court in 2010 overturned the Appeals Court decision that had voided the statute.[25] This ultimately unsuccessful restrictionist action on the issue of who gets to pay what level of tuition was brought under a larger WLF program initiative, "Protecting America's Freedom: National Security and Defense."

While these groups and many others carve out large swaths of public policy across different areas, none of them focuses exclusively on higher education legal issues. Rather, they turn their attention to colleges and universities predominantly as exemplars in their larger agendas, whether progressive or conservative. Thus, LDF and MALDEF have been involved in a number of college law cases but primarily to defend affirmative action plans or to challenge restrictionist residency and immigration classifications. CEO and CIR have opposed college affirmative action plans and campus speech codes but have larger public policy strategies and do not focus exclusively on postsecondary institutions—or even on litigation. CEO does not actually undertake its own litigation but coordinates with affiliates. It does, on occasion, file administrative actions. It also has as one of its ongoing interests a focus on comprehensive immigration reform. The Foundation for Individual Rights in Education (FIRE) singles out campus speech codes and practices that, in its libertarian view, compromise free speech in the name of what it considers "political correctness." While its public campaigns have been visible and successful and while it has arranged for suits to be brought by third-party referrals, it does not undertake litigation.

In a useful and informative review of the last fifty years of higher education law, Barbara A. Lee identified the rise of "external groups," which she also characterizes as "watchdog" groups and advocacy organizations "seeking to impose their agenda on" colleges; she uses as an exemplar FIRE, which, she noted, "has not hesitated to sue on behalf of students"; it is understandable that she characterized them as litigators, given their representations over the years.[26] For example, on its September 5, 2003, article on its website, the group notes its "Lawsuit to Proceed" in a speech code case, the area in which it has been very active. It also maintains a "Speech Code Litigation Project."[27] But elsewhere on its website, it becomes clear that FIRE is more a search engine for cases, not a law firm that actually files suits. Rather, it coordinates with lawyers through a FIRE "Legal Network": "Since its incorporation as a nonprofit foundation in April 1999, FIRE has intervened successfully in defense of liberty-related issues on behalf of hundreds of students and faculty members at colleges and universities across America. While many of the cases we accept can be resolved quickly and amicably by our office staff, other cases require the intervention of an attorney. Because FIRE does not undertake direct litigation, these cases must be referred to outside attorneys who share our principles, values and goals."[28] Even without actually litigating, FIRE is among the most visible conservative groups in teeing up litigation and in tracking college issues, particularly those it considers "political correctness" and threats to free speech, especially for wronged conservatives.

Increasingly, organizations devoted to religious accommodation issues and religious freedom of expression have undertaken extensive higher education litigation and may be among the most attentive and purposive groups suing colleges, with a wide range of cases that have addressed access for religious worship on campus, recognition of religious student groups, and the defense of religion in the curriculum and admissions policies. Indeed, religious legal organizations such as the Alliance Defense Fund (ADF) have become very involved in legal challenges against postsecondary institutions, and it has become arguably the most important player in this genre of purposive or ideological litigation.

ADF litigated *Christian Legal Society Chapter of the University of California, Hastings College of the Law v. Martinez (CLS)* before the U.S. Supreme Court in 2010, seeking recognition for a CLS student chapter, which bars membership of gay and lesbian students in violation of the law school's nondiscrimination policies.[29] The Alliance Defense Fund describes itself as "a servant organization that provides the resources that will keep the door open for the spread of the Gospel through the legal defense and advocacy of religious freedom, the sanctity of human life, and traditional family values," but it has increasingly focused on secular practices and policies in postsecondary institutions that it feels threaten religious free expression and conservative values. Founded in 1994, one of its first victories was bringing *Rosenberger v. Rector and Visitors of the University of Virginia,* an important 1995 Supreme Court case that assured financial support for a religious student organization newspaper at a public college.[30] The Supreme Court upheld the Ninth Circuit in *CLS,* allowing the University of California, Hastings, to deny recognition to *CLS* on the grounds that its membership policy violated the university's nondiscrimination requirements as to religion and sexual orientation. As will be seen, litigation in these purposive fields of religious accommodation and free exercise in public institutions of higher education has grown into the topic attracting the greatest attention in the recent and current higher education Supreme Court docket and shows no signs of abating.[31]

PART II

The Traditional Model of Higher Education in the Litigation Spotlight: *United States v. Fordice*

While this book examines, in case study fashion, significant higher education litigation that did not make it to the U.S. Supreme Court, on the theory that many institutional forces combine to winnow them out, I begin with a study of a 1992 case that made it through the screens: *United States v. Fordice*.[1] True, it moved at a plodding pace, over a protracted span of more than a dozen years, revealing why these types of cases are largely anachronistic in today's climate, where the likelihood of a case's being accepted is substantially greater when an organized interest group throws its weight behind a particular case by various means. *Fordice* is also an example of why it is, on balance, more difficult for minority groups to bring systemic, large-scale lawsuits seeking equity than it is for conservatives, including religious conservatives, to challenge practices to which they object. Almost by definition, asserting minority rights will likely be more difficult in a majoritarian society. The United States is overwhelmingly religious and Christian, with the result that these conservative groups find themselves not in the minority but in the substantial majority. A conservative U.S. Supreme Court and the significant political resources channeled into such a purposive, strategic, higher education litigation agenda in the last several decades have resulted in this situation, making it difficult to understand protestations about victimization and outright prejudice aimed at Christians.

As noted, many of these organizations have stolen a march on the NAACP's Legal Defense Fund, which litigated many higher education cases in the U.S. Supreme Court over its history.[2] Elementary and secondary schools are often thought of as defining "place," and the "neighborhood school" is a fixture of U.S. home buying and educational policymaking, deeply etched into tradition and realtors' steering practices. In a sense, the iconic 1954 *Brown v. Board of Education* decision was also about place—whether Linda Brown and her black classmates could attend a neighborhood school for white children, or whether they would be consigned to geographically inconvenient and physically segregated school-houses for black children that had been stigmatized as inferior.[3] And the 1955 "implementation case" of *Brown II,* mandating "all deliberate speed" was a wink and nod to the Southern judiciary, signaling that there was no need for haste in mandating desegregation.[4] Few persons, however, consider the relation-ship between higher education institutions and place. And, as is often true in the United States, the relationship had a distinctly racial character to it, subordi-nating African Americans into inferior-caste educational institutions. At the end of the day, it is difficult to categorize the result in *Fordice* as a win or a loss for the black plaintiffs, or whether it was one step forward and one back. The best face to put on this case is that black plaintiffs won the theory stage but lost in the more important political implementation phase and remedy stages.

Although *Brown* concerned primary and secondary public education, the road to *Brown* ran through several higher education cases in which black stu-dents were denied admission to predominantly white colleges and universities. In these cases, the relevant universities crucially influenced place, as states phys-ically excluded blacks from these white public spaces. In response, states went to extreme and expensive measures to maintain the barriers. They erected black colleges, started black law schools, paid for scholarships for blacks in these states to attend colleges or professional schools in other states, or required blacks to sit, eat, and study in designated segregated areas within the white university's facili-ties.[5] A stunning 1948 *New York Times* photograph shows G. W. McLaurin, the first black student to attend class at the University of Oklahoma, sitting in an anteroom adjacent to the regular classroom, separated from his white class-mates. McLaurin was further assigned "a special desk in the library and a spe-cial room in the student union building [to] eat his meals."[6] While the U.S. Su-preme Court saw through this ruse and ordered it discontinued, clearly, space counts in college, and always has.

The original 1973 *Adams v. Richardson* litigation, which required college deseg-regation, initiated widespread changes in universities' admissions policies that influenced and continues to influence the racial dynamics of universities, par-ticularly in those northern and southern states that had, over the years, main-tained dual systems of historically black and white colleges.[7] For example, all the affected states, mostly but not exclusively Southern, were required to enact "*Adams* consent decrees" that promised goals and timetables on cross-racial enrollments, so that historically black colleges had to enroll more nonblack students, while majority colleges were required to enroll more black students. Several southern states acted slowly to implement the holding, particularly the provisions addressing white institutions' need to admit black students, even though the rise of standardized testing meant that few black students could present satisfactory test scores.

Under "*Adams* consent decrees," historically black colleges also had to encourage the enrollment of white students even though few white students wanted to attend black colleges where historical resource allocations did not make the undergraduate, graduate, or professional programs of these institutions more broadly attractive. When the Supreme Court held that Mississippi had to eliminate the vestige of its dual system of public higher education in *United States v. Fordice,* the issues of remedies played out with dramatic effect in terms of place and location. The Court ordered:

> If the State perpetuates policies and practices traceable to its prior system that continue to have segregative effects—whether by influencing student enrollment decisions or by fostering segregation in other facets of the university system—and such policies are without sound educational justification and can be practicably eliminated, the State has not satisfied its burden of proving that it has dismantled its prior system. Such policies run afoul of the Equal Protection Clause, even though the State has abolished the legal requirements that whites and blacks be educated separately and has established racially neutral policies not animated by a discriminatory purpose.[8]

The district court in the case attempted on remand to apply this standard in several respects: admissions policies, program allocations, and institutional mergers.[9] Although the relationship between higher education admissions and desegregation remains one area where extensive litigation and analysis continue, *Fordice,* the 1992 Supreme Court case (by the end of the long case, the original 1975 *Ayers* case had morphed into *Fordice*), illustrates the intersection of admissions policies, race, and place. The *Fordice* case in Mississippi is important both for its status as a belated, post-*Brown* implementation ruling addressing the obligations of white and black institutions of higher education and for its value in addressing race in the context of higher education admissions. Before remanding the case, the Supreme Court had looked carefully at schools' use of test scores and the racial consequences of differential test score cutoffs. *Fordice,* therefore, is a direct predecessor to *Regents of the University of California v. Bakke,* the first Supreme Court case brought by a white plaintiff to address race in higher education admissions and the only college admissions case decided by the Supreme

Court in the twenty-five years between the 1978 *Bakke* and 2003 *Gratz v. Bollinger* and *Grutter v. Bollinger* cases.[10] In *Fordice,* the Supreme Court determined that the near-absolute reliance on standardized scores constituted a vestige of *de jure* segregation that continued to have segregative effects.

Fordice logically extended *Brown v. Board of Education* to address Mississippi's 1963 imposition of an ACT requirement. Mississippi had not employed standardized admissions tests until 1963, the year after James Meredith's widely publicized denial of admission to the University of Mississippi (UM) in 1962. By using the ACT as an entrance standard, knowing that white students in Mississippi achieved significantly higher ACT scores than black students, UM clearly undertook to provide ground cover for its failure to recruit blacks or admit them into undergraduate programs. After the *Meredith v. Fair* court ordered UM to admit Meredith, UM and several other state institutions began to require ACT test scores of 15, a number between the state's median black ACT score of 7 and the median white score of 18. The *Meredith* decision also struck down UM's requirement of recommendation letters from UM alumni that had guaranteed, for all intents and purposes, that no black students could present a complete admissions portfolio.[11]

In *Fordice,* the Supreme Court was particularly skeptical of the ACT test requirement because of the segregative history of its use in Mississippi, because the ACT was used as a sole criterion in defiance of the ACT test-maker's recommendations, and because even institutions with similar academic missions and state-designated equivalence weighted ACT scores differently. For instance, the traditionally white Mississippi University for Women used an automatic cutoff ACT admissions score of 18, but the historically black Alcorn State University and Mississippi Valley State University—also state institutions—required a minimum ACT score of 13. Thus, "those scoring 13 or 14, with some exceptions, are [generally] excluded from the five historically white universities and if they want a higher education must go to one of the historically black institutions or attend junior college with the hope of transferring to a historically white institution."[12] Justice Byron White emphasized that the lower courts had not articulated an educational justification for disparities in ACT entrance requirements or suggested whether such requirements could practicably be eliminated. He further noted that the ACT requirements were traceable to a discriminatory purpose that "seemingly continues to have segregative effects[;] the State has so far failed to show that the 'ACT-only' admissions standard is not susceptible to elimination without eroding sound educational policy."[13]

The Court remanded the case for reconsideration in light of Mississippi's affirmative duty to dismantle its formerly *de jure* segregated system of higher education.[14] Even after the district court reviewed Mississippi's plan for remediation, historically white institutions maintained their ACT requirement of 15; the historically black institutions, however, lowered the bar from a score of 13 to 11, with provisions to admit students in exceptional cases with scores as low as 9, raising questions about the likely success of such applicants. On remand, using language from *Fordice* that struck down actions that would channel students into racially identifiable institutions by their race, the district court determined that differential ACT admission standards would resegregate students by their race. The court then ordered that UM adopt Mississippi's plan, which required higher scores overall, considered students' grade point averages, implemented a transfer plan with the community college system with some open admissions with respect to test scores, and offered a summer preparatory program for remediation purposes.[15] The Fifth Circuit affirmed these remedial provisions upon appeal by the black plaintiffs but reversed the district court's holding that the use of ACT cutoff scores to award scholarships had no discriminatory purpose, finding such cutoffs traceable to *de jure* segregation.[16]

In upholding the settlement agreement eventually reached between the parties, who were supported by the United States in trying to compel desegregation of Mississippi's higher education system on the one hand and the State of Mississippi on the other, the circuit court reviewed the agreed-upon program duplication efforts and program approval policies. At the operational level, the issue was the extent to which historically black institutions would be permitted to develop high-demand and desirable specializations, such as post-baccalaureate professional schools—engineering, business, law, pharmacy—and doctoral programs. Thus, Jackson State University was awarded attractive programs in allied health professions, engineering, social work, urban planning, and business. For Alcorn State University, the legislature ordered and the court approved the establishment of an MBA graduate program.[17]

These new programs were designed to be prestigious curricular additions that might attract nonblack students, whereas whites would not otherwise be likely to attend black colleges if they had alternative opportunities in the state's traditionally white institutions. Although there had been a study to determine whether a law school or pharmacy school should be established at Jackson State University, state officials determined that existing area programs (including the Mississippi College of Law, affiliated with Mississippi College, the oldest university in the state and a Christian college, located in Jackson, the state capital) in these two prestigious fields were sufficient for Mississippi's needs and purposes. The success of these new programs, of course, depended on adequate funding, and the state agreed to appropriate more than $245 million over seventeen years to fund new programs at the three historically black institutions. The circuit court was apparently impressed by this aggregate amount, characterizing it as "generous," yet the total annual amount to be divided among the several schools and unadjusted for inflation would have been less than $5 million per college per year. Moreover, the state established an endowment for "other race" marketing and recruitment in the amount of $70 million, to be paid over the course of fourteen years, with promised "best efforts" to raise another $35 million from private sources.[18] In the best of worlds, a fully funded $105 million endowment would generate only about $4.5 million annually to be split among the three colleges. It has never been funded.

In response to the testimony that historically black institutions are better able to attract white students when the same programs are not offered at proximate institutions, the district court had previously ordered that the state consider merging traditionally white Delta State University and historically black Mississippi Valley State. The state subsequently determined, however, that such a merger was not efficacious; the district court agreed, and the state added several new academic programs to Mississippi Valley State University instead. The total amount of money for all program allocations, including capital projects, was to have been approximately $500 million over seventeen years.[19] By January 2004, virtually all the technical features of the thirty-year case had been settled, including attorneys' fees, upon the Fifth Circuit's holding that the settlement agreement approved in the district court was valid. The plaintiffs appealed their case to the Supreme Court because they had requested far more than the decree accorded them, but the Court denied certiorari.[20] At the end of the day (actually, the end of many years), the case had a tortuous provenance: several named defendants—reflecting changes in political leadership—and the full run of a complex litigation history of decisions, remands, and a contentious final settlement.

Despite the efforts in *Fordice* to address Mississippi's segregated higher education system, the decision has been criticized for its asymmetric result. In the eyes of legal scholar Alex Johnson, "*Fordice* fails to mandate equal funding for Mississippi's predominantly or historically black colleges so as to provide African-American students with an educational environment that allows them to rise above their subordinated social status as 'them' and compete with Whites on equal terms within their own black colleges."[21] Given these unequal opportunities, black students receive dissimilar educational experiences at historically black colleges, contrasted with the resources available at Mississippi's predominantly white institutions. *Fordice* also incorrectly assumes that white and black students have similar educational experiences at the same white college. Johnson notes: In deciding "that society need only provide whites and African-Americans with one [well-financed,] publicly-financed school system based on the assimilationist model"—even if both sectors were available to members of all races—the court "implicitly rejected the view that true equality can be attained by maintaining predominantly or historically black schools, perhaps out of fear that allowing predominantly or historically black colleges to exist undisturbed would legitimate the existence of all white schools."[22] This fear would be unfounded if blacks and whites had genuinely free choices to attend predominantly white or predominantly black colleges, but the state had always controlled access both by racial practices and by deracinated practices that had residual racial features in their admissions and program DNA. Moreover, predominantly white institutions in Mississippi are likely to remain predominantly white, no matter the result in *Fordice*.

More than twenty years after this critique by law professor Alex Johnson, the result of *Fordice* seems a mixed bag—both sectors have and will likely remain racially identifiable, allowing black colleges to continue but with only modestly increased resources, amounts far less than those deceptively promised in the settlement. Jackson State clearly benefited and has done so at a higher level with the additional programs and program authority. The infusion of overall resources resulting from *Fordice*, however, is unlikely to alter substantially the trajectories of any of these schools.

When this case finally wound down in 1992, a massive realignment of Mississippi higher education had not occurred, and the fundamental hierarchy and racial character of the governance of the state's public institutions remained essentially undisturbed. The case had been brought by an African American lawyer from North Mississippi Rural Legal Services (NMRLS) in Oxford, Mississippi, Alvin O. Chambliss Jr., who, a dozen years earlier, had also taken a desegregation and zoning case (*Memphis v. Greene*) to the Supreme Court.[23] However, it became clear throughout that the NMRLS was not structured to bring such a massive and unpopular public interest lawsuit, with its many complex research questions, the need for experienced and available technical expertise, and the sheer cost of this extensive litigation, especially arrayed against the deep pockets of the state of Mississippi and the U.S. government. At the conclusion of the case, as it wound down more than a decade later to the endgame of whether or not the lower court judge would order the case to be over, the courageous Chambliss, who speaks with a Southern preacher's cadence, and the Ayers family simply had to accede. Chambliss was unceremoniously fired from his agency and became *persona non grata.*

Neither a private individual nor a governmental poverty agency is a likely source of litigation against the state, as it is difficult for individuals and legal services groups to mobilize the political and organizational wherewithal required to slay the Goliath of a widespread public system of higher education. Even Mississippi's black college presidents, who stood to gain the most from a successful lawsuit that would bring them additional resources previously unavailable to their institutions, finally undercut Chambliss's legal strategy. He did not want to settle, but their unwillingness to support him in the end stages fatally and cruelly undermined the leverage he had gained as a result of the original Supreme Court victory. Immediately after *Fordice* ground to a halt, he even failed to gain permanent employment as a law professor at two historically black public law schools in other southern states where he taught in temporary positions, earning him the dubious distinction of likely being the only lawyer ever to take two cases to the U.S. Supreme Court—winning one—who could not catch on as a law professor. As of 2012, he resides in New Orleans, writing and lecturing and practicing law.[24]

The requirement of substantive organizational capacity and deep pockets in complex and comprehensive public interest litigation is one of the reasons there are so few effective legal organizations and why they must bring only the cases that will most accurately and strongly advance their ideological, political, and legislative or litigation interests. That there are no legal groups focused solely on suing or defending colleges even with such substantial litigation is testimony to the rise of the more conservative ideological, political, and religious rationales that underpin and support the more established and successful comprehensive purposive public interest firms and organizations. It is simply not possible for most solo practitioners or small nongovernmental organizations to mount a successful systemic public interest action, no matter how meritorious the potential claim, at least not in today's higher education settings or the postsecondary universe. Even the increasing number of law school clinics, which are established to teach students how to litigate in the public interest, have limitations: They cannot, in most instances, sue their home school or state, and there are increasing political restrictions, as determined either by courts that control student appearances before the bench and bar licensure or by legislators and administrators who determine that the political economy of suing entities is a bad idea, especially when well-connected and powerful corporate or business interests or state and governmental agencies are the likely defendants.[25] For all of these reasons, *U.S. v. Fordice* is a case preserved in amber, a reminder of times past.

The lack of organizations solely focused upon higher education litigation is not, of course, a crippling impediment. To be sure, many 501(c)(3) organizations support and surround higher education as an industry, representing membership interests (such as the umbrella American Council on Education), institution-type groupings (Association of American Universities, American Association of Community Colleges, American Association of Law Schools), affiliational interests (Association of Jesuit Colleges, Hispanic Association of Colleges and Universities, National Collegiate Athletic Association, the College Board), professionalized groupings of occupations (National Association of Financial Aid Administrators, National Association of College and University Attorneys, American Association of Collegiate Registrars and Admissions Officers, National Association of College and University Business Officers, American Association of University Professors). To promote national interests and agendas, these are usually either headquartered in the D.C. area or maintain offices near there. Although these groups are exclusively focused on higher education issues and constituencies and can sue (*AAUP v. Bloomfield College,* a collective bargaining and financial exigency case)[26] and be sued (*NCAA v. University of Oklahoma,* an antitrust athletics suit over sports revenue),[27] they exist primarily to provide professional representation in regulatory and legislative matters—hence the location of most in Washington, D.C.—and to advance their interests and focus on their share of the enormous higher education-industrial complex. Further, the landscape is replete with public policy foundations, think tanks, and research institutes, many of which are devoted to higher education or related educational policy.[28]

Most if not all will refer cases or enter disputes as *amici,* either in specific litigation involving higher education or in collateral issues that implicate college issues. But none exist simply to litigate higher education cases. It is clearly accurate to note that higher education regularly defends its legal interests, but there is no single organized entity or "purposive organization" that serves the explicit function as a college litigation "policy entrepreneur" in the sense that Vanessa Baird and James Q. Wilson identified the phenomenon. Baird's careful analysis of cases appearing before the Court between 1953, the year before *Brown v. Board* was decided, and 2000 did not even include higher education (or any form of education) as one of the most salient "Policy Areas" or "Categories of Parties" by which her data were grouped, although several dozen higher education cases fit into the doctrinal areas that were identified.[29]

The sum of these concerns is that there are remarkably few higher education issues that come to the attention of the actors and organizations cued to messages of approachability from the Supreme Court that possess enough salience or juice to justify the investment required to undertake a major case, even if the facts are compelling and may warrant litigation. Given the relative resources and attention that can be paid to the universe of college subject matter, it has become evident that, more often than not, it is a conservative or libertarian policy actor that has colleges in its crosshairs, a phenomenon that explains why so much of the universe of higher education litigation in the late twentieth and early twenty-first centuries has this distinctive slant. Especially prominent have been challenges to affirmative action in the broad sense and claims for increased religious accommodation.

Of course, an alternative way to characterize this landscape might be to point out that the existing system of higher education favors minority interests and excludes persons of faith from their full share of secular benefits. To crystallize the differences in worldview, consider the briefs offered by the University of California, Hastings, in the 2010 case *CLS v. Martinez,* where as defendants, they posed the question to the U.S. Supreme Court in the following manner: "Whether a public university violates the First Amendment by creating a program through which public funds, use of the school's name and logo, and other modest benefits are made available to student groups that agree to open their membership to 'any student . . . regardless of their status or beliefs,' . . . thus ensuring that all students have equal access to all school-funded and school-recognized groups."[30] In its *amicus* brief on behalf of the plaintiff Christian Legal Society, the libertarian Cato Institute succinctly summarized its view that the case was, rather, about the following issue: "Whether individuals lose their right to freedom of association when they become students at a public educational institution."[31]

In a nutshell, the competing visions in this case—one nuanced and contingent, the other blunt and straightforward—perfectly illustrate why the disputes brought against colleges by conservative groups are on the ascendancy: The higher education sector has developed over a long period of time an ethos and resultant legalized regime of nondiscrimination and affirmative action, provoked by longstanding racial discrimination and the civil rights era efforts of minority and women litigants. Conservative groups decry the tilt toward racial minorities, even while claiming their own aggrieved status, characterizing themselves as persecuted for their outlying viewpoints, or positioning themselves as marginalized because they are persons of faith. Similar arguments advanced by students of color, women, and gays in the time leading up to the 1980s and 1990s have been picked up and turned back onto campuses by the political right and by religious groups, particularly fundamentalist Christians. White applicant Allan Bakke used the Supreme Court to claim his place in the University of California, Davis Medical School in 1978,[32] just as Heman Sweatt had done to assert his claim to admission into the University of Texas Law School in 1950.[33] The irony, of course, is that the Title VI statute Bakke employed to bring his suit arose indirectly as a result of the earlier case and others in the decades-long span of civil rights legislative history. When liberal student organizations such as the Students for a Democratic Society (SDS) were denied recognition in the 1960s and then given access by 1972's *Healy v. James*,[34] the same theory was available to be advanced later in *Widmar, Rosenberger,* and *CLS* by conservative religious groups seeking what they considered to be their fair share to redress the years of their exclusion due to secular intolerance and religious bias.[35] Even with their asymmetric advantages and majoritarian status in the United States, these groups feel aggrieved and discriminated against for their years of wandering in the secular desert.[36]

In short, no longer satisfied with rendering unto Caesar, the conservative religious groups, interpreting iconic liberal decisions in their favor, have appropriated them to advance their interests. While not all the religious organizations advance the same interests or adhere to the same litigation strategy, there is clearly a coordinated and tactical strategy employing careful, incremental, deliberate choices of the cases to bring to the Court, by way of geographic and other political alternatives. *CLS* is one example, following a 2006 Seventh Circuit case (brought in order to cause a circuit split and advance the case to the Supreme Court), *CLS v. Walker,* in which the organization prevailed on its free expression and free association rights claims.[37] Another such case is *Beta Upsilon Chi Upsilon Chapter v. Machen,* a student organization recognition case in federal court, before the Northern District of Florida and then the 11th Circuit.[38] In this case, the University of Florida (UF) had over 750 registered student organizations (RSO), including 60 religious groups, of which 48 were self-identified as Christian. The university denied recognition to Beta Upsilon Chi Upsilon (BYX), a national Christian fraternity, under UF nondiscriminatory time, place, and manner regulations: "Student organizations that wish to register with the Center for Student Activities and Involvement (CSAI) must agree that they will not discriminate on the basis of race, creed, color, religion, age, disability, sex, sexual orientation, marital status, national origin, political opinions or affiliations, or veteran status as protected under the Vietnam Era Veteran's Readjustment

Assistance Act."[39] Because BYX had a membership requirement that rendered it ineligible for RSO status under the university's guidelines, it sued for the recognition and benefits that went with that status. The Court found:

> BYX is a national fraternity founded in 1985. It has twenty-two chapters in nine states. According to its constitution, it "exists for the purpose of establishing brotherhood and unity among college men based on the common bond of Jesus Christ." BYX espouses a strict approach to the Christian faith, and membership in the fraternity is contingent upon what the fraternity deems "a credible profession of faith in Jesus Christ." This requires agreement not only with the traditional core Christian beliefs and values contained in such ancient expressions as the Nicene Creed, but adherence to a demanding view of the faith. In its doctrinal statement, BYX explains that members must "believe that the Bible is God's written revelation to man, that it is inspired, authoritative, and without error in the original manuscripts." . . .
>
> BYX also demands moral and "sexual purity." According to its code of conduct, BYX believes that "sex is a gift of God to be enjoyed inside the covenant of marriage between a man and a woman. Therefore, we will not condone such activity as homosexuality, fornication, or adultery."[40]

In footnotes, the Court also noted: "BYX considers Mormons and Seventh Day Adventists [to be] non-Christians,"[41] and this "rule applies to all homosexuals irrespective of whether they have ever engaged in homosexual conduct."[42]

The university, rather than risk protracted litigation, fecklessly capitulated after the circuit oral arguments had been heard, modifying its policy to allow a religious exception: "A student organization whose primary purpose is religious will not be denied registration as a Registered Student Organization on the ground that it limits membership or leadership positions to students who share the religious beliefs of the organization. The University has determined that this accommodation of religious belief does not violate its nondiscrimination policy."[43] By the new policy, agreed to in the wake of the litigation, BYX was allowed all the benefits it had sought and was treated like any of the university's other approved RSOs.

But having won, the fraternity was not mollified. Next, it contended that the University of Florida, a state institution, had done the right thing in granting full recognition and eligibility for the resources—but for the wrong reasons. As the circuit court noted:

> BYX is not satisfied with this result, however, and urges us to reach the merits of its constitutional claims. It ardently presses us to retain jurisdiction over this case

because the University has failed to change the regulation from which the CSAI Handbook nondiscrimination policy derived: UF Regulation 6C1-1.006(1) (the "Regulation"). Furthermore, BYX is troubled by UF's timing. It contends that "the timing of [UF's] motion to dismiss [this appeal] indicates that *it is motivated not by a genuine change of heart but rather by a desire to avoid liability.*" We are not concerned with UF's motivation for changing its registration policy, but only with whether a justiciable controversy exists. Finding that BYX has received the relief sought in its complaint, we reject its request that we reach its constitutional claims and dismiss this case, as we no longer possess jurisdiction.[44]

Thurgood Marshall may well have wished that the University of Texas Law School in 1950 had behaved better and that the NAACP Legal Defense Fund had not been required to spend precious resources bringing *Sweatt v. Painter* to have its client admitted into the real University of Texas Law School, not the inferior makeshift version that the state had offered in the alternative. But once he won the case and Heman Sweatt was admitted, Marshall neglected to go back to the courts to ensure that UT applied the ruling with a better attitude or "genuine change of heart." This extraordinary line of BYX reasoning, even when a mainstream Christian group had already prevailed on the merits of the case in federal court, shows the extent to which such organizations are on a crusade or jihad and will settle not for mere accommodation or even tolerance, but for no less than winning hearts and minds—and then only according to their own, narrow terms.

Moreover, the LDF would never have litigated that Homer Plessy was not fully black and was therefore, on that basis, entitled to sit in New Orleans public transportation's whites-only sections, nor would it have reasoned that Colin Powell was not African American for affirmative action purposes because his people were from the Caribbean rather than from Africa. It surely has come as a shock to Mormons (after all, members of the "Church of Jesus Christ of Latter-day Saints"), Seventh-day Adventists, and other Protestant faiths that a "Christian" fraternity has expelled them from Eden and deemed them ineligible for CLS or BYX membership. And it begs the extremely troubling question of who is entitled to trademark Christianity or to dictate who is a Christian. Or, for that matter, who is gay or lesbian. As became evident in the Republican presidential primaries in 2011–12, candidate Mitt Romney's Mormon faith became a major bone of contention with evangelical and conservative Christians, some of whom engaged in ugly public displays of intolerance.[45]

Legal scholar Erwin Chemerinsky in his incisive 2010 book *The Conservative Assault on the Constitution,* taking note of the Christian demographics in the

United States, where most persons profess a religious preference—for the over-whelming majority, Christian—has summarized:

> The increasingly conservative Supreme Court has been undermining the rights of religious minorities. The Court has narrowly interpreted the protection of free exercise of religion in the First Amendment and has said that religious minorities must rely upon the [Christian] majority through the democratic processes for protection of their religious freedom. The conservative majority on the Court [which in 2012 includes six Catholics and three Jews] is on the verge of largely leaving the limits on the establishment of religion to the political process. The court is jeopardizing the central vision of the religious clauses in the First Amendment that protect religious minorities in their free exercise of religion and assure a separation of church and state.[46]

These conservative, religious, and restrictionist pressures will likely increase. Organized interests regularly monitor educational programs and benefits that appear to have gender or racial/ethnic restrictions, and groups such as the Center for Individual Rights and the Center for Equal Opportunity will continue to challenge programs that single out underrepresented students. As a result, many institutions have folded their tents and abandoned their modest equity efforts, even in colleges that have had very few minority initiatives or successful programs. For example, Texas A&M University, a school that chose not to implement *Grutter v. Bollinger* in admissions, even after *Hopwood v. Texas* had been reversed by the U.S. Supreme Court and even after establishing a long record of historical underachievement in a state with rapidly increasing minority populations, was sued by CIR over a small, HHS/NIH/USDA-funded summer minority apprenticeship program. Texas A&M University settled before trial and agreed to discontinue the effort. CIR filed a similar action to end a journalism program at Virginia Commonwealth University, intimidating the institution into pulling the plug on its small minority summer journalism program, partially funded by a foundation.[47] In 2005, the Center for Equal Opportunity convinced the U.S. Department of Justice to sue minority fellowship programs at Southern Illinois University (SIU), and SIU blinked, dismantling the minority-specific programs, including one that had received federal funding from the National Science Foundation.[48] Coincidentally, the same year, SIU was also the defendant in another Christian Legal Society case, in which the SIU Law School lost at the Seventh Circuit and chose not to appeal to SCOTUS.[49] For CIR, FIRE, CEO, and similar conservative purposive organizations, no minority child is to be left behind—nor a program serving them.

Conservative advocacy groups also set their sights even on programs such as the 1997 Texas Top Ten Percent program, a race-neutral initiative that granted automatic admission to public colleges and universities for the state's graduating students who were in the top 10 percent of their classes. When Texas A&M University surfaced a plan to extend its admissions percentage to 20 percent, beyond that required of all state colleges and universities, the Center for Equal Opportunity (CEO) and the American Civil Rights Institute (organizers of the California anti-affirmative action Prop. 209) kicked up so much dust that Texas A&M backed away, even though there was no legal prohibition against the university if it had chosen to do so.[50] The state statute was a percentage floor, not a ceiling. Indeed, some public colleges and universities in Texas *have* extended their automatic admissions criteria (required by statute for all institutions to be set at 10 percent) to 20 percent, just as Texas A&M had considered doing. The conservative opposition to affirmative action is so reflexive, automatic, and pervasive that these organizations have sought to dismantle race-neutral plans that also assist white students and that do not use racial classifications—just because they look like traditional race-based affirmative action or were enacted as legitimate responses to previous challenges based on race—as the Texas Top Ten Percent Plan was a deracinated response to *Hopwood*. And some courts have stoked this fire, as in *Fisher v. UT*, where the Fifth Circuit upheld the lower court decision and the constitutionality of the state's Top Ten Percent plan—but with obvious reluctance:

> The Top Ten Percent Law was adopted to increase minority enrollment. That it has done, but its sweep of admissions is a polar opposite of the holistic focus upon individuals. Its internal proxies for race end-run the Supreme Court's studied structure for the use of race in university admissions decisions. It casts aside testing historically relied upon, admitting many top ten percent minorities with significantly lower scores than rejected minorities and nonminorities alike. That these admitted minorities are academically able to remain in the University does not respond to the reality that the Top Ten Percent Law eliminated the consideration of test scores, and correspondingly reduced academic selectivity, to produce increased enrollment of minorities. Such costs may be intrinsic to affirmative action plans. If so, *Grutter* at least sought to minimize those costs through narrow tailoring. The Top Ten Percent Law is anything but narrow.
>
> In short, while the Top Ten Percent Law appears to succeed in its central purpose of increasing minority enrollment, it comes at a high cost and is at best a blunt tool for securing the educational benefits that diversity is intended to achieve.

We cannot fault UT's contention that the Top Ten Percent Law is plainly not the sort of workable race-neutral alternative that would be a constitutionally mandated substitute for race-conscious university admissions policies. We are keenly aware that the University turned to the Top Ten Percent Law in response to a judicial ruling. Yet we cannot agree that it is irrelevant. To the contrary, that the Top Ten Percent Law, accounting for the vast majority of in-state admissions, threatens to erode the foundations UT relies on to justify implementing *Grutter* policies is a contention not lacking in force. "Facially neutral" has a talismanic ring in the law, but it can be misleading. It is here.[51]

Thoughtful readers will note the exquisite irony in the circuit's abject and bothersome reluctance to accept *Grutter* and the percentage plan, inasmuch as it was the Fifth Circuit decision in *Hopwood* that occasioned the eventual percentage plan, that arrogated to itself the determination that *Bakke* no longer applied, and that held affirmative action to be dead. It is truly extraordinary that this circuit would lament the appearance of a legitimate and deracinated admissions remedy and chafe under the nonracial policy, even after the stinging rebuke that *Grutter* represented.

In a sense, this line of judicial reasoning is breathtaking, for it was not the University of Texas that created the percentage plan but the Texas Legislature and the sitting governor, George W. Bush. The court gets this provenance wrong ("We are keenly aware that the University turned to the Top Ten Percent Law in response to a judicial ruling") and misplaces the governance of admissions policy in the state. Moreover, the percentage plan was so successful that its numbers grew to more than two-thirds of each entering UT-Austin full-time, first-time freshman class. Considering that judges must regularly determine whether policies are narrowly tailored, it is disconcerting that the court finds the straightforward percent plan to be "anything but narrow." At the urging of the campus, in 2009 the legislature revised and "narrowed" the statute to accommodate fewer such students so that more students could be admitted from conventional pathways.[52] This legislative change was enacted, despite UT-Austin's own data and other scholarly research indicating that percentage plan students had lower attrition rates than freshmen enrolled outside the plan, due to a narrative of crowding and loss of control over admissions policy.[53]

And there is a convergence with nativists and immigration restrictionists in their higher education efforts, particularly among groups that oppose comprehensive immigration reform or who lobby against the regularization of undocumented immigrants and programs that address undocumented college students.

Immigration reform is a complex subject, where reasonable persons can disagree about the scope of the problem, the principles that are affected, and the legislative remedies that may be enacted—chiefly, that the parents of these children may not have "clean hands" and may have violated federal immigration law to bring their children to this country without authorization or, while in this status, gave birth to U.S. citizen children.

But the rhetorical devices used to characterize this phenomenon are significantly disproportionate to the small number of such undocumented college students.[54] No study has ever revealed more than 50,000 to 60,000 such students enrolled in the entire country, even with accommodations by major receiver states, such as resident tuition for long-term but undocumented high school graduates who enroll in public colleges.[55] Even in California and Texas, the two largest states *and* the states with the largest number of immigrants, a small percentage of all enrollments were found to be undocumented; in both states, the legislation designed to accommodate undocumented students and accord them in-state tuition has also been widely used by citizens. Yet restrictionist lawyers have attempted in both states and elsewhere to strike down the statutes that had been enacted under federal law.[56]

These nativist efforts have been unavailing, as have similar efforts in other states with even fewer undocumented college students, but such litigation has been brought by the same conservative groups. This record shows the extent to which they are purposive organizations, with aims to reform higher education's progressive strains.[57] For example, successful efforts to enact tuition legislation in Wisconsin in 2009 and Maryland in 2011 have been reversed and halted: In the former case, fewer than two hundred students had used the provisions in the Wisconsin campuses when the two-year-old law was overturned by Republican Governor Scott Walker, who made national news in 2011 by rescinding benefits to unionized state workers.[58] In Maryland, a ballot measure introduced for the voters to decide whether to rescind the just-enacted Maryland tuition measure "froze" the statute until the voters could weigh in.[59] In California, when Governor Jerry Brown signed AB131 into law in late 2011, according state financial aid to undocumented college students, efforts began immediately to recall him and to put the issue on a ballot measure in the hopes of rescinding the law.[60]

Until there is comprehensive immigration reform, this issue will likely leach into discussions of educational equity and access for immigrant students and will remain a focus of conservative and restrictionist organizations. It is for these institutional reasons of limited resources and a vacuum in purposive organizations devoted exclusively to higher education law cases that such matters on the Supreme Court's agenda will be relatively few. But it is due to the intensity and focus of the litigation policy entrepreneurs that such college cases will be advanced and cultivated, aided by the infrastructure of well-resourced conservative study groups and policy institutes.[61] The thread that knits together many of the concerns of these groups is their continued insistence that race no longer matters and that 1954's *Brown* settled the issue once and for all, notwithstanding the massive resistance and visceral opposition by whites to the ruling at the K–12 and college levels. Given the circumstance of an African American U.S. president in office since 2008, these groups point to what they consider to be postracial progress and an unnecessary multicultural polity, desiderata they insist are their major concern and ones that, they believe, are the proper legacy of the civil rights movement. To counter this false and misleading perception of colorblindness, law professors Mario L. Barnes, Erwin Chemerinsky, and Trina Jones have noted:

> One could argue that racially disparate outcomes [in educational opportunity] might be expected given that there is no fundamental right to an education in this country, and that education funding is often tied to a local tax base—a factor that exploits the interconnectedness of race, geography and poverty. As such, it is not clear to what extent race versus other factors—including socioeconomic class or parental educational levels—contributes to disparities in educational attainment. Part of the educational attainment deficit, however, is likely tied to the "achievement gap." With this measure, critics have long claimed that both cultural bias and teacher expectations have hindered the performance of certain students of color.
>
> For the purposes of this Essay, we need not establish that racial disparities are proof of race-based discrimination, especially in the area of education where affirmative action may still be practiced. The point is that if we ignore these disparities—as recent Supreme Court cases and voter initiatives suggest we do—then these numbers will only worsen.[62]

Law professor Girardeau A. Spann, even more critical, calls out such critics and legal structures as protectors of white privilege:

> The Supreme Court has not only refused to recognize the legitimacy of disparate impact claims for constitutional purposes, but its recent *Ricci* decision seems intent on nullifying congressional disparate impact claims for statutory purposes as well. Because it is difficult to imagine a non invidious explanation for the Court's resistance to such a seemingly sensible precommitment strategy, one cannot help

but marvel at the genius of the regime that the culture has created for ensuring the preservation of white privilege. Although the institution of judicial review is sometimes viewed as reflecting an effort to ensure that our transitory baser motives are not permitted to override the more admirable values that are possessed by our better selves, in the context of race the Supreme Court appears to be serving precisely the opposite function. The Supreme Court seems to be the structural institution on which we rely to ensure that our transitory desires to promote racial equality are not permitted to override the less admirable value of white privilege that is possessed by our baser selves.[63]

Of course, not all of these conservative purposive groups are religiously oriented, but there is substantial overlap in their agendas, particularly their arrogation of victim status and their disdain for affirmative action. They appear to want to eradicate one regime (the progressive racial artifices) and to install another ("colorblind" and conservative values), to remove affirmative action, and to institute religious accommodation and mainstream Christian religious primacy as the legal ethos. This is why these groups are so easily able to appropriate the language and argot of civil rights but more importantly, also to appropriate the tactics and legal theories, however ironic and asymmetrical. And the groups reinforce and provide technical support to each other. Legal and human resources scholar Barbara A. Lee characterizes these "external groups" variously as "issue-oriented," "watchdog," and "advocacy" organizations that are increasingly "seeking to impose their agenda on colleges and universities."[64] As primary actors in the cultural and administrative state, colleges and universities will always have a place in traditional agenda-setting priorities and will claim their share of the polity's attention—and so will noncollege cases arising in other contexts that will have many implications for colleges, especially those involving employment discrimination and free speech.[65] Indeed, one of the cases with a profound effect on colleges is proving to be *Garcetti v. Ceballos*, the California case involving public speech and the protected interests of public employees such as lawyers working for district attorneys, which has begun to be used against faculty performing their teaching and writing duties who, if removed, will find themselves to have limited recourse.[66] As we shall see in chapter 10, *Garcetti* is a sword that will cut against both conservative and progressive faculty. If this thesis is correct, the cases that do come before the Court in the rough count of college litigation will likely be relatively few but will reveal far-reaching cultural, religious, and governance significance. And these disputes will likely be litigated and supported by conservative purposive organizations seeking to extend free religious exercise further than is evident even at the present, but only for the chosen few: Christians, whites, and conservatives.

One additional layer to this intersection of conservative political thought and evangelical Christian legal action is the longstanding cultural war that reactionary academic actors have waged, one that has been funded largely by conservative think tanks, educational organizations, and foundations. Intellectual historian Ellen Schrecker, who wrote critically of the ineffectiveness liberal groups showed in the face of McCarthyism in the 1950s, when the American Association of University Professors (AAUP) failed to mount aggressive campaigns against the systematic purging of academics tarred with Communism or other perfidies, has turned her attention to the ambitious sweep of the conservative backlash against liberal pieties in the academy since the 1960s:

> The right-wing foundations also subsidized organizations that challenged the supposed radical domination of the academy. Established in 1987, the National Association of Scholars claimed to represent those allegedly suppressed right-wingers within the professoriate who were upholding "what is admirable about Western civilization" and standing fast against such intellectual remnants of the 1960s as feminism, multiculturalism, and revisionist history. The NAS also opposed affirmative action, as did some other organizations (also funded by Olin et al.) that litigated against preferential admissions for minority groups. In a related area, the libertarian Foundation for Individual Rights in Education (FIRE) fought against the speech codes designed to make campuses more welcoming to women and people of color—a campaign that supported academic freedom but also undermined public support for higher education. And then there's the American Council of Trustees and Alumni (ACTA), founded in 1995 by Lynne Cheney and Senator Joseph Lieberman to encourage donors, trustees, and policy makers to take a more active role in pressing for such academic "reforms" as the restoration of the traditional curriculum.

> What is so striking about this conservative campaign against the academy is how self-conscious it was. In a 1989 speech at the Heritage Foundation, a former Reagan official openly acknowledged that he and his colleagues were seriously engaged in "a counteroffensive on that last Leftist redoubt, the college campus." That counteroffensive has paid off handsomely. Not only has the nation's intellectual discourse shifted noticeably to the Right, but by the time the mainstream media was promoting the so-called "political correctness" controversy in the late 1980s, the professoriate's reputation was in tatters. As the current economic crisis

intensifies the financial plight of the nation's colleges and universities, that loss of status has been devastating.[67]

Like water slowly and eventually eroding the Grand Canyon, this demonization of the American professoriate has taken its toll, especially as the corporatization of the postsecondary sector continues to erode public support for higher education. The organized legal right, brilliantly seizing on this opportunity, has managed to transform its majoritarian features into victimhood and special pleading.[68] As public support has declined, so has the cost of college escalated, at a time when applications are at an all-time high. The result has been a cascading disaster of overenrolled public institutions and extraordinarily competitive elite colleges. It is difficult to operationalize affirmative action, to take one example, when the spaces are so precious and when the cost of attendance is beyond most families' reach can accomplish the same end. One need not be of a conspiratorial bent to see the many facets at play and the many interlocking features.

Hopwood v. Texas: "A University May Properly Favor One Applicant Over Another Because of His Ability to Play the Cello, Make a Downfield Tackle, or Understand Chaos Theory"

Courts have decided a surprising number of college admissions cases in decisions that have turned largely but not exclusively on the American trope of race. Before the landmark 1978 Supreme Court case of *Regents of the University of California v. Bakke,* these cases included the postsecondary forerunners to *Brown v. Board of Education* and several college cases that followed *Brown.*[1] In the post-*Brown* cases, intransigent whites actively resisted college desegregation, manipulated admissions criteria to deny college or professional school admissions to minority applicants, or claimed that *Brown* was limited to public elementary and secondary schools. Since *DeFunis v. Odegaard,* a case that was dismissed as moot by the U.S. Supreme Court in 1974, causing a well-known dissent by Justice Douglas,[2] college admissions cases have largely concerned white challenges to practices that appear to favor minorities. The 1978 decision in *Bakke* has become an almost totemic holding, one that has been invoked in settings that range well beyond medical school admissions, from governmental set-asides for minority contractors and highway guardrails to 4H club membership rules. However, *Bakke*—which held that set-asides are unlawful in admissions but that race may be used as a "plus" factor—is still under assault, even though its holistic review procedures were affirmed by the Supreme Court in 2003's *Grutter v. Bollinger.*[3]

Many conservative commentators and a number of judges have acted as if *Bakke* had no continuing validity. In *Hopwood v. Texas,* a panel of the Fifth Circuit struck down a University of Texas Law School (UTLS) admissions program that had given preferences to black and Chicano applicants. The panel concluded that *Bakke* was no longer the law of the land and that it had been overruled *sub silentio* by the Supreme Court in a series of affirmative action cases. However, the Supreme Court had not overturned *Bakke,* notwithstanding its decisions in a trio of affirmative action cases: *City of Richmond v. J. A. Croson Co.*, *Metro Broadcasting, Inc. v. Federal Communications Commission*, and *Adarand Constructors, Inc. v. Pena*.[4] In a thorough review of these cases and of the argument contending that *Bakke* having been overruled explicitly or implicitly, Akhil Reed Amar and Neal Katyal summarized: "Since *Adarand* overruled *Metro Broadcasting* in part, and *Metro Broadcasting* relied upon *Bakke*, does this mean that the Court has overruled Bakke? No. The Court, we repeat, nowhere explicitly overruled *Bakke*, and so, under well established general principles, it clearly remains binding precedent for all lower courts, state and federal."[5]

By their reasoning, *Metro Broadcasting* was overruled by *Adarand* only insofar as it was " 'inconsistent' with the holding that 'strict scrutiny is the proper standard for analysis of all racial classifications, whether imposed by federal, state, or local actors.' "[6] Although the *Adarand* court held that minority set-aside contracting programs enacted by Congress were subject to strict scrutiny, it did not address the diversity premise of *Bakke*. One member of the *Hopwood* panel who voted to strike down UTLS's affirmative action admissions program demurred at considering *Bakke* to be lifeless: "If *Bakke* is to be declared dead, the Supreme Court, not a three-judge panel of a circuit court, should make that pronouncement."[7] He may not have wanted to declare the 1978 ruling dead by saying so, even if he were clearly considering the decision to turn it into a corpse.

Exactly how far did *Bakke* reach? How had judges ruled in admissions cases since 1978? Inasmuch as *Bakke* endorsed the Harvard admissions program for achieving diversity, was affirmative action permissible under the right circumstances? After all these years, and after *Grutter* upheld the earlier case in the University of Michigan's Law School admissions program,[8] and after *Gratz*, which applied to the Michigan undergraduate program,[9] it is still instructive to review *Bakke* and a sample of its progeny on this issue. In addition, a review of undergraduate admissions cases sheds light on the employment of standardized tests and other admissions measures in graduate and professional schools. Finally, looking carefully at these cases reveals how complex the admissions decision-making process is; many applicants and judges mistakenly assume that the process is simple, that individuals vie against other individuals in a joust-like tournament or that the use of modest racial criteria displaces many whites. My review reveals the complexities of the admissions process and shows how admissions criteria have been, and in some instances still are, racial gatekeepers to higher education.

In *Regents of the University of California v. Bakke*, white applicant Allan Bakke submitted his credentials for both the 1973 and 1974 hundred-member medical school classes at the University of California at Davis (UC-D). After a review of his admissions portfolio and "benchmark scores," which included his undergraduate grade point average, his standardized MCAT score, and his letters of recommendation, the UC-D committee chose to deny him admission both to the eighty-four general admissions places and to the sixteen affirmative action places reserved for applicants who were members of underrepresented groups.

After he was denied admission for the second year in a row, Bakke sued in California state court on the grounds that his equal protection rights had been violated and that UC-D had violated Title VI of the 1964 Civil Rights Act in maintaining the racially separate admissions policies. The trial court found for Bakke, holding that UC-D's separate admissions process was an unconstitutional racial quota and that his federal and state constitutional rights had been violated, as had his Title VI rights. However, because he could not show that he would have been admitted even if the separate admissions program had not existed, the trial court did not order that he be admitted to the medical school.[10]

He then appealed to the California Supreme Court, which did not rule on his state constitutional or federal statutory rights but did find that the UC-D program had violated his equal protection rights. The court also shifted the burden of proof regarding admissions, finding that UC-D had failed to show that, even in the absence of the minority program, Bakke would *not* have been admitted. The court held that race could not be used as an admissions criterion, and he was ordered to be admitted to the medical school.[11]

The U.S. Supreme Court granted certiorari and, in a complex and frustrating opinion, affirmed in part and reversed in part. The Court held that racial setasides such as the UC-D sixteen-seat plan could not operate lawfully, but the Court also held that race could be used as one of several factors in admissions. Justice Lewis Powell's opinion attracted the votes of Justices John Paul Stevens, William Rehnquist, and Potter Stewart and Chief Justice Warren Burger for the former holding,[12] and the votes of Justices William Brennan, Thurgood Marshall, Byron White, and Harry Blackmun for the latter. Justice Powell was the swing vote for each 5–4 holding, and he also affirmed that Bakke should be admitted to the UC-D medical school.[13]

The *Bakke* decision, particularly Part V-C, had lasted nearly two decades before *Hopwood,* and the Court's view on the permissibility of racial factors in admissions had held sway in judicial opinions and institutional practice. Following its mid-1980s attempt to rule out minority scholarships, even the George H. W. Bush administration beat a hasty retreat, citing *Bakke.*[14] Part V-C reads: "In enjoining [UC-D] from ever considering the race of any applicant, however, the courts below failed to recognize that the State has a substantial interest that legitimately may be served by a properly devised admissions program involving the competitive consideration of race and ethnic origin. For this reason, so much of the California court's judgment as enjoins [UC-D] from any consideration of the race of any applicant must be reversed."[15]

Further, Justice Powell identified the admissions criteria that could appropriately further this "substantial interest" in diversity: "The file of a particular black applicant may be examined without the factor of race being decisive when compared, for example, with that of an applicant identified as an Italian-American if the latter is thought to exhibit qualities more likely to promote beneficial pluralism. Such qualities could include exceptional personal talents, unique work or service experience, leadership potential, maturity, demonstrated compassion, a history of overcoming disadvantage, ability to communicate with the poor, or other qualifications deemed important."[16]

In addition, the four Justices who joined Justice Powell in supporting racial criteria as one part of a comprehensive admissions plan would have upheld even the UC-D plan. The program "[did] not, for example, establish an exclusive preserve for minority students apart from and exclusive of Whites. Rather, its purpose is to overcome the effects of segregation by bringing the races together."[17]

In their review of *Bakke* and more recent Supreme Court cases concerning affirmative action, Amar and Katyal concluded: "Our survey of the post-*Bakke* affirmative action cases will demonstrate an important distinction between contracts and schools. We want to persuade readers that a wall between these two domains exists, and that this wall—at the base of *Bakke*—has not collapsed under the weight of the various post-*Bakke* contracting cases."[18] Whether *Bakke* "hangs by a thread" or will have continued vitality and precedential value, it remains the touchstone case for college and graduate/professional school admissions, and its endorsement of racial and ethnic criteria as a part of selective admissions has driven this process since 1978 in public and private colleges and universities. If it were overruled, minority admissions and financial aid programs for nearly every college and graduate or professional school in the country would be affected.

As will become evident from the following review of other postsecondary admissions cases, no other criterion—even the alluring concepts of class and income preferences—delivers more efficacious racial results than does race itself. There is no good proxy, no more narrowly tailored criterion, no statistical treatment that can replace race. A movement away from *Bakke*, therefore, would have been likely to deracinate the admissions and financial aid processes, even in communities where racial minorities have become the plurality or majority populations. Meanwhile, in some special settings such as historically black institutions of higher education, whites who find themselves to be racial "minorities" or "historically underrepresented" students have access to court-ordered scholarships at the same time that black-only or minority scholarships have been struck down by courts.[19]

In the 1970s and 1980s, Texas and other southern states had to follow the court order in *Adams v. Richardson* that required the federal government to monitor postsecondary institutions more aggressively and to enforce Title VI at the collegiate level.[20] As a result of increased federal enforcement in the 1990s, Texas—like other *Adams* states—was required to produce a remedial plan that would increase the college enrollment of black and Latino Texans. UTLS's efforts to recruit black and Latino applicants led directly to *Hopwood*.

In 1971, UTLS did not admit a single black applicant, and it admitted only a handful of Mexican Americans. In order to increase the number of minority applicants and to give "fuller consideration"—that is, a full-file review extending beyond the stark numbers of the undergraduate grade point average and LSAT score—UTLS began to read its applications from minority and white disadvantaged students separately. By 1992, UTLS was attracting more high-scoring minority applicants than it had in 1971 and had developed a complex system of review that functionally resembled the original UC-D admissions process in *Bakke*: two separate admissions processes—one for blacks and Mexican Americans and one for whites. UTLS assigned a different "presumptive admission" score for each process. For whites, that score was a combined LSAT/UGPA index of 192; for minority applicants, it was 179. Moreover, all minority applicants, regardless of their LSAT/UGPA index scores, were reviewed by the "minority subcommittee"—but some white applicants who fell below a certain LSAT/ UGPA index score were not reviewed. Although there were no minority set-aside places, a provision that the *Bakke* Court had rejected, UTLS invited trouble by having a separate decisionmaking process for minority applicants and different admissions decisionmakers and standards for minority applicants than it was using for white applicants.

In 1992, Cheryl Hopwood and three other white plaintiffs applied for admission to UTLS. Hopwood's UGPA of 3.8 and LSAT of 39 (83rd percentile) gave her a combined index score of 199, which placed her in the "presumptive admit" category. (By this time, the Law School Admissions Council had re-normed and re-numbered LSAT scores on a different scale.) However, because she attended an undergraduate institution that the chair of the admissions committee considered "non-competitive" (California State University-Sacramento), the chair moved her from the "presumptive admit" category to the "discretionary" category. When Hopwood did not receive enough committee votes to move her application higher in the queue of applicants, she was offered a place on the waiting list. She ultimately was not admitted from the waiting list, nor were the other three white applicant plaintiffs.[21]

The district court judge first held that *Bakke* was the controlling precedent: "Absent an explicit statement from the Supreme Court overruling *Bakke*, this Court finds, in the context of the law school's admissions process, [that] obtaining the educational benefits that flow from a racially and ethnically diverse student body remains a sufficiently compelling interest to support the use of racial classifications."[22] To the extent that the UTLS process accorded extra points to minority applicants, he found the process to be constitutional. However, because the four plaintiffs were compared only with other white applicants and not with the entire group of applicants, the judge found that the process was not narrowly tailored and thus violated the plaintiffs' equal protection rights.

Although he struck down UTLS's original admissions process, which UTLS changed after the start of the litigation, the judge declined to order UTLS to admit the plaintiffs. He found that white applicants had been admitted with very low indices, that many whites with indices lower than Hopwood's had been admitted, and that the number of whites admitted in this fashion exceeded the total number of minorities admitted. He awarded one dollar in damages to each plaintiff and ordered that they be allowed to reapply without any charge the following year, noting: "The Court simply cannot find from a preponderance of the evidence that the plaintiffs would have been offered admission [even] under a constitutional system."[23]

The Fifth Circuit panel saw it differently. Judge Jerry E. Smith, writing for the majority, rejected *Bakke*'s diversity rationale and called Justice Powell's holding a "lonely opinion."[24] The majority opinion read *Bakke* as having no bearing on *Hopwood*: "Justice Powell's view in *Bakke* is not binding precedent on this issue [of diversity as an acceptable goal]. While he announced the judgment, no other Justice joined in that part of the opinion discussing the diversity rationale. In *Bakke*, the word 'diversity' is mentioned nowhere except in Justice Powell's single-Justice opinion."[25] Further, the panel interpreted the Supreme Court's subsequent decisions in *Adarand*, *Wygant*, and *Croson* to mean that *Bakke* either "[did] not express a majority view" or that it was "questionable as binding precedent."[26] They then reached this sweeping conclusion, cleverly wording it as if their hands were tied: "Accordingly, we see the caselaw as sufficiently established that the use of ethnic diversity simply to achieve racial heterogeneity, even as part of the consideration of a number of factors, is unconstitutional. Were we to decide otherwise, we would contravene precedent that we are not authorized to challenge."[27] Thus, they ruled that even the revised UTLS program, which the district judge held to be constitutional, was unconstitutional for relying upon "diversity" as it did: "We do note that even if a 'plus' system were permissible, it likely would be impossible to maintain such a system without degeneration into nothing more than a 'quota' program."[28]

In his special concurrence, the third panel member, Judge Jacques Wiener, agreed that the revised program was unconstitutional, finding that it was not narrowly tailored. However, he disagreed that race as a single criterion among many could not be used for diversity reasons: "I would assume *arguendo* that diversity can be a compelling interest but conclude that the admissions process here under scrutiny was not narrowly tailored to achieve diversity." He also scolded his colleagues for their overreaching: "[The panel's] conclusion may well be a defensible extension of recent Supreme Court precedent. . . . Be that as it may, this position remains an extension of the law—one that . . . is both overly broad and unnecessary to the disposition of this case. . . . [I]f *Bakke* is to be declared dead, the Supreme Court, not a three-judge panel of a circuit court, should make that pronouncement."[29]

Despite the clear invitation to do so and increase the chances of the Supreme Court to take up the affront, the Fifth Circuit declined to take up the case *en banc,* or as a whole. Yet the U.S. Supreme Court denied certiorari in 1996, with terse language from Justices Ginsburg and Souter declaring that the whole case had been moot because UTLS had abandoned the original program under which Hopwood and the others had been considered.[30] This left the two-judge panel (with the concurring judge) as the authority for the Fifth Circuit.

The states of Louisiana and Mississippi, the other two Fifth Circuit states, were involved in litigation concerning the desegregation of their own public higher education institutions and so were not bound by *Hopwood.* Moreover, the Texas attorney general had advised his client colleges to expand *Hopwood*'s admissions decision to minority scholarships, leading public and private colleges as well as state agencies to dismantle or reorganize their minority scholarships and targeted financial assistance programs.[31]

Was Judge Wiener correct? Did the two-judge panel overreach? Can a circuit court declare a Supreme Court decision overturned? The simple answer is that it cannot. First, neither a panel nor a full circuit can expressly overrule the Supreme Court; for *Hopwood* to have effect, it had to treat *Bakke* as explicitly or *sub silentio* no longer in force. Second, to the extent that *Hopwood* might have controlled, it would have done so only in the narrow area of college admissions. There was no precedent to extend it to minority scholarships, as the Texas attorney general did, following *Hopwood.* Unlike the Texas attorney general in this instance, attorneys general in most states strive hard to narrow decisions and to contain damage done to state agencies or institutions, if any. Indeed, the Texas attorney general's expansive reading of *Hopwood* led another state's attorney general to apply *Hopwood* to his college clients even though the clients were in another circuit.[32] It also prompted virtually every public and private college in Texas and also the state's postsecondary agency (the Texas Higher Education Coordinating Board) to dismantle longstanding and legally unchallenged financial aid programs, including some established by the legislature with proper statutory foundation.

By selectively citing from Supreme Court opinions in *Croson* and *Adarand,* the Fifth Circuit panel of Judges Smith and DeMoss treated *Bakke* as either overruled or nonbinding. This is an incorrect reading of *Bakke,* and it poisoned the reasoning that flows from it. In Part V-C of *Bakke,* in which Justices Brennan, Blackmun, Marshall, and White joined, thus constituting a five-Justice majority, Justice Powell wrote: "In enjoining [UC-D] from ever considering the race of any applicant, . . . the courts below failed to recognize that the State has a substantial interest that legitimately may be served by a properly devised admissions program involving the competitive consideration of race and ethnic origin. For this reason, so much of the California court's judgment as enjoins [UC-D] from any consideration of the race of any applicant must be reversed."[33] In Part V-A, Justice Powell explained that the "substantial interest" was diversity; in Part IV-D, he asserted that admitting a "diverse student body . . . clearly is a constitutionally permissible goal for an institution of higher education. . . . [I]t is not too much to say that the 'nation's future depends upon leaders trained through wide exposure' to the ideas and mores of students as diverse as this Nation of many peoples."[34]

Although the two-judge panel treated the *Bakke* holding (derisively termed Justice Powell's "lonely opinion") as questionable precedent, the U.S. Supreme Court at that time had neither overturned *Bakke* nor accepted for review any higher education affirmative action case since its 1978 decision in *Bakke.* Justice O'Connor, in her concurring opinion in *Wygant,* noted that "although its precise contours are uncertain, a state interest in the promotion of racial diversity has been found sufficiently 'compelling,' at least in the context of higher education, to support the use of racial considerations in furthering that interest."[35]

In the Fifth Circuit's *Hopwood* opinion, Judges Smith and DeMoss simply omitted mention of Part V-C, the authentic, five-member central opinion, and ignored its "substantial interest" holding. Moreover, in *Adarand*, Justice O'Connor had held, "When race-based action is necessary to further a compelling interest, such action is within the constitutional constraints if it satisfies the 'narrow tailoring' test this Court has set out in previous cases."[36] These holdings hardly sounded like the death knell for well-crafted admissions programs, which proved to be the case in *Grutter* (in which the Court upheld the University of Michigan's law school affirmative action plan) as well as in *Gratz*, which struck down another type of plan, but also revealed that nuance and narrow tailoring were being applied to different admissions approaches, even in the same institution.

While the *Hopwood* panel misread *Bakke* and struck down the UTLS racial admissions criteria, its opinion was even more curious for the criteria it *would* have allowed. In its laundry list of acceptable criteria, the panel judges would allow alumni privilege, which they termed the applicant's "relationship to school alumni"[37]; they also concluded that a college could consider "whether an applicant's parents attended college" (a first-generation preference).[38] In the context of UTLS, consider these two criteria: one that rewards applicants fortunate enough to have parents who were allowed to attend the law school, and one that rewards applicants who were fortunate enough, in this narrow sense, to have parents who did *not* attend college. If implemented at public institutions, the former criterion would likely exclude substantial numbers of African Americans, Mexican Americans, and Asians, whose families had not been welcomed in the colleges. At the University of Houston, which became a public institution in 1963–1964, the first black law student did not graduate until 1970; fewer than a dozen Mexican Americans had graduated before 1972.[39] Even as recently as 1971, UTLS had enrolled no black students in its first-year class. Children of early 1970s UTLS minority graduates, if born while their parents attended law school, would now be eligible for the alumni preference—but they would be in competition with the thousands of white applicants who could also invoke the privilege. While it is true that the latter criterion—first-generation preferences—would more likely favor minority children whose parents were denied admission or were unable to attend college, many uneducated white parents would likewise be in a position to transmit this "advantage," simply because there were so many Anglos in the population, including those who never attended college. A Texas Coordinating Board study group, which reviewed alternative admissions criteria, determined that there is no good proxy for race. Deracinating the racial criterion simply cannot work.[40] In 1997, the first year under post-*Hopwood* procedures, minority applications to UTLS were down by more than 40 percent for blacks and by 15 percent for Mexican Americans; offers of admission fell from 65 to 5 for blacks and from 70 to 18 for Mexican Americans. Not a single black first year law student was scheduled to enroll at UTLS and only a handful of Chicanos—this despite their majority status in the Texas K–12 school system.

One of the *Hopwood* plaintiffs actually presented a letter of recommendation from a professor who described the student's academic performance at his small college, where he graduated 98th in a class of 247, as "uneven, disappointing, and mediocre."[41] That such a student could obtain high scores on the UTLS index, which uses only UGPAs and LSAT scores, demonstrates why law schools should consider more than standardized scores and grades in assessing applicants. Any professional school would be wary of applications whose letters of recommendation singled out a student for "mediocre" performance.

To return to a question I raised before—the validity of *Bakke*—the answer is that even articulate critics of *Bakke* and race-based affirmative action, such as Professor Jim Chen, believed that *Bakke* remained good law after *Hopwood*.[42] Until the Supreme Court accepted another such admissions case (as it declined to do following circuit decisions in *Podberesky*[43] and *Hopwood*), *Bakke* governed admissions to professional schools and to other postsecondary institutions of higher education. Unfortunately, UTLS and other public law schools in Texas had to play upon a very uneven surface, as no other circuit had struck down *Bakke*'s holding in admissions. Of course, this situation changed in 2003, when the U.S. Supreme Court decided both *Gratz* and *Grutter,* the University of Michigan admissions cases, on the same day and upheld *Bakke,* allowing racial criteria when properly applied.

These cases, and many others that could have been analyzed, show that the distribution of scarce benefits remains a contentious issue, one that divides American society along fronts of race, class, ethnicity, gender, and other dimensions. Like immigration cases that define who we are as a polity or as a people, so do college admissions cases define us as a nation. Inasmuch as higher education is the great engine of upward mobility in our society, how we constitute our student bodies is an important consideration. Unfortunately, due to historical racism and unequal educational opportunity, race remains a fugue in postsecondary education to this day. Therefore, understanding the admissions process and the cases that form its common law is an important key to understanding our country's complex racial history.

In the subtitle of this chapter, I quoted the *Hopwood* panel decision, which singled out students with special talents, even though I believe Judge Smith and

DeMoss used the articulate metaphors of talented athletes and musicians in a cynical fashion. Justice Blackmun, in his *Bakke* opinion, also was being cynical, but in the opposite direction, in noting that college admissions had historically been the preserve of the wealthy and powerful, even when the official story is that the criteria were meritocratic.[44] Truth be told, selective admissions have always been the preserve of the advantaged. Had I been a UTLS faculty member, I am certain that I would have voted for Cheryl Hopwood, had I known her entire record. At the very least, I assuredly would not have marked her down for attending the California State University, a school that reserves its places for the top 25 percent of high school graduates in the state and enrolls many minority and working-class students.[45]

The plaintiffs in *Hopwood*, as well as other white beneficiaries of admissions standards, assumed that they reached their station in life on their own merits and that members of minority groups have advanced only because admissions procedures have been bent to accommodate them. The friends and family of one plaintiff who was denied admission based on his 197 UTLS index were sure that a less worthy minority student had taken his place; the plaintiff's father wrote the law dean accusatorily saying just that.[46] However, blacks admitted to UTLS had a median UGPA of 3.3 and a median 158 on the LSAT; for Mexican Americans, the medians were 3.24 and 157, respectively, making them extremely qualified to do the work at UTLS and other elite law schools. Indeed, those indices would be medians for the entire student bodies at other very good law schools, then and today.[47]

Yet critics of affirmative action, especially the conservative higher education purposive organizations, and many federal judges have become convinced that higher scores on tests translate into more deserving and more meritorious applications and that reliance on "objective" measures and statistical relationships constitutes a fair, race-neutral process. The evidence for this proposition is exceedingly thin; indeed, a substantial body of research and academic common practice refutes it. Heavy reliance on solitary test scores and cutoff marks and the near-magical properties accorded to them inflate the narrow, modest use to which any standardized scores should be put. Accepted psychometric principles, testing-industry norms of good practice, and research on the efficacy of testing all suggest that the uses of test scores should be limited, whether they are considered alone or in conjunction with other imperfect measures such as grades or class rank. Recognizing this, federal judges in Mississippi and Alabama, among others, have struck down the misuse of tests as cutoffs for admissions and as a method for determining an applicant's fitness to become a teaching major.[48]

Conservative organizations that challenged the Texas Percentage Plan have averred that a single criterion (rank in class after four years of schooling, often used as a marker of quality) was unfair, even as they touted the near-absolute reliance on high-stakes exam scores, taken on a Saturday morning and coachable, as meritorious. These critics have the burden of persuasion: How is one regime that they would dictate more effective or efficacious or fair than the other in use?

Also, importantly, the same standardized test score means different things for different populations. For example, careful studies of predictive validity consistently show that scores from standardized tests are less predictive of Latino college students' first-year GPAs (both over-predictive and under-predictive) than the scores of white students. Similarly, the SAT measures less well for math ability and better for verbal ability for females than it does for males.[49] If research consistently shows that test scores for one population predict differently and less effectively than they do for other populations, it could weaken the claim by affirmative action critics that the LSAT or other standardized tests should be given more weight in the admissions process.

The *Hopwood* plaintiffs and the Fifth Circuit panel treated the revised UTLS admissions procedures as though they allowed many undeserving students of color to take places that rightfully belonged to deserving whites. Law school enrollment data rebut this viewpoint. The number of white students studying law at the time of *Hopwood* was at an all-time high: in 1995–1996, more than 110,000 students, or almost 81 percent of the total enrollment in ABA- accredited law schools, were white.[50] Blacks and other minorities, even including Puerto Ricans in the three Commonwealth law schools, then comprised approximately 20 percent of the total. The numbers have remained disproportionate: In 2010, white applicants took 60 percent of the LSAT exams administered and applied to law school—66 percent of those who were admitted and 66 percent of all new law students enrolled that year were white. Meanwhile, the figures for self-reported minorities constituted 28 percent of all applicants, 22 percent of all who were admitted, and 22 percent of those who eventually enrolled. That year, there were more LSATs administered—171,500—than at any other point in recent history.[51] (The overall percentages changed due to new self-reporting for race, which allowed persons not to designate a racial category.) But there is an equipoise evident among the white test takers, the white admitted applicants, and the white enrollees. There is no evidence of displacement here, no hint of unfairness. Further, no law school can afford to admit students who cannot do the work; the transaction costs are too high, and the spaces are too precious.[52]

Moreover, in *Hopwood*, it was not "lesser-qualified" minorities who displaced the plaintiffs. At UTLS, the number of whites accepted from the waiting list exceeded the total number of all minority group students enrolled that year. Given the expense of applying and the self-selection factor, virtually all the applicants to UTLS could do the work that would be required of them as law students. This feature is surely evident in the undergraduate ranks, where there is tremendous compression and competition in such elite programs. At an elite college such as Harvard, after the original freshman class is carefully chosen, another full class could be admitted from the waiting list without losing a single digit on the mean GPAs and SAT scores. During this period, at UC-Berkeley, more than 9,000 students with GPAs of 4.0 or better (achievable by means of honors classes) vied for the 3,000 freshmen slots.[53] And these are not static processes: California's Proposition 209 and the University of California Regents action to deracinate admissions to the University of California, although initially put on hold pending court challenges to both actions, were allowed by the Ninth Circuit.[54] Almost immediately, minority University of California applications and admissions dropped sharply. They have never fully recovered, especially after tuition rates increased sharply due to the state's fiscal crisis in 2009–2011.[55] The compression remains, especially at the elite institutions and law schools but also at the open-door, two-year colleges and other less elite schools.

At all colleges and professional schools, admissions procedures today are more thorough and better administered than ever. The survival of selective and open-door colleges depends on competence and fairness in the admissions process. The sheer crush of applicants—Georgetown Law School received more than 10,000 applications at the time of the *Hopwood* decision, Harvard College received 18,000 (including 2,900 valedictorians), and University of California-Berkeley received more than 25,000—allows admissions officers to choose from among thousands of exceptionally qualified people.[56] Even with periodic fluctuations, the year 2009–2010 saw the greatest number of test takers and law school applications in history: over 602,000 applications were submitted by 87,500 persons. More than 51,000 One Ls enrolled in 2009–2010.[57] This is a key point. When admissions committees choose from among thousands of applicants, nearly all of whom have the credentials to do the work, they are doing exactly what they are charged to do: They are assembling a qualified, diverse student body. *Bakke* and now *Grutter* sanction this approach; common sense dictates it; and no anecdotal horror stories or isolated allegations can change this central fact. There is no evidence that whites are displaced in the process, and those few who are affected likely have many alternatives. Using *Bakke* and *Grutter* reasonably, the surprise is not that the system works fitfully, but that it works so well in light of the current crush of applicants and costs of applying.

Prior to the 2003 decisions, when I was asked if *Bakke* could survive, I answered that its longevity is proof that there is a God. Of course, I did not think so earlier, when the Court's 1977 order that Allan Bakke be admitted to the UC-D Medical School led me to believe that he had won. He did win admission to medical school, but the carefully nuanced Powell opinion has proven surprisingly resilient and supple over the intervening decades, even with the attempts at revisionism by Fifth Circuit judges and unyielding conservative purposive organizations that characterize whites as hapless victims. *Grutter's* rule of law ensures that affirmative action remains a vital tool in admissions. As demographic changes occur and historical discriminatory practices are changed, the argument that race preferences in admissions are necessary to combat the vestiges of racial discrimination will likely lose its force. Few legislatures are likely to confess racial prejudice or to acknowledge it in their state agencies. Thus, affirmative action must be theoretically and operationally grounded in the First Amendment, in academic freedom, and in the four tenets of autonomy, which include the freedom to choose students.[58] To the extent that doing so will justify diversity as an admissions consideration, it will only do so in a modest way that uses race among a mix of other criteria.

However, Anglo plaintiffs and their organizations will not be appeased and will continue to make the unsuccessful argument that even the slight use of race is unconstitutional. As one of the responses to *Hopwood,* and in light of the enrollment damage evident to its undergraduate programs and professional schools, the Texas Legislature enacted a race-neutral program, the Texas Top Ten Percent Plan, in 1997. This plan allowed all graduates of the state's high schools to attend any public college, provided that the applicant had graduated in the top 10 percent of his or her class. This provision broadened the number of schools that sent students to the state's public colleges, particularly to the University of Texas at Austin, and all internal UT studies and other scholarship have revealed that full-time, first-time freshmen admitted under the Top Ten Percent Plan remained in school longer, performed better, and graduated in greater numbers than their nonplan counterparts.[59] Indeed, the plan became so successful that it threatened to swamp the Austin campus. As a result, the legislature reluctantly granted an escape valve at UT-Austin to trim back admissions under the percentage plan to the top 7 percent of high school graduates in the state.[60]

Since its inception, this plan had no racial component; while it mitigated some of the earlier *Hopwood* losses, its participants were of all races, predominantly white. Even so, in *Fisher v. University of Texas*, another generation of white applicants sued the university, arguing in a 2008 federal district court case and a 2011 circuit appeal that, with the percentage plan in use, the university should not be permitted to use the tools that *Grutter* had constitutionalized—the admissions practice occasioned by the many years of *Bakke*:

> Appellants do not allege that UT's race-conscious admissions policy is functionally different from, or gives greater consideration to race than, the policy upheld in *Grutter*. Rather, Appellants question whether UT *needs* a *Grutter*-like policy. As their argument goes, the University's race-conscious admissions program is unwarranted because (1) UT has gone beyond a mere interest in diversity for education's sake and instead pursues a racial composition that mirrors that of the state of Texas as a whole, amounting to an unconstitutional attempt to achieve "racial balancing"; (2) the University has not given adequate consideration to available "race-neutral" alternatives, particularly percentage plans like the Top Ten Percent Law; and (3) UT's minority enrollment under the Top Ten Percent Law already surpassed critical mass, such that the additional (and allegedly "minimal") increase in diversity achieved through UT's *Grutter*-like policy does not justify its use of race-conscious measures.[61]

In other words, these white applicants claimed, the percentage plan has already been adopted, so further efforts to diversify were unnecessary, notwithstanding *Grutter*. If the Fifth Circuit had accepted this line of reasoning, it would have taken the polity back to *Hopwood*'s step one, where circuit judges were all but declaring *Bakke* dead. As it turns out, rumors of its demise were exaggerated. Ironically, the Texas Legislature's race-neutral percentage plan would have been allowed to thwart the use of race by UT. The Fifth Circuit did not find for the plaintiff applicants, but the language of the decision reveals that the circuit has only grudgingly given ground to the Supreme Court in the intervening years since *Hopwood*:

> In short, while the Top Ten Percent Law appears to succeed in its central purpose of increasing minority enrollment, it comes at a high cost and is at best a blunt tool for securing the educational benefits that diversity is intended to achieve. We cannot fault UT's contention that the Top Ten Percent Law is plainly not the sort of workable race-neutral alternative that would be a constitutionally mandated substitute for race-conscious university admissions policies. We are keenly aware that the University turned to the Top Ten Percent Law in response to a judicial ruling. Yet we cannot agree that it is irrelevant. To the contrary, that the Top Ten Percent

Law, accounting for the vast majority of in-state admissions, threatens to erode the foundations UT relies on to justify implementing *Grutter* policies is a contention not lacking in force. "Facially neutral" has a talismanic ring in the law, but it can be misleading. It is here.[62]

This extraordinary concession is as disturbing for the circuit's reasoning as it is for the tone, as in its earlier autopsies on *Bakke*. First, the ruling misconstrues the provenance of the plan itself, suggesting that it was a UT-Austin institutional initiative ("We are keenly aware that the University turned to the Top Ten Percent Law in response to a judicial ruling"), when it was a state statute, enacted, as all are, by the Texas Legislature. The statute required all the state's public institutions to employ the plan, with no exceptions. After several years, it became clear that only UT-Austin, the state's largest and most popular flagship campus, was affected to a major extent and filled such a substantial portion of its freshman class with these automatic admits. Indeed, UT-Austin accepted the plan at first, to its credit, but then chafed under the plan's alleged inflexibility. After several years of special pleading, its leaders convinced the legislature to roll back its reach and reduce the effect of the plan.[63]

But more importantly, the *Fisher* applicants had never called into question the constitutionality of the percentage plan—nor could they do so on any racial fulcrum, inasmuch as it was entirely race-neutral—so the circuit's back was up for no good reason. This factor caused Circuit Judge Carolyn Dineen King to "specially concur" but not to adopt the backhanded reference to the percentage plan: "I concur in the judgment and in the analysis and application of *Grutter* in Judge [Patrick] Higginbotham's opinion. No party challenged, in the district court or in this court, the validity or the wisdom of the Top Ten Percent Law. We have no briefing on those subjects, and the district court did not consider them. Accordingly, I decline to join Judge Higginbotham's opinion insofar as it addresses those subjects."[64]

Not only were some members of the circuit distressed that the plan had been implemented; but in another special concurrence, Circuit Judge Emilio M. Garza wrote to show his special disdain even for *Grutter*: "Today, we follow *Grutter*'s lead in finding that the University of Texas's race-conscious admissions program satisfies the Court's unique application of strict scrutiny in the university admissions context. I concur in the majority opinion, because, despite my belief that *Grutter* represents a digression in the course of constitutional law, today's opinion is a faithful, if unfortunate, application of that misstep. The Supreme Court has chosen this erroneous path and only the Court can rectify the error. In the meantime, I write separately to underscore this detour from constitutional first principles."[65] In this round of deciding the constitutionality of Texas public college admissions standards, the circuit was once again calling into question the legitimacy of the Supreme Court's decisionmaking, as it had done in *Hopwood*, even as it followed its requirements in this instance. What is extraordinary is that no legal challenge to the percentage plan or even to *Grutter* was on the table. On their own gag reflexes, they choked.

To the extent that race is accounted for in the process, it should be one of many considerations: I have argued that Justice Powell's opinion was the correct route for the Supreme Court to follow when it took up *Bakke*'s progeny, and *Grutter* has settled that issue for the foreseeable future. The use of affirmative action in college admissions has been the constitutional law of the land as determined by the U.S. Supreme Court at least since 1978. For consistency's sake, I have not relied on race as the trump card in my own reading of admissions files. I use it as an asterisk, to highlight and add nuance. Someday, I hope even this consideration will not be necessary. But having conservatives, and especially federal judges, cursing the darkness does not help matters; one can only ask why white purposive organizations continue to litigate settled matters and to protest, methinks, too much. Under traditional rules of civil procedure, before one can go to court, there must be a demonstrable harm to be remedied, and the admissions evidence clearly shows that whites are not harmed by affirmative action in the aggregate. There are substantial civil penalties for litigants frivolously employing federal courts to bring unwarranted or inappropriate actions, and the jurisprudence of admissions challenges on race—*Bakke* in 1978, affirmed by *Grutter* in 2003—has been resolved to the point where these sanctions should be leveled at such claims.[66] In Spring 2012, SCOTUS granted cert to the Fifth Circuit decision in *Fisher*,[67] setting up this important subject matter once again. After I heard this from a reporter—and finished weeping—I cursed the darkness: Where was the Supreme Court in *Hopwood*, when there was a case in controversy, a circuit split, a quarter century of settled law, and disrespect from the circuit? Why now: when the case was moot (Fisher ended up enrolling elsewhere), no circuit split, and less than a decade since *Grutter* and more disrespect from the Circuit?

CHAPTER SIX

Abrams v. Baylor College of Medicine: Jews Need Not Apply

If there had been no formal record, it would have been hard to conjure up a better set of facts to challenge the prejudicial practices of a medical school in hiring faculty and other medical personnel than the 1984 case of *Abrams v. Baylor College of Medicine*.[1] Jewish anesthesiology faculty members at Houston's Baylor College of Medicine (BCOM) were denied participation in a prestigious and lucrative summer rotation in Saudi Arabia, and the trial court found that the reasons for excluding Jews were both pretextual (alleging that "the Saudis did not want any Jews in their country" and that BCOM had " 'concern' for the safety of Jews traveling to Arab lands") and also, in any event, unlawful. Normally, I would not quote so extensively from the trial record of a case, for both stylistic and substantive reasons. However, I have taken the unusual liberty of citing substantial portions of this case, both because it is so extraordinary, given how few plaintiffs prevail in academic discrimination claims, and because the trial judge went out of his way to articulate the unbelievable examples of the practices and to pin down the discriminatory details of the program and personnel assignments:

> The objective criteria established by Baylor for participation in the program (regarding anesthesiologists) are that (1) the person must be a member of the Baylor Department of Anesthesiology faculty; and (2) that the person must be certified by the American Board of Anesthesiology or hold an equivalent foreign certification recognized by the American Board of Anesthesiology.
>
> The evidence clearly establishes that both Plaintiffs met the objective criteria set forth immediately above during times material to this lawsuit.
>
> In addition to the objective criteria, Baylor has posited what may be labelled as the "team player criteria" as being necessary to qualify for the program. (We note

that this "team player" qualification was raised at trial but was not put before the EEOC [Equal Employment Opportunity Commission].) The Court is not convinced that a requirement of being a "team player" is in any way objective in nature. "Team player" requirements are innately subjective and amorphous. As such, the Court finds that the "team player criteria" are not objective occupational requirements. . . . [2]

BCOM's doctors never gave good reasons why Jews were not involved in the Saudi program, and the Saudis never indicated that Jews could not participate. Indeed, other medical schools involved in the Saudi program not only involved Jews but also insisted on nondiscrimination clauses in the comprehensive contracts negotiated over the years with the Saudis.[3]

District Judge James DeAnda's decision in Abrams was upheld: "The Court concludes the exclusion of Jews from the King Faisal program was not justified by either a business necessity or by a BFOQ. In any event, the Court concludes that the Plaintiffs have amply met their burden of showing discrimination . . . which is the ultimate issue in a Title VII case."[4] The Court of Appeals called Baylor College of Medicine's assertions "A Theoryless Theory":

One of the chief difficulties in this case is that Baylor simply never arrived at a theory of its case. There was at least a theoretical possibility that Baylor could assert that "non-Jewishness" was a bona fide occupational qualification (BFOQ) for the Faisal Hospital rotation program, notwithstanding the fact that the exclusion of Jews as Jews would normally be prohibited from discrimination under Title VII. Baylor just danced all around this; it never zeroed in on this as a BFOQ. In order to substantiate that defense though, Baylor would have to prove that the official position of the Saudi government forbad or discouraged the participation of Jews in the program. That would have meant that Baylor would have to obtain formally an authoritative statement of the position of the Saudis. Yet [BCOM Chancellor and Heart Surgeon Dr. Michael] DeBakey testified that it was not until 1983, more than a year after suit was instituted, that Baylor attempted to obtain such a statement. While the failure to seek or obtain such a critical determination is puzzling— and goes a long way toward knocking the props from under the BFOQ defense— a good explanation may well be the District Court's finding that Baylor's inaction was motivated, in part, by its desire not to "rock the boat" of its lucrative Saudi contributors.[5]

I attended much of this bench trial in the Houston federal courthouse and had been alerted in advance when BCOM president Michael DeBakey would be testifying. It was an electric moment when he was asked whether he knew about the discrimination that, by that time, had been so clearly established in the courtroom. He said, "May I indicate to you that one of the reasons that I had not asked for a policy before was because we never had a problem. It has never come up before, and I have on occasions had Jewish physicians go [to Saudi Arabia] to see special patients I wanted them to see. And we had no difficulty getting visas for them."[6] It was a sad sight to see such a distinguished heart transplant surgeon in a tangled web of his own institutional making. Which would be sadder: if he were telling the truth and did not know, or if he were not telling the truth and did know? After all, he had been president or chancellor of the elite institution for more than a dozen years. The special Saudi summer program was his brainchild and existed largely because he had made the cardiac unit among the best in the world. Given the substantial number of Jewish medical personnel who would have been affected and the prominence of the Baylor program, it is hard to believe that he or the senior administrators could have thought that such a policy would pass muster, or whether it was the proper thing to do, at the least. Readers could plausibly wonder: How could it have gotten to this point late in a complex federal trial, when an institutional CEO plaintively testified under oath, "We never had a problem"? I witnessed the BCOM lawyers visibly sag in this highly cinematic moment.

Doctors Abrams and Linde had the good fortune to find their compelling case in the trial court of Judge James DeAnda, who had a long and distinguished plaintiff's trial practice and civil rights background.[7] At the time of the trial, he was the only Mexican American federal judge in the Southern District of Texas, Houston bench. Recall Judge DeAnda's careful and nuanced delineation of the genuine, formal job requirements for the Saudi medical faculty personnel and his demonstration that the Baylor College of Medicine had instead substituted inappropriate subjective criteria—what he labeled "innately subjective and amorphous" "team player criteria" that excluded only Jews from selection.

Even the Fifth Circuit judges, normally known to be quite hard-nosed toward the range of employee discrimination claims[8] were dubious of BCOM's assertions, characterizing the defense as "just danc[ing] all around this."[9] It is difficult to discern if this metaphor was employed as a veiled gibe at Baylor University's prohibition on its students dancing on the Waco campus of Baylor University, several hundred miles north. In 1996, when the university changed this policy, it issued a tongue-in-cheek press release: "Stop the Presses! Dance Fever to Hit Baylor April 18. The Berlin Wall has fallen, Big Macs have invaded Russia, and there are lights at Wrigley Field. Mankind's last great resistance is about to be history: There will be dancing at Baylor University. It's true. Boogie Fever has hit Waco. The 'D' word will no longer be taboo at the world's largest Baptist university."[10]

Following the careful and detailed record established by Judge DeAnda at trial, the circuit court was required to deal with the clearly pretextual defense offered by the medical school's lawyers. The "team player" defense is sometimes invoked in higher education collegiality cases, but prevailing on the theory is difficult for the proof reasons and technical reasons noted earlier, and because most judges defer to academic decisionmakers on the theory that faculties have the necessary authority and expertise. Judges also assume bona fides and objectivity unless there is clear evidence otherwise, as was the case here.[11]

The straightforward case actually had several unusual procedural twists to it, both before the trial and after the Fifth Circuit's affirmation. Before the trial, on August 5, 1983, Judge DeAnda ruled on three motions: the "Defendant's Motion to Dismiss or in the Alternative for Summary Judgment" (which he granted in part and dismissed in part), the "Plaintiffs' Unopposed Motion for Continuance" (which he granted), and the motion of Marcee Lundeen, a Jewish nurse in the unit, to "Intervene as a Plaintiff" (which he denied, inasmuch as she had not filed in a timely fashion).[12] Stuart Nelkin, the plaintiffs' lawyer, on behalf of Nurse Lundeen, had filed several causes of action, and BCOM sought to have them all dismissed before trial. In its "Motion to Dismiss," BCOM argued that Dr. Abrams and Dr. Linde had failed to plead all the necessary elements of a *prima facie* case as required by Title VII and that he had filed his charge with the Equal Employment Opportunity Commission too late. Judge DeAnda determined that the plaintiffs had pled the elements of a *prima facie* case, and because the "discriminatory system" persisted, he permitted Dr. Abrams and Dr. Linde to pursue the Title VII claim.[13]

The college also challenged the right to sue under the Export Administration Act, arguing that the statute—which also regulates U.S. companies that conduct business with countries that boycott Israel (such as Saudi Arabia)—did not allow a private right of action. Judge DeAnda concluded: "A private right of action is appropriate under the circumstances and in light of the legislative history of the statute."[14] This was the first time that a private right to bring suit had been allowed under the EAA, and another federal district court had ruled earlier in the same year that there was no private right to sue under the EAA.[15]

Interestingly, Judge DeAnda did accept the argument by BCOM that Abrams could not bring an action under civil rights statute Sec. 42 U.S.C. § 1981, on the grounds that the legislation required "race" as a predicate. DeAnda ruled, "While the term 'race' is rather unscientific, Jews as a group are not a 'race' protected under this law."[16] This ruling was interesting, in part because Jews have been historically racialized and demonized in a racially-stigmatizing fashion[17] and also because cases were working their way through to the Supreme Court (and which were decided together on the same day in 2007), including a college law case that would have allowed the judge to rule differently. In *St. Francis College v. Al-Khazraji*, the Court determined that persons of "Arabic ancestry" may file § 1981 claims, even if they were considered "present-day Caucasians"[18]; in *Shaare Tefila Congregation v. Cobb*, the Court held that Jews could state § 1982 claims.[19] If there had been any lingering doubt about the existence of institutional anti-Semitism, the detailed facts in this BCOM matter surely removed those doubts. And the defendants dodged a worse bullet because Judge DeAnda also chose not to venture into the ugly thicket of who should have known what and when they should have known it—including Dr. DeBakey. Thus, he could write: "The discriminatory actions of Baylor were, as noted above, the result of intentional discrimination, together with indifference and insensitivity. However, the Court does not find that the conduct was so wilfully malicious and egregious as to support the imposition of punitive damages."[20]

While he thoroughly detailed the case against BCOM, it was ironic that he would have ruled in this narrow fashion on the racialization issue. In 1954, *Hernandez v. Texas*, the first civil rights case taken to the U.S. Supreme Court by Mexican American lawyers—including the young James DeAnda, only recently graduated from law school—determined that the equal protection doctrine applied to Mexican Americans, legally considered "white" by the state of Texas. DeAnda and the team were successful in convincing Justice Earl Warren and the Court that their Mexican American client tried in criminal court and convicted by an all-Anglo jury had not received a trial judged by his peers. The case reversed a murder conviction and required that the defendant be re-tried with Mexican jurors.[21]

While the BCOM lawyers may have had reason to believe that the Fifth Circuit would not have agreed with the findings of the trial court, the decision was both very detailed and straightforward. But the trial was very tense, with sharp elbows thrown by both sides. One of the Baylor lawyers, in all apparent seriousness, observed that "the safety of the doctors themselves could be considered and there could conceivably be 'judicial notice of the fact that Saudi patients might not want a Jewish doctor' treating them."[22] After losing at the Fifth Circuit, the medical school did not seek certiorari to the U.S. Supreme Court, in part because prolonging the dispute could have seriously jeopardized its ability to receive federal funds for medical research, and because losing in such a conservative appellate venue likely convinced them that they would not have prevailed at the U.S. Supreme Court, particularly in such a case, where Jewish and other civil rights groups would undoubtedly have entered the fray.

The BCOM lawyers may have thought that, if the Fifth Circuit had been incredulous about the behavior of Chancellor DeBakey and BCOM's "see no evil" senior administrators, the Supreme Court would be equally likely to hold that the doctors had acted as fools—or worse, knaves. After all, the circuit had raised a substantial eyebrow at the medical school's behavior: "Both Dr. Abrams and Dr. Linde were informed, by various Baylor officials, that there were problems securing visas for Jews. Yet, Baylor never attempted to substantiate that 'problem,' and the veracity of those assertions is called seriously into question by the . . . testimony of Dr. DeBakey."[23]

Abrams's attorneys, husband and wife Stuart Nelkin and Carol Nelkin, had tried to get Jewish organizations on board at the trial level but could convince none to do so until the appeal, when the Anti-Defamation League of B'nai B'rith filed an *amicus* brief; it was the only *amicus* to appear in the proceedings. Behind the scenes, Jewish friends of the lawyers had sussed out the lesser-known case of a Jewish nurse (Marcee Lundeen) who was also precluded from service in the Saudi program, but this information came too late for her to be certified,[24] and she decided not to litigate the matter further and delay the main trial. Ironically, she later became a lawyer in Houston, where she practices today.

The last laugh in this sad matter went to Stuart Nelkin, who had his lawyer's fees reduced by the circuit but who later prevailed in the final order, where Judge DeAnda spelled out his extraordinary trial skills and awarded him the larger amount. When the final check was issued for his clients Abrams and Linde, Nelkin was summoned to the downtown Houston high-rise where the firm of Baylor's lawyer William R. Pakalka was located and where he commanded a majestic view of downtown Houston. In front of a phalanx of firm lawyers involved in the case, Pakalka dismissively threw the check at Nelkin across his desk and told him to take it and leave. Nelkin picked up the check, and in a move that justified his reputation as a skilled litigator and antagonist, insisted that Pakalka produce a driver's license for identification purposes. He could have laughed again when he was awarded the higher level of attorney fees from BCOM for the work performed in the trial and appeal.[25]

Attorneys Stuart Nelkin and Carol Nelkin continue to practice civil rights law and employment law in Houston, joined by their son. Dr. Linde and Dr. Abrams received substantial damages, and both eventually left BCOM—Dr. Abrams soon after the case went to trial and Dr. Linde at a later date. At the time of the trial, Abrams was still on the BCOM staff, although he was punished by moving him to a lesser-ranked hospital assignment;[26] he eventually left Texas and became an associate professor of clinical anesthesiology and director of cardiothoracic anesthesiology at the SUNY Downstate Medical Center, in Brooklyn, New York, and currently is in private practice in New Jersey. Linde remains in private practice as an anesthesiologist in the Houston area.

After a decade of service as Baylor's president, Dr. DeBakey served as the medical school's chancellor from 1979 until early 1996, after which time he served as chancellor emeritus. He continued to perform cardiac surgery there until just before his death in 2008, at the age of ninety-nine. In 2009–2010, BCOM attempted a complex merger with nearby Rice University, but the affiliation talks collapsed in January 2010, when the Baylor debt ballooned and long-standing clinical relationships with Methodist Hospital and St. Luke's Episcopal Hospital, its former partners at the Houston Medical Center, ended, leaving the medical school with no affiliated hospital facilities.[27]

Judge DeAnda died in 2006, and I was asked to speak at his funeral, where I recounted the details of the *Hernandez* Supreme Court case. His sister, who lives in Houston, came up and told me afterwards, "Michael, that was lovely. But I had not known Jimmy ever tried a Supreme Court case." My dear friend was such a modest and unassuming man that he had never even told his sister, with whom he was very close, about that important case. In February 2012, the Houston Independent School District dedicated a new school to honor him, the Judge James DeAnda Elementary school, in the heart of Mexican Houston.

Axson-Flynn v. Johnson: "Talk to Some Other Mormon Girls Who Are Good Mormons, Who Don't Have a Problem with This"

In 1998, Christina Axson-Flynn, a member of the Church of Jesus Christ of Latter-day Saints (a Mormon), applied to the Actor Training Program (ATP), a selective undergraduate major at the University of Utah, the state's flagship public institution. At the audition required for admission into the program, she was asked to recite a speech and indicated she had religious and personal preferences not to appear in the nude and not to curse by using God's name or saying "fuck." The trial court noted that "her refusal to use the words 'God' or 'Christ' as profanity is based on one of the Ten Commandments, which prohibits believers from taking 'the name of the Lord thy God in vain. . . .' Exodus 20:8. Plaintiff has also explained that her refusal to say the word 'fuck' is due to the fact that it is religiously offensive to her because she finds that it vulgarizes what Plaintiff, as a Mormon, believes is a sacred act, appropriate only within the bounds of marriage."[1] Her exact language was: "As for myself, I will not say the F word, take the Lord's name in vain, or take off my clothes."

She was admitted to the course of study and enrolled at the University of Utah that fall, in 1998. She participated in the course, sometimes substituting other words for words she found objectionable. One of her instructors admonished her about her word choices, but Axson-Flynn maintained her objections; when the professor challenged her, the student persisted, causing the teacher to offer begrudging admiration. She allowed Axson-Flynn to continue and finish the course, substituting other terms for class-exercise language she found objectionable. However, the full team of teachers, in reviewing Axson-Flynn's entire semester's worth of work, was more critical:

At the end of the fall semester, Axson-Flynn attended her semester review, at which Defendants Barbara Smith, Sarah Shippobotham, and Sandy Shotwell were present. Defendants confronted Axson-Flynn about her language concerns and said that her request for an accommodation was "unacceptable behavior." They recommended that she "talk to some other Mormon girls who are good Mormons, who don't have a problem with this." Finally, they told her, "You can choose to continue in the program if you modify your values. If you don't, you can leave. That's your choice." After the review, Axson-Flynn appealed for help to Defendant Xan Johnson, the ATP's coordinator, but Johnson told her that he supported the other Defendants' position on the language issue.[2]

In January 1999, after the start of the spring semester, Axson-Flynn dropped out of college. The next month, she sued the University of Utah in federal court for having violated her free speech and free exercise rights under the First Amendment. After a trial in Salt Lake City, she lost, as the district court granted the university's motion for summary judgment, finding no constitutional violations. It further found that, even if it had violated her rights, the University of Utah would have been entitled to qualified immunity on both claims.[3] She then appealed to the Tenth Circuit.

On appeal, she argued that the professors' forcing her to recite the language that she found personally offensive was an effort to force her to speak, in violation of her First Amendment free speech rights and furthermore that forcing her to say those particular words violated her First Amendment's religious free exercise clause. The circuit court held that her situation constituted "school-sponsored speech" or "speech that a school 'affirmatively . . . promotes,' as opposed to speech that it 'tolerates.'"[4] In doing so and grounding the decision in *Hazelwood*, a high school newspaper case, the court would, in most circumstances, have held in the university's favor: "'Expressive activities that students, parents, and members of the public might reasonably perceive to bear the imprimatur of the school' constitute school-sponsored speech, over which the school may exercise editorial control, 'so long as [its] actions are reasonably related to legitimate pedagogical concerns.'"[5]

The *Hazelwood* decision is one that has long been criticized by legal scholars both for its characterization of the school's newspaper and journalism class as "school-sponsored" speech—speech that a school "affirmatively . . . promote[s]" as opposed to speech that it merely "tolerate [s]"—and for its application to the postsecondary setting.[6] School-sponsored speech comprises "expressive activities" that "may fairly be characterized as part of the school curriculum, whether or not they occur in a traditional classroom setting, so long as they are super-vised by faculty members and designed to impart particular knowledge or skills to student participants and audiences." Because the newspaper was "part of the school curriculum," it was therefore school-sponsored speech. The U.S. Supreme Court had held that school officials may place restrictions on school-sponsored speech if they are "reasonably related to legitimate pedagogical concerns."[7] The Court then proceeded to find that the school's reasons for excising the two news-paper pages met that standard and that the educators' decision to do so should be upheld.

Communications law scholar Nicole Casarez, for one, has written persuasively that characterizing school newspapers, often organized as intramural or extra-curricular programs, as academic curricular speech virtually guarantees that the school will prevail, usually allowing it to censor or control the expressive activity, such as student articles—often articles or editorials critical of the school administration or the status quo:

> Although the Court distinguished *Tinker* as involving personal, political expres-sion that coincidentally took place on school premises, had *Tinker* come before the Court in 1989 rather than 1969 it is far from certain that the Court would have treated *Tinker*'s facts as beyond *Hazelwood*'s reach. The students in *Tinker* ex-pressed their opinions about the Vietnam War during school-sponsored activities because they wore their armbands to class—the quintessential supervised learn-ing experience. Parents or members of the public visiting the school could reason-ably have concluded that the armbands were authorized by the school, and thereby may have associated the school with a non-neutral position regarding a controver-sial political issue. The school board's finding that the armbands would disrupt classroom instruction would surely qualify as reasonably related to a legitimate pedagogical objective under *Hazelwood*'s deferential approach. . . . Recognizing that the Court in *Hazelwood* intended to go beyond the public forum doctrine to classify the school-sponsored newspaper as the school's own speech—government speech—clears the confusion: when the government speaks, it is entitled to ad-vance its own viewpoint.[8]

Moreover, acceptance of *Hazelwood* is not widespread across the various cir-cuits, and several have rejected its application at the postsecondary, noncompul-sory higher education level. In a footnote to *Axson-Flynn*, the circuit acknowl-edged this limitation: "We acknowledge that some circuits have cast doubt on the application of *Hazelwood* in the context of university *extracurricular* acti-vities. However, because Axson-Flynn's speech occurred as part of a *curricular* assignment during class time and in the classroom, we need not reach any analysis of university students' extracurricular speech."⁹

But any readers who thought that merely framing Axson-Flynn's objections as a *Hazelwood* situation would allow the University of Utah to prevail, as it had at the trial court level, would be wrong. First, the circuit laid the predicate by insisting that it was upholding the right of professors to make classroom judgments:

> *It is the essence of the teacher's responsibility in the classroom to draw lines and make distinctions—in a word to encourage speech germane to the topic at hand and discourage speech unlikely to shed light on the subject.* Teachers therefore must be given broad discretion to give grades and conduct class discussion based on the content of speech. . . . It is not for us to overrule the teacher's view that the student should learn to write research papers by beginning with a topic other than her own theology. . . . [Thus,] we hold that the *Hazelwood* framework is applicable in a university setting for speech that occurs in a classroom as part of a class curriculum. Although we are applying *Hazelwood* to a university context, we are not unmindful of the differences in maturity between university and high school students. Age, maturity, and sophistication level of the students will be factored in determining whether the restriction is "reasonably related to legitimate pedagogical concerns."¹⁰

That said, the court switched gears and applied the school case reasoning with a vengeance, first establishing the authority of professors to have wide latitude in fashioning their teaching methods and establishing their curricular goals:

> In their pleadings, Defendants rely on the ill-defined right of "academic freedom" when they reference this principle of judicial restraint in reviewing academic decisions. Although we recognize and apply this principle in our analysis, we do not view it as constituting a separate right apart from the operation of the First Amendment within the university setting.
>
> In her amended complaint, Axson-Flynn posits that Defendants forced her to adhere strictly to the script not because of their educational goals as described above, but rather because of "anti-Mormon sentiment." During her deposition, she queried, "They respect other kids' freedom of religion that aren't [Mormon]. Why won't they respect mine?" Additionally, the program's insistence that Axson-Flynn speak with other "good Mormon girls" and that she could "still be a good Mormon" and say these words certainly raises concern that hostility to her faith rather than a pedagogical interest in her growth as an actress was at stake in Defendants' behavior in this case. Viewing the evidence in a light most favorable

to Axson-Flynn, we find that there is a genuine issue of material fact as to whether Defendants' justification for the script adherence requirement was truly pedagogical or whether it was a pretext for religious discrimination. Therefore, summary judgment was improper.[11]

As to her free exercise claim, Axson-Flynn also argued that by attempting to force her to say words whose utterance would violate her strongly held religious beliefs, the University of Utah professor, who had been on notice that she held the beliefs and had partially accommodated them throughout the semester, violated the free exercise clause of the First Amendment. The trial court had rejected this argument and had granted summary judgment to the defendants. However, the circuit once again reversed the decision of the trial court, revealing how strongly it felt that the university had behaved badly in this instance. The court held that for this analysis, *Employment Division v. Smith* was the controlling case, particularly the *Smith* standard of whether or not the rules or behavior were pretextual—neutral in form but discriminatory as applied. Despite the deference language, it became evident that the court had not believed the testimony of the professor:

> We find a genuine issue of fact in the record as to whether Defendants' requirement of script adherence was pretextual. Therefore, we remand for further proceedings on whether the script adherence requirement was discriminatorily applied to religious conduct (and thus was not generally applicable). Unless Defendants succeed in showing that the script requirement was a neutral rule of general applicability, they will face the daunting task of establishing that the requirement was narrowly tailored to advance a compelling governmental interest. . . . [12]

There remained a question as to whether the case was covered by the second *Smith* exception, which held that "in circumstances in which individualized exemptions from a general requirement are available, the government may not refuse to extend that system to cases of religious hardship without compelling reason." The court then reviewed the Utah calendar, which allowed absences on holy days, and held:

> Axson-Flynn argues that Defendants' willingness to grant an exemption to [a Jewish student who observed Yom Kippur] demonstrates that the ATP had a system of individualized exemptions in place. That Defendants did not grant her an exemption, Axson-Flynn argues, constitutes "discriminat[ion] among members of different religious faiths" that violates the Free Exercise Clause.

When this evidence is coupled with the fact that Defendants sometimes granted Axson-Flynn herself an exemption from their script adherence requirement, we find that the record raises a material fact issue as to whether Defendants maintained a discretionary system of making individualized case-by-case determinations regarding who should receive exemptions from curricular requirements.[13]

Thus, the very accommodations and exemptions Axson-Flynn had been given in class to substitute other words for the ones she found objectionable came back to haunt the professors and mousetrap the university, the academic equivalent of no good accommodation going unpunished. Nowhere was this more evident than in the final issue: whether the university and its professors could claim qualified immunity as to her free speech claim, on the grounds that any reasonable belief that their behavior was allowable would shield them from judgment and provide them immunity. The trial court had found that even if she had been discriminated against—it did not find she had been harmed—the university was immune, as the professors had acted in good faith and within their allowable professional norms. The Tenth Circuit very much disagreed on this argument as well: "Because the law is clearly established and there exists a material factual issue as to the objective reasonableness of Defendants' actions, the qualified immunity defense to the free speech claim must fail on summary judgment."[14]

The final nail was that even if the remand and rehearing were to show that the behavior had not been grounded in religious intolerance or animosity, the university would have to rebut the evidence offered by Axson-Flynn under strict scrutiny, the most exacting standard, and one it would be unlikely to rebut, given the extraordinary reading of the facts by the appeals court: "Even if the court does conclude on remand that the rule is a neutral one of general applicability, there remains a genuine dispute of fact as to the individualized exemption to *Smith*. If *Smith* does not apply either because the rule is not a neutral one of general applicability or because the rule invoked a series of individualized exemptions, then Defendants would have to defend their conduct under the strict scrutiny standard on Axson-Flynn's free exercise claim. Under such a strict scrutiny standard, Defendants have not established a right to qualified immunity."[15]

When the smoke cleared, the university was devastated. The circuit had reversed the district court on all three issues: the summary judgment on both her free speech and free exercise claims and the finding of qualified immunity, which would have to be proven under the strict scrutiny standard. The freshman had beaten the university on all her major claims, and a new trial would have to be held in the original court. After much internal discussion, the university chose not to appeal, fearing worse damage should the decision be affirmed upon remand or, worse, ratified by the U.S. Supreme Court. The university had been held up to harsh light during the trial, and the local papers had hammered the university, making it seem as if Axson-Flynn had been singled out for anti-Mormon animus. This was especially true in the LDS-owned media, including the *Deseret Morning News*, which regularly featured the case in a fashion sympathetic to Axson-Flynn. Not only was the case kept in the public eye by both Salt Lake City papers but, among several examples of how the language became slanted in favor of the disgruntled student, the *Morning News* also characterized the matter as a "profanity case" and freshman theater student Axson-Flynn as a "thespian."[16]

In addition to a requirement that the state pay her attorney's fees, admit her to the ATP program, and pay her tuition, the university agreed to fashion a policy that would accommodate students who raised bona fide claims to religious content accommodation. In 2005, it promulgated such a policy:

> Content Accommodations: Students are expected to take courses that will challenge them intellectually and personally. Students must understand and be able to articulate the ideas and theories that are important to the discourse within and among academic disciplines. Personal disagreement with these ideas and theories or their implications is not sufficient grounds for requesting an accommodation. Accommodations requested on such grounds will not be granted. The University recognizes that students' sincerely-held core beliefs may make it difficult for students to fulfill some requirements of some courses or majors. The University assumes no obligation to ensure that all students are able to complete any major . . .
>
> Instructors who believe that course materials may conflict with students' deeply held core beliefs may include a statement in the syllabus for the course that advises students that some of the writings, lectures, films or presentations, or other requirements in the course include materials that may present such conflicts. However, this policy recognizes that Faculty will not always be able to predict in advance which if any materials may conflict with the beliefs of a given student or group of students.[17]

The University of Utah has enacted this extraordinary and extraordinarily detailed "Content Accommodation" policy and has separate policies for accommodating disabilities under federal law and for accommodating class attendance, such as holidays for religious purposes and other school-related issues, such as intercollegiate events; in a number of states, all public colleges must provide such exceptions for religious holidays, but it seems a stretch to determine, as the circuit did, that the act of granting religious attendance requirements could constitute proof that there was a categorical precedent for accommodating all requests labeled "religious." Moreover, this religious holiday provision was not a discretionary matter but Utah law, and as such it applied to all public college instructional staff. However, it would be one thing to force a student to perform classwork on a traditional Sabbath or holy day and quite another to turn such mandatory flexibility into evidence that any religious objection must be accounted for in the classroom, especially one occasioned by a professor's reasonable curricular choices.

Christina Axson-Flynn never returned to the University of Utah, although the settlement would have required the university to readmit her and pay her tuition. After withdrawing from the University of Utah, she enrolled as a theater major at Utah Valley State College. The content accommodation policy was adopted in 2005; through 2012, seven years later, not a single case had been adjudicated under its provisions.

Two cases with similar facts and Christian plaintiffs have been proceeding through federal courts in Georgia and Michigan in 2012. In the first, *Keeton v. Anderson-Wiley*, a graduate student in a counseling program at Augusta State University (ASU) who was morally opposed on biblical grounds to homosexuality was placed on "remedial status" and required to receive supplemental training regarding the counseling of gay, lesbian, bisexual, transgender, and queer/questioning (GLBTQ) clients, all in accord with the American Counseling Association's (ACA) Code of Ethics, guidelines adopted by the program for its professional certification.[18] In 2010, Jennifer Keeton sued her professor advisor and ASU, alleging First Amendment violations of viewpoint discrimination, compelled speech doctrine, right to belief of her choice, and retaliation. She sought a preliminary injunction, but the judge ruled that she had failed to show a "substantial likelihood of success on the merits."[19]

In another 2010 case, *Julea Ward v. Wilbanks, et al.*,[20] another graduate student, at Eastern Michigan University (EMU) had the same personal objection to the graduate program in counseling, and she also was dismissed, due to her unwillingness to complete a remedial plan required by her professors who were charged with implementing the curricular requirements. In both instances, the graduate program certification was contingent on their adoption of the ACA and the American School Counselor Association (ASCA) Ethical Standards for School Counselors. The ASCA certificate was required for Ms. Ward's eventual

eligibility to be licensed in Michigan to become a high school counselor, her occupational goal. To be fully accredited through the Council for Accreditation of
Counseling and Related Educational Programs (CACREP), EMU students were
required to gain "curricular experiences and demonstrated knowledge" in the
ACA and ASCA Ethics Codes. Additionally, Michigan approves CACREP accreditation standards and requires that all professional counselors and school
counselors be trained in ethics.[21]

In 2010, both Keeton and Ward lost in the preliminary stages of their cases,
as did another student in a California public college who raised similar issues in
a complex grade and classroom management dispute. Now that several years
have passed since the *Axson-Flynn* case was decided and then settled, it has
proven to be a decision cited by many students and their lawyers, particularly at
the K–12 level, and by others who feel aggrieved over religious liberties issues.
Shepardizing the 10th Circuit *Axson-Flynn* decision on the commercial Lexis-
Nexis tool shows its interesting reach. By December 2011, it had appeared in
more than 181 "Citing References," a rough shorthand for the reach of the case.
In actual court decisions, it has been "distinguished" (3 times); "followed" (12);
in a "concurring opinion" (1); and in a "dissenting opinion" (2). In secondary
references, it has had broader influence, included in law reviews (72 times), statutes (5), treatises (2), and court documents (50, including 35 *amicus* or party briefs
that have raised it). But its actual doctrinal or substantive influence has been
negligible, rather like the University of Utah's policy, which has never been invoked in its history. Despite its fifty-one "citing decisions"—that is, all the cases
that have cited the appellate decision—the holding has only been "followed" in
four college cases, one of them incidentally litigating a college building permit
and the other three involving curricular disputes such as that in *Axson-Flynn*.
But, extraordinarily, in all three disputes—two of which were certification-
related—the student lost, and all three were dismissed at early stages. Thus, not
a single college law case in which *Axson-Flynn* was followed as a precedent on a
curricular matter has been won by a student litigant. At the end of the day, its
great potential effect has been exceedingly modest.[22]

Because both Keeton and Ward are represented by the Alliance Defense
Fund, there will, at some point, almost certainly be appeals on the merits.[23] The
parallels to the *Axson-Flynn* case are obvious, even with the differences between
certification requirements and the elective drama class; with the Alliance Defense Fund involved, there will be litigation as far as the cases can proceed.[24] On
its website, this purposive organization throws down: "By God's grace, ADF has
fought and won nearly 100 percent of all university legal matters—but the battle

is far from over. ADF has identified more than 270 public universities in America where Christian students may be hindered from freely living out their faith without fear of censorship, discrimination, indoctrination, or dismissal because of unconstitutional policies and university administrators who are intolerant of your sincerely held religious beliefs."[25] This crusade will continue, and there will be many battles in this holy war.

Location, Location, Location: *Richards v. League of United Latin American Citizens* and the Cartography of Colleges

A large number of life's advantages and opportunities are parceled out by residence, duration, domicile, and location. There is an extensive legal and sociological literature—and literally hundreds of relevant court decisions on the varieties of legal rights and opportunities that vary by residence.[1] The concepts of "neighborhood schools," voting districts, tax obligations, in-state tuition, eligibility for certain resources, exposure to certain regulations, eligibility for office, and many other legal statuses derive from varying applications of place. Although there is a system of comity among states in the United States for reciprocal arrangements and full faith and credit among political entities, there is an important issue of federal jurisdiction that can preempt various state laws, such as a uniform immigration policy or national security regime or voting rights practices that can trump state residency matters.

In higher education, this complex algebra of "place" traditionally delegates the statewide coordination of the governance of higher education to the institutional boards of trustees and statewide higher education agencies who execute the legislative and corporate requirements to establish and locate colleges. And where a college is located can apportion access in a way that benefits or harms certain citizens. For Mexican Americans in Texas, "place" counts, especially in determining who goes to local colleges. Consider the "border": forty-one counties form the border between Texas and Mexico, from El Paso in the west to Brownsville in the east, where the Gulf Coast begins. This swath is almost a thousand miles long and stretches from Ciudad Juarez to Matamoros, along the Rio Grande River/Río Bravo; it is widely referred to as "the Borderlands," "the Valley," or "la Frontera."[2] (In geopolitical if not exact cartographic terms, this frontier might also include San Antonio, approximately 150 miles from Mexico, although it is the country's seventh largest city and has more than a dozen public and private colleges.)[3]

There is a long history of conflict along the border, not only with regard to its national security and immigration dimensions, but as the state's poorest and least developed region—especially over its provisions for higher education. The Mexican American Legal Defense and Educational Fund (MALDEF), founded in San Antonio in 1968, has long been involved in various cases and efforts to improve the region's educational achievement, especially for the schooling of the children in the Valley. The litigation has included *Plyler v. Doe*,[4] the 1982 MAL-DEF case in which the U.S. Supreme Court struck down the Texas law that allowed school districts to charge tuition for undocumented school children, extensive school finance litigation (particularly complex multi-year cases such as *Edgewood v. Kirby*, which stretched from 1984 to 1995), desegregation cases, voting rights issues, and various topics such as challenging local ordinances regulating immigration.[5]

Inspired by the early litigation and legislative successes in the *Edgewood* case; the lower court cases in *Fordice*, which later culminated in the 1992 Supreme Court case in Mississippi, discussed in chapter 4; and what seemed its promise for redistributing college political resources, MALDEF San Antonio lawyers Albert Kauffman and Norma Cantu, he a native of Galveston and she a native of Brownsville, undertook to challenge the constitutionality of the state's system of higher education locations in state court, filing *LULAC v. Clements*. (After a change in governors, the case became *LULAC v. Richards*.)[6] The plaintiffs contended that the policies and practices of state officials and regents of public universities denied Mexican Americans who resided in the border area of Texas participation in quality higher education programs and access to equal higher education resources, even in light of an earlier federal Office for Civil Rights (OCR) Consent Decree that had set out goals and timetables for improving minority enrollments in the state's colleges.[7]

Cantu and Kauffman mounted their challenge on a geographic theory of "dollars, degrees, and distance," charging:

(1) about 20% of all Texans live in the border area, yet only about 10% of the State funds spent for public universities are spent on public universities in that region; (2) about 54% of the public university students in the border area are Hispanic, as compared to 7% in the rest of Texas; (3) the average public college or university student in the rest of Texas must travel 45 miles from his or her home county to the nearest public university offering a broad range of masters and doctoral

programs, but the average border area student must travel 225 miles; (4) only three of the approximately 590 doctoral programs in Texas are at border area universities; (5) about 15% of the Hispanic students from the border area who attend a Texas public university are at a school with a broad range of masters and doctoral programs, as compared to 61% of public university students in the rest of Texas; (6) the physical plant value per capita and number of library volumes per capita for public universities in the border area are approximately one-half of the comparable figures for non-border universities; and (7) these disparities exist against a history of discriminatory treatment of Mexican Americans in the border area (with regard to education and otherwise), and against a present climate of economic disadvantage for border area residents.[8]

To bring the case, which required massive research and technical expertise, the MALDEF lawyers had a tangle of difficult tasks and technical procedural litigation issues, each almost unique to Texas and to Mexican American plaintiffs. Chief among them was the issue of standing and the issue of whether the lawyers could even prove that their clients were a discrete group, a legal prerequisite to qualify them for the harder issues of whether the actual legal theory could work or what relief would look like if they were to prevail. There was no doubt that the border was disproportionately poor in terms of its number of institutions, their quality and range of programs, and their facilities. In the north, a small college town such as Denton, outside Dallas, had two large doctoral-degree–granting universities (University of North Texas, formerly North Texas State University, and Texas Women's University), each with dozens of doctorates and academic programs, and the flagship schools such as Texas A&M University in rural College Station and the University of Texas, in the state capital of Austin, were far from the Valley, as were other major public institutions located in Dallas, Houston, and panhandle Lubbock and other communities.

Thus, defining the who-and-where of the case was the key strategy, and it was not clear that the courts would certify such a farflung, inchoate class under the group umbrella of "the border." Did San Antonio, with its large University of Texas-San Antonio campus, its large University of Texas Health Sciences Center medical school, several other two-year and four-year public colleges, and large Mexican American population count as being along the border for this purpose?

It also was problematic, inasmuch as it adopted in part *Fordice*'s African American litigation strategy, premised on the *de jure* Jim Crow system of higher education. Mexican Americans, clearly disadvantaged and subordinated by *de facto* "Jaime Crow" practices in Texas—the one southern state that included substantial numbers of both Mexican Americans and African Americans—were not black, although the state's regime of racial subordination clearly implicated both groups. The predominant theory of the case borrowed from MALDEF's *Edgewood* school finance strategy, but followed the 1973 U.S. Supreme Court ruling in *San Antonio v. Rodriguez,* which thwarted equal protection challenges to K–12 school finance mechanisms and also held that education was not a fundamental right. This theory of the case would have reversed the burden of proof in the case, as a postsecondary *Rodriguez* was even less likely to gain constitutional favor for a postcompulsory educational setting. Complicating these alternatives was the fact that the demographics surrounding these institutions were often in flux. An area's growth could be so pronounced that several racially distinct institutions could coexist, which appears to have happened in Houston with Texas Southern University, the University of Houston, and UH-Downtown. Furthermore, the demography could change so substantially that a college of one race could morph into a college with a different racial character. For instance, Bluefield State College in West Virginia, a historically black school, became a predominantly white institution over time; the University of Houston changed from a private white college to a public institution without a predominant undergraduate racial majority. An area's racial calculus could also change so dramatically over time that its local colleges simply reflected changes in their communities. For example, the rise of Asian student enrollment in California colleges, particularly the University of California at the Berkeley and Irvine campuses, is surely due to changes in immigration policy, Asian academic achievement, and other historical and sociological developments in the years following shameful World War II internment practices.

Texas Rio Grande Valley institutions such as Laredo State University, Corpus Christi State University, Kingsville A&M University, Pan American University, and Texas Southmost College became predominantly Mexican American or Mexican, although the original institutions were not historically Latino. In addition, each of these institutions was absorbed into the larger University of Texas or Texas A&M University systems, creating TAMU-Laredo International University, TAMU-Corpus Christi, TAMU-Kingsville, UT-Pan American/Edinburg, and UT-Brownsville. In 1914, the Texas State School of Mines and Metallurgy was established in El Paso, morphed into Texas Western College, and then into UTEP. (It remains the only Texas institution to have won the men's national basketball championship and was the first team in the country with an all African American starting lineup that did so, defeating the all-white team from the University of Kentucky in 1966.) A similar pattern of being reconstituted held true for many other institutions, particularly community colleges that have become predominantly minority campuses, as the urbanization of minority populations in the twentieth century affected higher education.

For Mexican Americans, contesting the politics of place, including college place has taken a different route than that occasioned by the separate-but-equal route of *Brown* and its progeny, *Fordice*. Education was poor and inadequate for Mexican Americans in the twentieth century, and although *de jure* segregation affected Mexican Americans in ways different than the racism aimed at blacks in Texas, the end results were very similar.[9] As one example, very few Mexican-origin children graduated from high school or attended college; fewer attended professional schools, such as law school or medical school, even in large cities like Houston, Dallas, or San Antonio.[10] Even Catholic institutions performed poorly in serving Mexican Americans, despite the fact that the overwhelming majority of Mexican Americans are Catholic. Further, there was no Mexican American equivalent to the network of historically black institutions. Against this demographic backdrop, MALDEF attempted to carve out as its class "all persons of Mexican-(Hispanic) ancestry who reside in the Border Area consisting of these forty-one contiguous counties along the border in Texas and who are now or will be students at Texas public senior colleges and universities or health related institutions (or who would be or would have been students at Texas public senior colleges and universities or health related institutions were it not for the resource allocation policies and practices complained of in Plaintiffs' petition). This class does not include persons with claims for specific monetary or compensatory relief."[11]

The trial judge in the 107th state district court in Brownsville, across the border from Matamoros, Tamaulipas, agreed to this class and enabled the trial to proceed.[12] The defendants were the governor of Texas, the state's commissioner of higher education, the chair and each individual member of the Texas Higher Education Coordinating Board, and the chancellors and regents of eleven universities or university systems in Texas. Before the trial could proceed, the state appealed the class certification; in December 1990, the 13th Judicial Court of Appeals upheld the class certification, allowing the trial to go forward. During an extensive and complex jury trial that lasted from September 30 to November 20, 1991, the plaintiffs entered into the record "certain statistical matters" that showed substantial disparities in the higher education resources available to the area's residents.

On January 20, 1992, MALDEF lawyers had alleged first that the allocation of resources to the border colleges was discriminatory and unconstitutional under the state constitution, because the state had located academic programs and physical facilities where they were largely inaccessible to border-area residents and second, that the state funded institutions in the border area at lower levels than it funded other institutions. After noting that "these disparities exist against a history of discriminatory treatment of Mexican Americans in the border area (with regard to education and otherwise), and against a present climate of economic disadvantage for border area residents," the trial court held that the Texas system of higher education discriminated against Mexican Americans, depriving them of equal educational opportunity by spending fewer state resources in areas significantly populated by Mexican Americans, particularly the border area.[13]

The first question placed before the jury asked whether the defendants had treated the border institutions "differently, to their detriment, at least in part because Plaintiffs are Mexican Americans, in the process that leads to program approval or allocation of funds for Texas public institutions of higher education." The court defined the higher education system in the jury charge as "the laws, policies, practices, organizations, entities and programs that have created, developed or maintained Texas public universities and professional schools" and instructed the jurors that, if the higher education system treated plaintiffs differently at least in part because they were Mexican American, then the defendants had done so for that reason. The jury answered "No" to each of these questions. (There were approximately eighty named and ex officio defendants in this complex case, including various elected officials, trustees, and others; the jury likely did not think that they each had individually discriminated, even if they might have felt that the system did discriminate in the aggregate, collective sense.) However, on the larger issues and more important questions, the Brownsville jury did find that (1) the legislature had "failed to establish, organize or provide for the maintenance, support or direction of a system of education in which the Plaintiffs have substantially equal access to a 'University of the First Class'"; (2) the Texas Legislature had "failed to make suitable provisions for the support or maintenance of an Efficient System of public universities"; and (3) the state could "have reasonably located and developed university programs that provided more equal access to higher educational opportunities to Mexican Americans in the Border Region."[14] The court rendered a declaratory judgment that the higher education system was unconstitutional under the Texas Constitution. Although the case had been tried before a jury, at the close of evidence the trial judge granted the plaintiffs' motions for an instructed verdict (notwithstanding the jury's determination, called a JNOV, or "judgment notwithstanding verdict") and for uncontroverted fact findings on certain statistical matters. The trial court stayed its injunction until May 1, 1993—seventeen months later—to allow the state time to enact a constitutionally sufficient plan for funding the public universities. This stay was later extended by the Texas Supreme Court until final resolution of the appeal.[15]

On October 6, 1993, the Texas Supreme Court unanimously reversed the trial court decision, holding that a claim for equal rights violation based on a "geographical classification" could not be sustained, nor could a claim based on race or national origin classification. The court denied the trial court's reasoning, holding that the plaintiffs "failed to establish that the Texas university system policies and practices are in substance a device to impose unequal burdens on Mexican Americans living in the border region." The court determined that the plaintiff's theory was both under-inclusive and over-inclusive: "Whatever the effects of the Texas university system policies and practices, they fall upon the entire region and everyone in it, not just upon Mexican Americans within the region. Conversely, they do not fall upon Mexican Americans outside the region. The same decisions that plaintiffs allege show discrimination against Mexican Americans in the border area serve, at the same time, to afford greater benefits to the larger number of Mexican Americans who live in metropolitan areas outside the border region."[16]

The Texas Supreme Court also found that the *Fordice* case was not applicable, as Texas had never maintained a *de jure* discriminatory system that applied to Mexican Americans. In fact, the court did not grant that any of the theories advanced by the plaintiffs were persuasive: "Because we hold that plaintiffs' evidence of impact in this case is insufficient under any standard to prove an equal protection violation, we do not need to consider the effect, in this case, of the jury's finding of no purposeful discrimination or intent. Nor do we need to address plaintiffs' many arguments as to why that finding by the jury is inconsequential." MALDEF appealed for a reconsideration of the verdict, but the court denied the rehearing on February 2, 1994. Without a federal issue to appeal to the U.S. Supreme Court, the case ended.

However, the final result was actually a different and surprising endgame. Although the plaintiffs were unsuccessful in the Texas Supreme Court, which sat on the case for almost a year before it actually released its decision, the war was won in the Texas Legislature, where border-area legislators directed substantial resources to border colleges, including doctoral and other graduate programs, established a pharmacy school in Kingsville, and substantially upgraded facilities and programs. In its opinion, the Texas Supreme Court commented on these legislative developments.[17] Unlike the one-time infusion of dollars and modest increases involved in the Mississippi *Fordice* settlement, this initiative brought substantial program resources, program authorization, and political prestige to the border-area institutions.

Some of the results were clearly tradeoffs. For example, colleges that had been small institutions with their own boards of trustees were admitted into the larger and more powerful flagship University of Texas and Texas A&M University systems with greater political regional-distribution requirements, which meant a smaller number of local area residents actually served on the consolidated boards. Given the distribution of power in the state and the significant likelihood that the south Texas region would never catch up with the state's flagships and urban colleges in the statistical sense, it seems clear twenty years later that the region has benefited from the political settlement, even if the case originally seemed lost, an ironic and Janus-faced result. The facilities portion of what came to be known as the "Border Initiative" gave rise to genuine gains. As one of many such examples of inadequate facilities before the litigation, the Laredo State University, as it was known at the time, had leased space on the Laredo Junior College campus. One perceptive reporter who followed the story over its several years noted its successes but also characterized the initiative in an arid metaphor: "South Texas absorbed the $500 million like a desert does a brief rain, leaving the schools shortchanged in many ways."[18]

The state's chief lawyer was Jay Aguilar, a Mexican American attorney in the attorney general's office; after leaving government practice, he became a corporate lawyer in San Antonio. At the time of the trial, Daniel C. Morales was the Texas attorney general, serving from 1991 to 1999 and overlapping the administrations of Governors Ann Richards and George W. Bush. In 2003, he admitted to having falsified documents in the Texas tobacco settlement and served time in federal prison and a release facility until 2007. He surrendered his law license in 2003 to the Texas Supreme Court less than a decade after his team won *LULAC* in the same court. Kevin O'Hanlon and Richard Gray also argued the state's case at various stages. O'Hanlon, who went on to a successful private trial practice in Austin, had also argued against MALDEF in earlier school finance litigation, while Gray had been aligned with MALDEF in the same litigation, representing other low-income districts; he had also litigated Texas redistricting and voting rights cases.

The two key MALDEF lawyers who conceived and litigated the South Texas Initiative, Albert Kauffman and Norma Cantu, later left the organization. Cantu served as President Bill Clinton's assistant secretary of education for civil rights and then became an education and law professor at the University of Texas at Austin. Kauffman succeeded her as the San Antonio MALDEF regional counsel and then left in 2002 to conduct research with several university research institutes. He is now a law professor at St. Mary's University Law School in San Antonio.

In a second case turning on geography, MALDEF filed suit in 2004 to challenge the admissions practices of California State Polytechnic University, San Luis Obispo (CSU-SLO), which combined standardized test scores and regional criteria based on residence in certain geographic "service areas." The plaintiffs charged CSU-SLO with using a "rigid mathematical formula" that heavily weighted the SAT and awarded "250 points to students living within a specific geographic area around the CSU-SLO campus—its so-called 'service area.'" The complaint further claimed:

> Cal Poly SLO's geographical preference for applicants living within its "service area" also results in an adverse disparate impact against Latino, African American, and Asian American students. For high school aged individuals residing within Cal Poly SLO's designated "service area," whites are overrepresented, while Latinos, Asian Americans, and African Americans are underrepresented in comparison to their populations statewide. Therefore, Latinos, Asian Americans, and African Americans are eligible for the "service area" bonus at lower rates than whites. These differential rates result in a discriminatory effect on Latinos, African Americans, and Asian Americans.[19]

The data did, in fact, reveal that the chosen "service area" was disproportionately white at the time of the case. Of all the high school–age students in California at the time, 37.5 percent were white (55.0% in the CSU-SLO service area), 40.1 percent Latino (35.3%), 10.8 percent Asian (3.4%), and 7.0 percent black (2.4%). In the SLO-designated service area resided 1.9 percent of all white students statewide, 1.2 percent of all Latino students, 0.5 percent of all African Americans, and 0.4 percent of all Asians. As with the "geographical classification" strategy attempted in Texas, political factors undoubtedly underpinned the admissions cartography at CSU-SLO.

In *Garcia v. Board of Trustees*, the California State Court of Appeals found for the university in 2005,[20] handing MALDEF another setback in its geographic access litigation strategy, which has proven to be a difficult theory to sell to courts in the two states with the largest Latino populations. Here, unlike the scenario that played out in Texas, the court held standing and the right to sue on behalf of indefinite plaintiffs to be fatal flaws, but not before invoking an unusually sympathetic architecture metaphor:

[In California,] Government Code section 11135 prohibits a state agency from discriminating on the basis of race, national origin, and ethnic group identification, among other things. Recently, the Legislature has amended section 11135 a few times. Amending a statute is like adding a room to an existing house. A successful architect must ensure that the addition be integrated into the whole. In amending section 11135, the Legislature drafted plans that call for a shower in the living room. We cannot remove the shower, but we can cap the water pipe to prevent damage to the furniture. Here we hold that the California State University is not subject to section 11135. We leave it to the Legislature to remove the shower. Its presence is anomalous, if not disquieting.[21]

Those designated schools in the San Luis Obispo service area may or may not have been chosen for their racial characteristics (or their plumbing, as in the court's metaphor), but it is hard to imagine that race was not a factor. High-achieving schools are not necessarily required to be predominantly white or Asian, but the complex calculus of high school attendance line drawing is rarely race-free, just as race is often a leading factor in the checkerboard of underlying housing patterns. School board politics, the degree of parental participation, and individual school trajectories constitute the site of substantial local politics, and these often have racial, class, and, increasingly, religious overtones.[22] And California's financial problems, especially evident in its public college sector, have affected overall attendance policies.[23]

While the *LULAC v. Richards* litigation has not been examined carefully by many scholars, Richard Valencia's authoritative study of the history of Mexican American education litigation devotes a chapter to the case. He characterizes the Texas Supreme Court ruling as "unsound" due to the way it ignored "the centrality of race and racism and the intersectionality of racism with other forms of oppression."[24] Indeed, not to put too fine a point on it, the same critique must be made of many cases that are about race but that are pleaded in deracinated or nonracial form, due to the technical requirements of litigation, the racial bona fides of the various decisionmakers, and the majoritarian assumptions of so many of the structures that support schooling or any other establishment sector. In the chronology of *LULAC* and the later *Hopwood*, many of the players on both sides of the matter were themselves Mexican American, including a Texas Supreme Court justice and the state attorney general, evidence that it is not always possible or useful to employ reductionist assumptions. In *LULAC*, a Jewish lawyer for MALDEF argued the case at the trial level before a Mexican American judge in a border town, with another Mexican American as the state's lead lawyer in this case and with white co-counsel. In 2011, the University of Texas System chancellor was a Mexican American academic physician from Laredo, Dr. Fernando Cigarroa. Chancellor Cigarroa was among the defendants in the 2012 SCOTUS case *Fisher v. UT.*

In virtually every state, a relatively small number of feeder high schools routinely send their graduates to certain colleges, and this channeling process has a powerful racial and ethnic influence as well. In its response to the *Hopwood* case that banned the use of affirmative action in Texas, before 2003's *Grutter* decision, Texas acknowledged this "channeling" effect by its enactment of the Top Ten Percent Plan that broadened the number of high schools that send graduates to the state's flagship public colleges. Moreover, some of the colleges have broadened their recruitment efforts beyond the traditional schools to reach a wider array of schools with promising applicants.

Quite apart from the difficulty of litigating "place" in a postcompulsory schooling context, legal challenges to the politics of resource allocation are theoretically and technically difficult, especially in the many states where the institutions are variegated by history and mission, hence by historical funding patterns and support.[25] As another example, the complex political resources across campuses in the large City University of New York system were challenged unsuccessfully in *Weinbaum v. Cuomo,*[26] but the court deferred to the political process and did not find constitutional grounds on which to allow the challenge to proceed. In that 1995 case, the New York Appellate Court held that the funding differences among a state's public institution systems did not give rise to any sustainable legal theory, whether grounded in intentional racial animus, disparate funding, equal protection, or state civil rights laws: "The complaint does not set forth any facts tending to show that in making their decisions regarding [the] funding of the two systems, the defendants acted with a discriminatory purpose or were motivated by the race or ethnic background of the student bodies [and] plaintiffs point to no particular 'civil right' which has been denied them based on race or other protected basis. As the court below correctly recognized, there is simply no 'right,' constitutional or statutory, to a State financed higher or college education."[27]

Geography has proven to be a difficult and complex theory in search of traction in federal and state courts, and very few geographical challenges have ever prevailed, such as in the siting of new campuses in a multi-campus system, which occurred in the longstanding *Geier* cases in Tennessee. There the state successfully blocked the predominantly white University of Tennessee from establishing a new Nashville campus hundreds of miles from its home in Knoxville.[28] When the dust settled in this unusual case, the historically black Tennessee State University was in charge of the downtown Nashville venue.[29] But neither the historically black institutions in Mississippi nor the south Texas border colleges would have made up any ground had it not been for the political solutions occasioned by the *Fordice* and *LULAC* cases.

To the extent that some legislative attention to a systemic issue is a desirable feature, such cases may be characterized as efficacious, even as partial successes. Using the courts for specific legislative change is a two-edged sword, one that can cut in either direction. Winning the *LULAC* case, even at the lower courts and for a short period of time, gave Mexican American plaintiffs and their organizations the political leverage and wedge that was needed in the legislature, where regional and other political considerations provided a substantial but not transformative remedy. And it may be impossible to calculate the odds against a legislative strategy, minus that leverage.

Attempting such a strategy requires enormous resources, both political and legal; just as one can lose in court, so an issue can become worse in the shifting fortunes of securing change by a legislature, especially a body, such as that in Texas, that meets only every other year in regular session. The timing, especially in such a biennial legislature, is impossible to control when a case takes longer to try. The players are more numerous, and the state always holds more of the home field advantage and for a longer number of innings. The number of moving parts is even greater than they would be in a relatively straightforward trial. Even so, for many issues that will have to be resolved by appropriations or other statutory or regulatory changes, an overarching policy strategy will consider both legal remedies and political approaches in tandem. In this matter, no lasting, permanent, systemic change resulted, and it did not substantially redraw the Texas postsecondary map, but it was not effort exerted for nothing. Such an event is the antonym for a pyrrhic victory—perhaps a victory notwithstanding the verdict.

CHAPTER NINE

Clark v. Claremont University Center:
"I Mean, Us White People Have Rights, Too"

Job descriptions can both reveal and mask additional criteria, informal industry practices, and mythologies pertaining to each profession, particularly one as elite as choosing professors and colleagues. As legal scholar Elizabeth Bartholet observed in her classic 1982 piece critiquing the "Application of Title VII to Jobs in High Places":

> Recent legal developments call into question whether the principles applied to open up blue collar jobs to blacks will be applied to upper level jobs. The courts have tended to show far greater deference to upper than to lower level employ-ers.... While the Supreme Court has not explicitly differentiated between upper and lower level employment systems, it has hinted, just as upper level job issues are coming to the forefront, that it may be prepared to relax [T]itle VII standards for employers on all levels.
>
> Courts have tended to obscure the extent to which they have applied a differen-tial standard, presumably because ... [T]itle VII appears to provide no basis for distinguishing between lower and upper level jobs. The message that blacks may be excluded from proportionate participation in upper level jobs has consequently been communicated in a singularly obnoxious form. Because the courts have been reluctant to state that upper level employment should be subject to a more lenient standard, they have tended to endorse racially exclusionary upper level selection systems by finding that these systems meet the stringent standards applied to lower level jobs. Employer policies that exclude blacks from positions of respon-sibility in the most important institutions in our society have been found reason-able and necessary to maintain the quality of those institutions. Demands for

access by blacks have been rejected as equivalent to demands for the lowering of standards.[1]

Who has not seen this rarified reasoning articulated or assumed in faculty hiring decisions, either at the small committee level or in the larger faculty meeting setting? While many observers have noted that we need to look beyond basic hiring and admissions issues to establish improved or ideal college and departmental environments, I suggest that the most exclusionary practices occur in the distribution of the highest level of prestige resources, those of the various merit badges earned or handed out in the daily business of academia, especially in the award of tenure. There are many hidden assumptions and distributive inequalities in these prestige resources, and those inequalities are usually socially constructed, often highly competitive, and almost always racially significant.

To begin with, I note that this phenomenon of the inequitable distribution of merit badges has been widely observed and recorded. In addition to the important pioneering work of Professor Bartholet, who so carefully delineated the widespread failure of courts to accord satisfaction to minorities in high places, more recent employment law scholarship by Professors Pat Chew and Robert Kelley carefully examined hundreds of federal cases involving racial harassment from 1976 through 2002 and confirmed what Bartholet found in her study published fifteen years earlier. In "Unwrapping Racial Harassment Law," they found that there were many procedural hurdles and technical roadblocks to plaintiffs in successfully bringing Title VII, section 1981, and section 1983 claims, and that only 21.5 percent of all reported decisions—itself a winnowing process—were decided for the plaintiffs.[2] Their comprehensive database revealed a number of features that exceed the more modest scope of my project, but particularly striking were the various informal means by which judges manage such cases and narrow their scope.

Indeed, their study found that plaintiffs in racial harassment cases won only 20.8 percent of federal district court cases and 24.5 percent of their appellate cases; in contrast, sexual harassment plaintiffs win nearly half the time: 48.2 percent, with 51.2 percent at the district level and 39 percent at the circuit courts.[3] While the databases and definitions vary across studies, it is clear that this is a rough apples-to-apples comparison. It is difficult to win harassment cases, and the more elite the profession, the more discretion is accorded the employers. Again, drawing from Chew and Kelley, the data show that the higher the occupation status, the less likely employee-plaintiffs are to win. Their conclusions are complex but seem intuitive; the more blue-collar the position, the more blatant or obvious the nature and type of harassment are. In higher-end occupational status positions, such as general management or faculty, the norms and behaviors are less obvious and more subtle. They note:

> While the existence of both blatant racism and subtle racism has been recognized by social scientists, a number of legal scholars argue that the courts do not recognize more subtle discrimination. This study supports this contention: judges are slightly more likely to recognize blatant racial prejudice than more contextual or subtle racial prejudice. In perusing the plaintiffs' presentation of facts and particularly when evaluating whether the harassment is "because of race," judges tend to deem relevant only those allegations of harassment that are overtly race-linked. Thus, judges make reference to racial epithets such as "nigger" and to "noose" incidents, but tend not to find relevant plaintiffs' allegations of their exclusion from professional or work-related activities; social isolation; or hostile, rude, and demeaning comments that do not expressly include a racial epithet. Most judges do not know, do not find applicable, or do not find persuasive the relevant social science research on subtle and contextual racial harassment.[4]

Nooses and specific racial epithets are concededly less likely to occur in high places, especially on campuses, so what do racial harassment and insensitivity look like at this level in the academic workplace? The best example may be *Clark v. Claremont University Center and Graduate School*,[5] a rare example where a traditionally white college actually lost a discrimination claim, brought by Reginald Clark, a faculty member of color who was treated very badly by his clueless colleagues. Such cases are all the more rare because they are more blatant than one would normally find in boorish departmental behavior or institutional rough and tumble. After all, cases where colleagues are simply boors or even sons-of-bitches occur more commonly than most of us in this field care to acknowledge in public.[6]

However, these garden-variety cases do not often shock the conscience or rise to the level of both specific and casual racism that occurred here. This case even involved racial epithets and graffiti: "The 1982 term, however, was marred by the racial vandalism and ransacking of some faculty offices in the education department. Clark's office was broken into, ransacked, and spray painted with a 'nigger inscription' on the wall. Several other offices were also damaged."[7] But rather than treat Professor Clark as the victim, his colleagues interrogated him and accused him of somehow prompting the crime. The court noted, "Upon discovering the vandalism, Clark's colleagues questioned Clark. Professor Weeres asked Clark if he knew anything about the incident. Similarly, Chairman Briner questioned Clark and remarked that 'this never happened before you came.' Professor Kerchner said to Clark, 'God damnit, Reg, now, look what you have done.' Later that evening, Professor Dreyer dropped by Clark's house with some beer, ostensibly to see how Clark was doing. However, Dreyer also questioned Clark about his movements the previous day. According to Clark, Dreyer said 'someone had taken a valuable plaque of his. He did not know who was behind it. He was hoping it was not some jealous person who would do that to him. He did not know who did it. He asked me again, are you sure you did not go out at all last night?' "[8]

In *Clark*, the African American assistant professor of education at Claremont Graduate School (CGS—later renamed Claremont University Center) brought suit under the State's Fair Employment and Housing Act after being denied promotion and tenure. After hearing evidence of the extraordinary goings-on at CGS, the jury believed his compelling trial narrative and found for him. The appeals court upheld the judgments.[9] Much of the case was ordinary legal skirmishing about academic norms and quality judgments and the like, but what was most unusual (in addition to the result, which was unprecedented) was the way that the tenure review committee behaved and how Clark became aware of their reasoning. I cite at length from the appellate decision, and I indicate for the record that—even at my most cynical bad self—I could not make up this kind of thing:

> While Clark's tenure request was in the departmental review stage, Clark, who was viewing a tape in the audio-visual room, happened to hear loud voices next door. It turned out that the department was holding a faculty meeting on Clark's tenure request. Clark overheard Professor Kerchner say, "Who in the hell does he think he is anyway. Let's make him wait a couple of years and show him how we do things around here." Clark then heard Kerchner say, "Yeah, we don't have to review his request for a raise, do we? I mean, us [sic] white people have rights too." Then a voice said, "No, we are not here to review his request for a raise. He's asked the dean for the dean's review. What we are here to do is talk about his request for tenure."
>
> Clark then heard Professor Dreyer say: "Well, you know, let's review where we are. Now, we are all agreed he's got the potential for greatness, perhaps. But you know I just don't know how I would really feel. I have been giving that a lot of thought going to these conferences with him, and I have been thinking about it seriously. I don't know how I would feel working on a permanent base [sic] with a black man."

By this time, Clark had started taking notes of the conversation. He then heard Professor [Shuster] say, "Well, we are not under any obligation to have any blacks because we are a private college. It's the public universities that are under that constraint right now."

Professor Drew then said: "Well, one thing is for sure. If we keep him around here, we will have to do what it takes to help him succeed."

Professor [Shuster] said: "Well, one thing I will say. We won't find another black with as much an effect as he has."

An unidentified person said: "Well, let's tell Conrad [Briner]. Let's tell him his teaching is bad. And let Con be the one that tells him. He trusts Con the most. He will accept it if it comes from Con."

In response, Professor Weeres said: "No, he won't. He's too proud. He won't buy it. He thinks he's a fantastic teacher. He wouldn't go for it."

Clark testified that the discussion then turned to the question of whether President Maguire would "go along with this." Someone said, "First, we know what we will do at the [next] level. We will take care of that. Then it is in the hands of Maguire. Then we think he'll go along with it."[10]

The court felt that there was no reason to question the record or the jury's verdict: "There was ample evidence to support an inference that Professor Dreyer felt uncomfortable working with Clark due to his race. According to Clark's testimony, Dreyer told Clark he was against admitting a 'critical mass' of minority students; Dreyer resisted Clark's efforts to deemphasize test scores in order to admit more qualified minority students; Dreyer admitted to Clark he had problems getting along with black women and spoke disparagingly about a student who used the term African-American in her work. The jury could reasonably infer from this evidence that Dreyer resented Clark's presence at Claremont because of his race and his activism."[11]

The remarkable tone of this detailed opinion is staggering, and in many respects, resembles the anti-Semitic *Abrams* decisionmaking chronicle discussed in chapter 6. But this judicial review turns on an even more comprehensive record and important features than a Saudi summer program with its short-term financial rewards. It is clear that CGU's casually racist language and derogatory attitudes convinced the court that the faculty had acted in a discriminatory fashion:

Claremont places great reliance on the fact that the discriminatory remarks were only made by Education Faculty members, and not by either the APT Committee members who voted against Clark or President Maguire. However, Clark is not required to prove intentional discrimination at each level of the review process. The jury was entitled to rely on: the evidence that Chairman Briner misled Clark concerning publication requirements and gave him a discriminatory review; the conceded remark by Professor Kerchner ("us white people have rights, too") who wrote a negative letter to the APT Committee; the evidence that Dreyer's luke-warm support for Clark before the APT Committee was a subterfuge for discrimi-nation; the statistical evidence that Claremont had never granted tenure to a mi-nority professor; the testimony by other scholars concerning the excellence of Clark's work and the ground breaking nature of Clark's book; the granting of tenure to other nonminority professors (Professors Dreyer and Weeres) who had less substantial publishing records; and Claremont's use of changing, unwritten publication standards to justify its denial of tenure to Clark.[12]

This is riveting academic theater and very unusual evidence in such a trial. Only extremely rarely do plaintiffs, even those with substantial reason to suspect that they are not being treated fairly, have firsthand evidence of what actually was said in a closed-door meeting about their own case. The stunned Professor Clark surely rejoiced to have been so proximate to the deliberations, while pre-paring AV materials for class right next the very room where his personal and professional fate was being decided. Very few courts will allow wide-ranging depositions and discovery to recount confidential discussions in meetings, so without some convincing evidence, such as a witness who is stricken by con-science or some incriminating records that leak out, almost no plaintiff will have access to the information sufficient to discover the blatant racism that appeared to have occurred here. Clark was also helped by the sheer implausibility of the CGS claims that he was unqualified. The court notes that his record exceeded those of other recent comparators (who happened to be on the same small fac-ulty, some of whom were in that room), that the book in question was to be published by the prestigious University of Chicago Press, that at the time of the case in 1992 CGS had never tenured a black faculty member, and that another black faculty member had also been denied tenure. In recounting her situation, Professor Dreyer had conceded in a public conversation that "he seemed to al-ways have trouble with black women." Then there was that racial graffiti, for which his colleagues actually had blamed Clark for having attracted it to their campus or something even more sinister.

Clark filed a complaint against Claremont with the California Department of Fair Employment and Housing, alleging that he was a victim of race discrimina-tion. On May 5, 1985, the department gave Clark a right-to-sue letter. After waiting almost a year in hopes that Claremont would reconsider and award him tenure, on May 2, 1986, Clark filed an action in state court for damages for racial discrimination against Claremont under the Fair Employment and Housing Act (FEHA), alleging disparate treatment and disparate impact theories of employment discrimination.

The first trial in March 1989 ended in a mistrial due to juror attrition on the sixth day of deliberations, after an outbreak of flu struck several jurors. Here, Claremont played hardball, refusing to accede to a continuance so that the jurors could recover, necessitating a second trial almost a year later. There may have been a hope that Clark would run out of money or the will to pursue the matter, as several years had already elapsed. The trial judge granted the university's motion for a directed verdict on the disparate impact theory and certified several questions to the jury, which they were required to decide by at least nine of the twelve members. They found that Claremont was liable for racial discrimination and awarded Clark $1 million in compensatory damages and $16,327 in punitive damages; he was also awarded attorney's fees of $419,633.13.

On the issue of punitive damages, the jury had wanted to find Claremont liable for a greater amount, but the Claremont lawyers cleverly argued that the $16,000 was all that the university had available—that any more would not be covered by insurance and would, in effect, take scholarships from future students. A fascinating contemporaneous newspaper account detailed the claims by Claremont:

> A school accountant testified that the graduate school had $79 million in assets and $10 million in liabilities. [Claremont attorney Catherine] Hagen told the jury that "$1 million is a whole lot for the school. You already sent them a message, and they have been humbled and saddened by it. Please don't punish them any more."
>
> The jurors spent another 45 minutes deliberating and then voted 11 to 1 to award Clark an additional $16,237 in punitive damages—the [entire] amount Claremont had in its cash account. They said later in interviews that they heeded Hagen's warning that the school would have to raise students' tuition to pay for any punitive damages. Such awards are . . . not covered by any liability insurance that the school may hold.
>
> "We didn't want to increase tuitions for students," jury foreman Sean Reaney, a 23-year-old airline flight attendant, said. "So we thought that, by draining the college's active cash account, they would get the message."[13]

Of course, in order to make such a claim of poverty, CGU had only to make cash transfers out of that particular account and leave the change on the table.

The annual multi-million dollar budget clearly would have allowed the institution to pay more punitive damages than this single account indicated. After the damages portion of the trial, the judge entered judgment for Clark and denied Claremont's motions for a new trial and request for a judgment notwithstanding the verdict. The university then appealed to the state appellate court, which, after reviewing all the issues raised on appeal by the institution's lawyers, from the merits to the inferences drawn by the jury to the jury instructions, held: "At the outset, we note the trial court denied Claremont's motion for judgment notwithstanding the verdict. We agree with the trial court's determination that the evidence, viewed in the light most favorable to Clark, was sufficient to support the verdict."[14]

In a very detailed review, the appellate court sifted through the voluminous and complicated trial record and upheld the entirety of the earlier result, except for a remand on attorney's fees. (In this and in other respects, this case eerily resembles the *Abrams* trial and its aftermath, especially on the egregious fact patterns, the detailed and damning trial record, and the acceptance by the appellate courts. Both also involved additional determinations on the issue of the attorney's fees.) The appellate court was very sure that the jury and trial judge had committed no error in the original complete trial, which was actually the do-over after the illnesses that had occurred on the second week of the first trial: "We must add we are not surprised by the jury's verdict. Many employment discrimination cases do not even survive to trial because evidence of the employer's improper motive is so difficult to obtain. This case is unusual, not because of Clark's claims, but because of Clark's strong evidence of improper motive. Our own computer-assisted research of tenure denial cases across the nation revealed none involving university professors who made such blatant remarks as in this case. We hold the jury's verdict is supported by substantial evidence."[15]

The university's lawyers appealed to the California Supreme Court, which denied the appeal on July 23, 1992, and the matter was ended. Professor Clark never again held a permanent position at another college, although he taught part-time over the years in the California State University system. He became a successful consultant and evaluation specialist in the Los Angeles area, working with many school districts and foundations.

His team of lawyers has gone on in unusual ways. Steven Friedman, who briefed the appeal of the case before the California Court of Appeal and California Supreme Court, practices employment law in Los Angeles, as does Godfrey Isaac, whose original case it was; he is now in his mid-eighties. Most interestingly, co-counsel Ellen Rabiner left the practice of law to become a contralto at the Metropolitan Opera; several summers ago, I heard her sing a glorious Gaea in Richard Strauss's *Daphne* at the Santa Fe Opera. Her email address contains a combination of the two strands of her life as a contralto and a lawyer, and is a version of *altoesq.* Attorney Catherine Hagen Pepe tried the case as the university's attorney, as outside counsel from the Los Angeles law firm O'Melveny & Myers, where she was a partner and from which she retired in 1994. In 2008, she was appointed to serve as an independent diversity monitor for Morgan Stanley's Global Wealth Management Group.

What surprised the appellate court twenty years ago remains essentially undisturbed since 1992: "This case is unusual, not because of Clark's claims, but because of Clark's strong evidence of improper motive. Our own computer-assisted research of tenure denial cases across the nation revealed none involving university professors who made such blatant remarks as in this case."[16] To many observers, particularly to women and persons of color, this case will ring true, with the devastating and telling details of the locker-room dialogue in the tenure committee conference room. I knew several of the participants in this sad matter and found the proceedings that led to the case hard to fathom. Even so, cases in academe where faculty win tenure and promotion are exceedingly rare, and Clark was not awarded tenure, even in this instance with its remarkable and unique optics. To paraphrase the Chew-Kelley findings, many are claimed, but few are chosen.

Chapter 6 suggested substantial and widespread evidence of anti-Semitism in the Baylor College of Medicine's summer Saudi program, perhaps even more open and evident than this focused private example at Claremont, as it had penalized and stigmatized an entire people. The short list of reported discrimination cases that have awarded either tenure or promotion due to systemic and blatant sexism and/or racism would include *Brown v. Boston University* (1989),[17] *Bennun v. Rutgers* (1990),[18] and *Jew v. University of Iowa* (1990),[19] a particularly ugly race and sexual harassment case in a medical school anatomy department that may have set the low bar for institutional indifference and sheer hostility. Professor Jean Jew, an accomplished neuroscientist, was treated so horribly in the Iowa matter that I could not even believe the published details, which included over a dozen years of vicious racial and sexual innuendo, graffiti, lewd taunts, and slander. More, I could not believe that a major institution would not only tolerate such behavior but would also act so badly in its legal resolution. Law professor Martha Chamallas, one of Jew's University of Iowa defenders, has written sorrowfully of this case:

This case has taught me a host of potentially conflicting lessons. Sometimes I consider Jew's case to be a complete victory; she won in the courts, she changed public opinion in our [Iowa City] community, while insisting that she should not be forced to find a new job in a more hospitable environment. Sometimes, however, I regard Jew's case as a warning that legal claims of sexual harassment offer only very limited prospects for social transformation.

Jew's victory was exacted at an extremely high cost. Jew fought the University for more than a decade and was treated cruelly by an institution which, during the lengthy ordeal, professed a commitment to sexual and racial equality. As Jew acknowledged, her public stance was made possible only because she was relatively privileged in terms of education, economic and social position and had no partner or child who might also suffer from the stress and ostracism that accompanies such a lawsuit. I also regard Jew's case as special because certain unusual factors, including grassroots organization and extensive press coverage, combined to overcome the formidable institutional resistance to her claims.[20]

I had Jean Jew's incredible story on my list of possible candidates for case studies in this book project but decided that Professor Chamallas's insider work on the case had flushed out the departmental and institutional behavior, as had legal scholar Amy Gajda's recent book *The Trials of Academe,* where she characterizes the "vile conduct" in the case.[21] I could not improve on these and other treatments of the case.[22] Read together, these pieces do not allow the matter to be swept under the rug. Anyone using Google Scholar can find the case and the commentary. Reginald Clark's case is not as well known.

Another study I considered was that of my University of Houston colleague Ignacio (Tatcho) Mindiola's case, also from 1990, which eventually led to an out-of-court settlement for his award of tenure in sociology. In a very unusual resolution, the case ended happily for him and resulted in his actually remaining at the same university all of these twenty-plus years since. He wrote about the matter,[23] employing the disinfectant of sunlight on his trial, which also involved *Abrams v. BCOM* federal judge James DeAnda. In addition, I was a footnote in the institutional treatment of his review, so I did not include his trial in this book, where it would have seemed like too much insider baseball (or autobiography). Professor Clark did not win tenure and left college teaching, and his case has been largely untold, the proverbial zen tree falling in the forest, away from observers.

It is a good thing that there are relatively few cases in this ugly race to the bottom, although there are more cases than most people think, and many more examples of unfortunate and discriminatory behavior in colleges than the actual cases would indicate. One thing is clear: the costs for such litigation—the literal, institutional, and personal—are incalculable.

CHAPTER TEN

The Developing Law of Faculty Discontent: The *Garcetti* Effect

In 1993, Professor Michael S. Adams began his career as an assistant professor of criminology in the Department of Sociology and Criminal Justice at the University of North Carolina-Wilmington. He gained tenure and was promoted to associate professor in 1998. The Fourth Circuit describes succinctly what happened next to change the trajectory of his career at the institution:

> In 2000, Adams became a Christian, a conversion that transformed not only his religious beliefs, but also his ideological views. After his conversion, Adams became increasingly vocal about various political and social issues that arose within both the UNCW community and society at large. He became a regular columnist for Townhall.com and appeared on radio and televisions broadcasts as a commentator. In 2004, he published a book entitled *Welcome to the Ivory Tower of Babel: Confessions of a Conservative College Professor,* a collection of previously-published columns and new material. Throughout this time, Adams continued to receive strong teaching reviews from students and faculty.
>
> As Adams cultivated his conservative standing beyond the UNCW campus, some tension evolved within the UNCW community. Some UNCW employees indicated discomfort with Adams' views and his manner of expressing them. From time to time, UNCW officials fielded complaints from members of the Board of Trustees, the faculty and staff, and the general public about Adams' public expressions of his views. Correspondence about the complaints indicates that while UNCW officials, some of whom are named Defendants, occasionally expressed personal disagreement with the content of Adams' columns, they uniformly recognized that the First Amendment and principles of academic freedom protected Adams' writings and other expressions of his views. At one point, defendant Levy,

then interim chair of the Department, suggested that Adams alter the tone of his speech to be less " 'caustic' " and more " 'cerebral' " "like William F. Buckley" in order to " 'make things a whole lot more pleasant around the office.' "[1]

At the outset, it is not at all clear how behaving like William F. Buckley would have made Adams more pleasant to be around—I always found Buckley to be a pompous prig in his public persona, with a grating voice and accent. But no matter. It is clear from the details of this case that Professor Adams found himself at odds with his department. Matters came to a head in 2004 when he applied for promotion to full professor and his promotion was denied. He sued in federal court, claiming discrimination for his religious and political beliefs; he lost when the judge granted summary judgments for the university on all counts.[2] He appealed to the Fourth Circuit, which held that Adams had failed to show religion was a "motivating factor" in the departmental and university decision not to promote him to full professor or that he was denied his promotion due to unlawful discrimination. This ruling upheld part of the trial court's verdict. However, Adams did prevail upon a separate *Garcetti* issue: His protected speech was not transformed into unprotected speech in his promotion review. On this theory, the Fourth Circuit remanded the case to the trial court for further review in 2011.[3] It has not yet been finally resolved.

The lawyers bringing his case were from the Alliance Defense Fund, one of the purposive organizations most active today in higher education litigation, representing conservative and Christian clients such as Professor Adams in the United States and internationally. A case such as this, where a faculty member feels aggrieved due to his or her Christian beliefs, lies squarely within the ADF litigation agenda, as defined in the notably stark and strident language of its website: "We *must* continue the fight for religious freedom and the right of conscience, so that the life-changing message of Jesus Christ can be proclaimed and transform our culture. Each win for the Body of Christ is a loss for the opposition. It's that black and white."[4]

Well, I studied to be a priest for eight years in high school and college seminaries and consider myself to be a cultural and practicing Catholic and a person of faith. But I have found myself on the opposite side of the Alliance Defense Fund and its fellow organizations on almost every issue concerning higher education institutions. Even writing this autobiographical reference makes me uncomfortable and reticent, for I believe strongly in a sharper separation of church and state, and I believe that it is proper to render to Caesar on virtually every issue pitting one against the other, reserving religious faith to private spheres.

One of my brothers, a Ph.D. in religious history and a college professor and fundamentalist minister in a Los Angeles immigrant church, once called me a "hopeless secular humanist former seminarian." I took it as loving praise, whether he intended as such or not.

Yet as a member of the American Association of University Professors (AAUP) Litigation Committee, I found myself endorsing our participation as *amici* in Adams's appeal to the Fourth Circuit. For me, it was an easy call: In our brief, we emphasized the academic freedom exception promised in *Garcetti* and asked the court to rely in large part on the Supreme Court's recognition in *Garcetti, Sweezy,* and other cases of the value and special nature of academic speech. We did not take a position on Professor Adams's speech in this matter or on his promotion but urged the circuit to look more carefully at the operations of academic promotions and why faculty produce scholarship for our own intrinsic reasons, and not at the behest of our employer institutions. In the AAUP view, we believe that the district court erred by even applying *Garcetti* to the facts of this case, especially in the Fourth Circuit.[5]

The U.S. Supreme Court reserved the issue of *Garcetti*'s application to "scholarship and teaching," and the Fourth Circuit is one of the circuits that has not applied *Garcetti* to college academic freedom disputes; rather, it has employed the *Pickering-Connick* doctrines, concerning whether a matter is of "public concern."[6] The district court confused the common law of academic decisionmaking, wrongly concluding that Professor Adams's publications in his promotion application were written "pursuant to his official duties" and that they merited no First Amendment protection, based upon *Garcetti*.[7] Not only are promotion-related materials dictionary definitions of the category "scholarship and teaching," but the district court should also have applied Fourth Circuit law, holding that *Garcetti* is not the controlling law for academic speech.

Of course, all this sturm and drang is due to the dreadful SCOTUS reasoning in *Garcetti v. Ceballos,* where the trial judge had dismissed Assistant District Attorney Ceballos's claim, ruling that his professional memo was unprotected by the First Amendment because he had drafted it as a function of his employment duties.[8] The Ninth Circuit reversed the trial court, ruling that the *Pickering-Connick* lines of reasoning required balancing and, because Ceballos had exposed governmental misconduct, his speech should be characterized and protected as "inherently a matter of public concern," no matter how disruptive to the good of the order in the district attorney's office.[9] U.S. Supreme Court Justice William Kennedy, writing for the majority, rejected the Ninth Circuit's reasoning and found for District Attorney Garcetti: "When public employees make statements pursuant to their official duties, the employees are not speaking as citizens for First Amendment purposes, and the Constitution does not insulate their communications from employer discipline."[10] In reaching its decision, the Court characterized a public employee's official speech as a product "commissioned or created" by the employer.[11] Justice David Souter wrote a dissent, fearing and hoping that the decision "does not mean to imperil First Amendment protection of academic freedom in public colleges and universities, whose teachers necessarily speak and write 'pursuant to official duties.' "[12] In response, Justice Kennedy noted: "There is some argument that expression related to academic scholarship or classroom instruction implicates additional constitutional interests that are not fully accounted for by this Court's customary employee-speech jurisprudence. We need not, and for that reason do not, decide whether the analysis we conduct today would apply in the same manner to a case involving speech related to scholarship or teaching."[13] From his lips to God's ears— a prayer that seems particularly appropriate in the matter of Professor Adams.

The Fourth Circuit followed the AAUP's urging in the Michael Adams matter and applied its circuit law to the matter:

> We are also persuaded that *Garcetti* would not apply in the academic context of a public university as represented by the facts of this case. Our conclusion is based on the clear reservation of the issue in *Garcetti*, Fourth Circuit precedent, and the aspect of scholarship and teaching reflected by Adams' speech. . . .
>
> There may be instances in which a public university faculty member's assigned duties include a specific role in declaring or administering university policy, as opposed to scholarship or teaching. In that circumstance, *Garcetti* may apply to the specific instances of the faculty member's speech carrying out those duties. However, that is clearly not the circumstance in the case at bar. Defendants agree Adams' speech involves scholarship and teaching; indeed, as we discuss below, that is one of the reasons they say *Garcetti* should apply—because UNCW paid Adams to be a scholar and a teacher regardless of the setting for his work. But the scholarship and teaching in this case, Adams' speech, was intended for and directed at a national or international audience on issues of public importance unrelated to any of Adams' assigned teaching duties at UNCW or any other terms of his employment found in the record. Defendants concede none of Adams' speech was undertaken at the direction of UNCW, paid for by UNCW, or had any direct application to his UNCW duties.
>
> Applying *Garcetti* to the academic work of a public university faculty member under the facts of this case could place beyond the reach of First Amendment

protection many forms of public speech or service a professor engaged in during his employment. That would not appear to be what *Garcetti* intended, nor is it consistent with our long-standing recognition that no individual loses his ability to speak as a private citizen by virtue of public employment. In light of the above factors, we will not apply *Garcetti* to the circumstances of this case.

The Defendants nonetheless contend that because Adams was employed as an associate professor, and his position required him to engage in scholarship, research, and service to the community, Adams' speech constituted "statements made pursuant to [his] official duties." In other words, the Defendants argue Adams was employed to undertake his speech. This argument underscores the problem recognized by both the majority and the dissent in *Garcetti*, that "implicates additional constitutional interests that are not fully accounted for" when it comes to "expression related to academic scholarship or classroom instruction." . . . Put simply, Adams' speech was not tied to any more specific or direct employee duty than the general concept that professors will engage in writing, public appearances, and service within their respective fields. For all the reasons discussed above, that thin thread is insufficient to render Adams' speech "pursuant to [his] official duties" as intended by *Garcetti*.[14]

I am not an expert in the field of criminology and so cannot assess Adams's bona fides and the proper subject matter measure for such a promotion. No matter, as I stand shoulder to shoulder with Professor Adams in this matter, because the trial court used the wrong analysis and misapplied the vexing *Garcetti* doctrine to pour his claim out of court. But my final observation on this case is to note the civil rights, equal protection claim employed by Adams—that "he is the *only* Christian conservative in his Department"[15]—reasoning that neither the trial court nor the Fourth Circuit accepted. Because he never convinced the courts that his promotion denial had any nexus at all to his status or viewpoint as a conservative or a Christian, much less a "Christian conservative," this claim failed.

But it is instructive to note that his claim was essentially the same theory as that of Professor Lawrence M. Abrams in the Baylor College of Medicine case and that of Professor Reginald Clark in the Claremont matter, where they both prevailed, largely due to institutional perfidy—and institutional perfidy beyond that which most plaintiffs have traditionally been able to demonstrate. Regrettably, Mormon student Christina Axson-Flynn prevailed in her religious claim as well, using existing University of Utah religious accommodations in class scheduling to convince the Tenth Circuit that her Christian principles should extend to her classroom instructional assignments and class requirements. The good news in this case is that the circuit ruling is so wide of the mark that it has been cabined to its narrow facts and has not been followed in many other cases. It also died before getting to the Supreme Court, where it would have been the law of the land, either way it might have come out. Thus, it is limited to the 10th Circuit and the Rockies. *Garcetti,* however, has let slip.

My Friends, Special Programs, and Pipelines

Of course, I do not expect that only my aggrieved friends and allies—categories that are not always clear or consistent—should be able to use civil rights laws and theories. In fact, I reject this favoritism viscerally, both because I do not require my friends to hold my views (else I would have even fewer friends) but also because it is only fair that if I get to use all the tools, so should others, even those with whom I vehemently disagree, such as conservatives—especially radical conservatives and Christian activists—and immigration restrictionists. Audre Lorde famously remarked, "The master's tools will never dismantle the master's house,"[1] but I have a more modest agenda than dismantling any house: I want the restrictionists and the conservatives to acknowledge what I willingly concede to them—my use of all the legitimate tools and full participation in the discourse. Also on my wish list are two items: that they stop re-litigating the civil war of *Grutter* and accept its modest reach and that they start thinking constructively about how to help undocumented students, who someday will be members of our community, after the adults in Congress bring about comprehensive immigration reform.

For example, over the years, I have worked with and organized specialized programs and "pipeline" projects—the various programs undertaken to improve the flow of students into professions, such as high school newspaper editors working with newspapers, pre-med students working in labs with scientists, or pre-law students attending court with attorneys or observing judges. In my heart, I have always been somewhat skeptical of these programs, even as I have been involved in them much of my professional life, as I made my way to law school and the law profession without ever having known a lawyer as I was growing up. That I live in Texas much of the year leads some observers to think that

I must be an advocate for pipeline programs, but I have objected to the metaphor for many years, and once wrote:

[A pipeline] is a foreign mechanism introduced into an environment, an unnatural device used to leach valuable products from the earth. It requires artificial construction; in fact, it is a dictionary-perfect artifice. It cuts through an ecosystem and can have unintended and largely uncontrollable, deleterious effects on that environment. It can, and inevitably does, leak, particularly at its joints and seams. It can also rust prematurely, and if any part of it is blocked or clogged, the entire line is rendered inoperative.

For the admissions process, I prefer the metaphor of the "river." It is an organic entity, one that can be fed from many sources, including other bodies of water, rain, and melting snow. It can be diverted to create tributaries without altering its direction or purpose, feeding streams, canals, and fields; it can convey goods, drive mills and turbines, create boundaries, and irrigate land—all without diminishing its power. . . .

The metaphor chosen to describe the admissions process is important for its characterization of the problem, for the evidence mounted to measure the problem, and for the solutions proffered to resolve the problem. Let me illustrate briefly. Characterizing the problem of minority underenrollment at any level as a "pool problem" suggests a supply shortage or, at best, a failure to cast one's line in the right fishing hole. The pipeline metaphor reinforces this view of the problem, suggesting that minority enrollment is simply a delivery glitch, or that admissions committees would admit minorities if they only used better conveyances. After all, pipelines do not produce anything of value; they only carry or convey products. While both the supply function and the conveying function are important, they are not, individually, rich enough metaphors to portray the complex phenomenon of both functions intertwining to produce undergraduates and transform them into graduate or professional students.

A river, in contrast, provides nutrients and conveys resources, unlike its more static counterparts that do one or the other, but not both. . . . It constantly changes form, seeking new flows and creating new boundaries. It can even wear down rock, as observers of the Rio Grande Gorge and Grand Canyon can attest. This is what I wish to convey; that demography and efforts by schools to do the right thing will inevitably lead to improvement over time.[2]

Perhaps because of my religious training, I hold the view that anyone can be saved, and I am almost always the most optimistic person in the room. Having said that, I may be one of the few observers who does not think of these programs in purely legal terms but in cultural or organizational theories or normative terms. Things come in threes for me, so I offer these three lenses to view these programs. Consider them as motivational, efficacy, and boundary-spanning grounds; they also are proxies for other questions: What are the real issues? Who are your friends? and Where do you look for guidance?

First, I do not look for help among scholars and observers who urge that "class-based" differentiation be employed rather than racial algebra, both because brahmins are likely to preserve their class-based privileges no matter the regime, as occurs with alumni preference programs, and because the operationalization of these approaches is fraught with technical and conceptual difficulties. Try and determine "need" for a need-based financial aid program in a law school, where most students have accumulated undergraduate debt—unless they were wealthy or had other social class advantages—and the only real differentiation is among those with more than $100,000 debt and those with less. As unfair and complex as undergraduate need-determination is for financial aid packaging—and the system is both—at least there is a definable "family" built into "expected family contribution" calculations. For every complaint that the rise of biracial or multiracial individuals has made it impossible to ascertain race, there is a thermodynamic parallel of the impossibility of employing other class- or need-based criteria for parceling privilege.

Well-intentioned commentators such as Richard Kahlenberg have attempted to finesse this issue by raising different questions. In citing the work of others, he notes:

> Academics tend to look at the issue of race and class in affirmative action differently than judges. For example, . . . Carson Byrd, Wornie Reed, and Ellington Graves of the Center for Race and Social Policy at Virginia Tech, argue that "conflating class and race will not solve the problem of racial inequality." The authors suggest that "even members of racial and ethnic minorities who achieve middle- or upper-middle class status face discrimination every day. Money does not shelter people from racism." They conclude, "Class cannot serve as a proxy for race and ethnicity, or vice versa." We should pursue "both race-conscious and class-sensitive approaches."

How are these types of arguments likely to hold up in the event that the Supreme Court decides to take the Fisher case? One immediate problem is that the Court has never suggested that racial preferences are justified as a way to combat societal discrimination. Going back to the 1978 *Bakke* case, which permitted universities to use race as a factor to promote diversity, a majority of the Court rejected the idea that racial preference is an appropriate response to general societal discrimination. Justice Powell noted that societal discrimination could not justify imposing disadvantages on white applicants like Allan Bakke, "who bear no responsibility for whatever harm the beneficiaries of the special admissions program are thought to have suffered."

In *Bakke,* Justice Powell did, of course, provide universities with a green light for using race where there was no race-neutral way to produce sufficient racial diversity. Here, Byrd, Reed and Graves make an argument that is likely to have more resonance with the Court. Poor white and Asian American students, they note, tend to have "higher GPA's and test scores than those of poor blacks, Latinos, and American Indians." As a result, "College-admissions policies based on socioeconomic status are unlikely to increase racial and [ethnic] equality in higher education."

But a skeptical Supreme Court may press this issue, noting that at the University of Texas, economic affirmative action and the top-10-percent plan produced a class that was 4.5 percent African-American and 16.9-percent Hispanic in 2004, a combined rate that was higher than the "critical mass" achieved through racial means at the University of Michigan Law School in the *Grutter* case (between 13.5 and 20.1 percent minority.) Likewise, research by Anthony Carnevale and Stephen J. Rose found that class-based affirmative action could produce classes that were 10-percent black and Hispanic at the most selective 146 colleges and universities, down from 12-percent when using race, but up from 4 percent if basing admissions strictly on grades and test scores. Employing additional factors not used by Carnevale and Rose—such as wealth—could boost racial diversity further.

By definition, socioeconomic affirmative action won't guarantee a degree of racial diversity as efficiently as using race, but here it's important to note that the Court won't be asking what will produce the greatest racial diversity—only a "critical mass." As the minority representation among high school graduates grows in this county, over time, race-neutral alternatives will become more and more likely to produce critical mass, making it harder to justify the use of race.

If this line of thinking is depressing to those who care about racial, ethnic, and socioeconomic diversity, consider this: While Byrd, Reed and Graves suggest preserving the use of race is an avenue for addressing "both" class and racial inequality, a growing body of evidence suggests that universities have for years been pursuing racial diversity without giving a thought to socioeconomic inequality. Ironically, only when universities are constrained from using race have they aggressively sought class diversity. They do so not for its in own sake, but as an indirect way of addressing race—effectively pursuing both goals at once.[3]

My own take on this line of reasoning is that the Virginia Tech authors get it more right than Kahlenberg, who has argued for what he characterizes as race-neutral, class-based, economic affirmative action measures. On the plus side, he is against alumni privilege and edited an important 2010 work on the subject, one whose title gives away its premise: *Affirmative Action for the Rich: Legacy Preferences in College Admissions.*[4] But anyone who elides whether the University of Texas actually employed "economic affirmative action and the top-10-percent plan" to "produce" its student body ignores whether financial aid is truly redistributive (his "economic affirmative action"). More to the point, this perception misunderstands how the percent plan actually worked before and after it was diluted from 10 percent to 7 percent and fundamentally ignores its nonracial implementation. The *Fisher* case also fundamentally misconstrues how the plan operates to help more whites than it does African American or Mexican American students. Because the changes to the plan have only taken effect in 2011–2012, the most recent data are not yet available for detailed analysis, but it is instructive to see how the plan worked in 2007, before the legislature recalibrated the requirements for the UT-Austin campus: at UT-Austin, first-time freshman enrollment included 48 percent white, 0.5 percent American Indian, 6 percent African American, 21 percent Asian American, 23 percent Hispanic, and 2 percent international.[5] In other words, in this program, almost half of the participants were white, a counter-story to all—including the Fifth Circuit judges who wrongly criticized the plan for its allegedly antimajoritarian features.

But perhaps worse is that Kahlenberg and others would characterize this situation as one of sufficient "critical mass" in the numerator where the denominator is Texas public schoolchildren—which I consider a fair measure, although there are others—and where white Texas schoolchildren have declined in total numbers and as a percentage of the total. In 2005–2006, they were down to 36.5 percent, having declined by more than 8 percent over the previous decade. By 2011, their percentage had declined to 31.2 percent. Is almost half of a remedial program such as the percentage plan, enacted by minority advocates in a predominantly white legislature to counter *Hopwood*'s devastating effect, sufficient "critical mass" in a state where whites were only 36.5 percent of the state's public schools? While the highly competitive University of Michigan Law School might plausibly characterize 20 percent of its class (including all minorities) as sufficient critical mass, can the flagship campus of Texas consider the same 20 percent mass to be sufficiently critical? Is it even a "mass" in Texas?

It might be fairly said that neither *Bakke* nor *Grutter* permit quota plans, but at some point the concept of a critical mass must mean something different in

Texas than it would mean in Maine without invoking the specter of quotas, especially when the trends are so demonstrable and when the discussion is enrollment management. In the larger canvass of complex admissions decisions for the millions of college applicants each year, decisionmakers must live and operate in a real world, not the parallel universe of a never-never land, where even the nonracial plans advantage whites. Worse, those very plans are offered as serious evidence that enough is being done or, more likely, too much is being done. Courts have to contextualize these enrollment figures, and schools must narrowly tailor their criteria.

It might be argued that the percentage plans, which operate differently in the various states that employ them or a version of them, have stanched the losses that *Hopwood* inflicted in the years following that case; once *Grutter* reaffirmed the *Bakke* precedent of twenty-five years earlier, it is difficult to see, even by squinting, that racial diversity can be achieved by anything other than racial means, however imperfect. If the biblical admonition is correct that we will always have the poor among us and if we cannot measure poverty in a more fair and equitable way, why does "economic affirmative action" warrant such strenuous support? If discussions about the taxation of millionaires at the national level drive political claims of "class warfare,"[6] how would using imprecise, shape-shifting, and non-efficacious class-based admissions be more acceptable to elites or to middle-class white parents who will still suspect that they are getting the short end—just of a different stick? And these class advocates are, arguably, in the same pews I find myself in, or the same choir in which I sing. Here, I do not want any more help from my friends, who cannot meet their burden of persuasion.

On the other side of the aisle, conservative organized interests regularly monitor educational programs and benefits that appear to have gender or racial/ethnic restrictions. In chapter 1, I detailed some of the aggressive tactics of those who oppose reasonable efforts to integrate college and university student bodies and faculties, even when the means are not racial, as in percentage-plan admissions. At the same time, even good-faith supporters of such efforts are not always as helpful as they could be, and sometimes they just make mischief. I would analogize these to the bumptious immigration reforms for undocumented drivers' licenses undertaken in a naive and unnuanced manner in 2007 by New York's governor Eliot Spitzer, only to have to beat a hasty retreat, soiling the nest.[7] As I saw these events unfold, I prayed: Please save us from our supporters.

For higher education examples, consider two good-faith efforts by credible and established organizations. In its recent efforts to help colleges and universities craft legally viable options, a group sponsored by the College Board issued a series of reports to respond to the *Gratz v. Bollinger* and *Grutter v. Bollinger* decisions and to the rise of statewide racial initiatives. The reports help sort out the complex issues, as the March 2007 *From Federal Law to State Voter Initiatives* concludes: "Attention to longer term investments (such as support for pipeline-building programs) and shorter term strategies (such as rigorous evaluation and pursuit of all available avenues—race-conscious and race-neutral—likely to advance institution goals) can frame a comprehensive and coherent action agenda that is compelling in the court of law, just as it is in the court of public opinion."[8]

In another 2007 report, *Echoes of Bakke,* three of the same authors write:

> It is important that institutions seeking to justify race-conscious policies in such ways [by using diversity practices] heed the Court's long-standing admonition (reaffirmed in the school assignment cases) that "societal discrimination" can never be a compelling interest justifying race-conscious measures by a discrete institution. The Court has observed consistently that interests unlimited in scope or time can never meet the threshold of strict scrutiny analysis. (Consider the following: At what point can a single institution pursuing broad social goals declare that its race-conscious policies have succeeded, and how would that institution establish such evidence?)[9]

The first recommendation (that schools pursue pipeline programs) suggests that these programs are somehow immune from purposive conservative organizational challenges and that such programs appreciably add to the sum. They are assuredly not immune and, overall, with few exceptions, have not added to the sum. I have monitored such programs across disciplines for years and have reluctantly come to believe that most of them are so small, transitory, soft-money-dependent, and contingent that they almost mask the failure of mainstream opportunity structures. Money and resources for these initiatives come and go, depending on foundation priorities, and the cycle rediscovers minority pipeline programs every few years, as the mandala turns. Virtually no institutional reward structures encourage senior faculty, especially the accomplished ones, to undertake pipeline programs, whether minority-specific or more generic. And while I have never considered doing this kind of work as a tradeoff against my more fundamental scholarship activities or teaching obligations, many colleagues do consider this work as less important and more peripheral. If you are in a public institution or in a college or university in a state with racially restrictive constitutional provisions (or governor initiatives, as in Florida), then the game may hardly be worth the candle. More importantly, I cannot in good faith identify a single institution in the country, at least not historically white ones or major producer schools, that could ever plausibly conclude that its race-conscious policies have succeeded and worry about what evidence could be adduced to extricate itself from litigation. If UT-Austin, with its embarrassing *Sweatt* legacy, its laziness that was evident in *Hopwood,* and its underachievement, doesn't give rise to a constitutional institutional remedy based on its historical record in court, virtually no school could muster such a defense.[10] Such admonitions strike me as counterproductive and chimerical, or, at the least, unnecessary.

The American Association for the Advancement of Science (AAAS) makes a very eloquent argument in *Standing Our Ground* for science, technology, engineering, and mathematics (STEM) programs to diversify those essential fields, but it is not clear to all observers that diversity programs can turn on perceived labor needs or national priorities.[11] I appreciate the efforts that some professional associations have played in undertaking and producing specialized programs to diversify their professions and to draw attention to the problems, but this supportive role and cultivation of the process cannot fundamentally alter the production function of campus-based efforts, where they really count. Various programs must affect and shape students (and junior faculty, for those programs that seek to develop the professoriate) in their academic programs to be truly transformative and meaningful; no peripheral agency or organization, however well-intentioned, can substitute for the home garden. I certainly think that professional associations and scholarly communities can cajole, shape, cheerlead, and assist, but at the end of the day, what counts is training and credentialing students (and faculty) where they are and where they will serve. Relying on the periodic and transitory attention of funders or the profession as a whole cannot provide the long-term, personal, and institutional commitments needed to remedy the serious problems. I applaud and recognize efforts by these well-meaning organizations, which are on the right side of the issue and of history, and many others, but I question the extent to which they can counter the systemic failure of graduate programs to recruit and graduate underrepresented U.S. minority students. Of course, there are institutionally based programs, including some that are well established and long-running.[12] But until the major elite feeder schools institutionalize these efforts to produce minority scientists, engineers, scholars, lawyers, and so on, such specialized and targeted programs cannot meet the increasing needs of society.

And rather than help with these underlying problems, restrictionist and conservative groups would rather challenge and dismantle them than add positively to the efforts. Where are they in offering initiatives to actually do something about the problems, rather than simply standing by and shooting the wounded on the battlefield? When will they sue an institution that is almost exclusively white or one that consistently underperforms by not enrolling minority students? When will they publicly challenge public college legacy admissions, such as, it turned out, were in existence at the University of Michigan? Where are their integrative and developmental efforts? When will they propose acceptable pipeline programs, rather than attacking them? Why advocate against race-neutral programs, such as percentage plans, especially when these challenges have not prevailed in courts and when white applicants prosper disproportionately by them? Why oppose state residency status to the undocumented, even when in California the major beneficiaries of A.B. 540 (the state statute according resident tuition for undocumented students) were the 80 percent who were U.S. citizens, largely whites? If they would undertake this line of inquiry, rather than acting in a nihilist and obstructionist fashion, we might engage in constructive action and discourse rather than seeing them simply sue every time they think a white Christian applicant has been slighted.

A number of progressive higher education advocates have held their breath since *Parents Involved in Community Schools v. Seattle School District No. 1*,[13] the Seattle and Louisville case decided in 2007 by the U.S. Supreme Court, as the racial attendance policies were held to be unconstitutional in the K–12 sector. Many decisions in one sector bleed into the other, but this decision may augur less for college and university law than it does in signaling how race cases will be decided by the Court in the future. It is true that there are college-siting and attendance cases that have clear racial consequences (as seen in the *LULAC v. Richards* case, examined in chapter 7), but *Parents Involved* will, in my estimation, not have substantial postsecondary implications, at least not for admissions cases, such as *Fisher v. University of Texas*, which, after *Grutter* and *Parents Involved*, upheld UT-Austin's modest use of race in its undergraduate admissions program. The *Grutter* holding is likely safe for the time being, more because the court will be unlikely to accept such a case for some time. *Regents of the University of California v. Bakke* held sway for over twenty-five years (eroding and losing force) before it was largely reaffirmed by the University of Michigan Law School admissions case.

In *Parents Involved*, the Court accepted that strict scrutiny was a legitimate interest in admissions and enrollment diversity, which had been upheld in *Grutter* "in the context of higher education."[14] It also differentiated the postsecondary context:

In upholding the admissions plan in *Grutter,* though, this Court relied upon considerations unique to institutions of higher education, noting that in light of "the expansive freedoms of speech and thought associated with the university environment, universities occupy a special niche in our constitutional tradition." The Court explained that "context matters" in applying strict scrutiny, and repeatedly noted that it was addressing the use of race "in the context of higher education." The Court in *Grutter* expressly articulated key limitations on its holding—defining a specific type of broad-based diversity and noting the unique context of higher education—but these limitations were largely disregarded by the lower courts in extending *Grutter* to uphold race-based assignments in elementary and secondary schools. The present cases are not governed by *Grutter.*[15]

But the U.S. Supreme Court and other courts have not always consistently identified a line between higher education and K–12 cases. For example, I list three (of many) examples where the differentiation has been clear and not-so-clear: high school newspapers and yearbooks, grooming standards, and inequities claimed on the basis of "regions" within a state. Where newspapers and yearbooks are concerned, *Hazelwood School District v. Kuhlmeier* reads: "We have nonetheless recognized that the First Amendment rights of students in the [K–12] public schools 'are not automatically coextensive with the rights of adults in other settings,' and must be 'applied in light of the special characteristics of the school environment.'"[16] A case involving grooming standards, *Lansdale v. Tyler Junior College,* held: "Today the court affirms that the adult's constitutional right to wear his hair as he chooses supersedes the State's right to intrude. The place where the line of permissible hair style regulation is drawn is between the high school door and the college gate."[17] One judge in the case dissented on this very issue: "I dissent, first, because I see no distinction between high schools and junior colleges under the *Karr v. Schmidt* holding, which is now the law of this Circuit."[18] In *Richards v. League of United Latin American Citizens,* on the issue of residence and attendance zones in higher education, another court differentiated between the sectors: "The constitutional directive to maintain 'an efficient system of public free schools' does not apply to higher education as that term is used in this case."[19]

I have made three observations and attempted to muster evidence for maintaining gains and increasing access for disadvantaged groups, particularly at the postbaccalaureate professional and graduate level, although my points apply with equal weight to the undergraduate experience and the transition from high school to college. First, restrictionist and conservative and religious pressures will likely increase, especially as the number and percentage of people of color increase and as immigrants and non-Christians grow in the U.S. polity and community. Second, mainstream and progressive groups offer advice and make suggestions that are unlikely to be efficacious. And third, the Supreme Court does not always make a fine distinction between K–12 and higher education.

On this point, it is true that the high wall between the two sectors has been observed in the breach by judges, but it is a line nonetheless. The Seventh Circuit, as one example, has ignored Justice Kennedy's admonition in leaching *Garcetti* into college cases, thereby confirming Justice Souter's warning, as regrettably occurred in 2008's *Renken v. Gregory*.[20] In *Isenalumhe v. McDuffie*, a U.S. District Court in New York in 2010 also extended the case to what it termed an "appointment [that] has become a nearly ten-year war of attrition."[21] Even when the Third Circuit has acknowledged *Garcetti*'s academic freedom reservation, it did so in a crabbed fashion in *Gorum v. Sessoms*, a 2009 ruling that left unclear whether faculty advising duties fall under its reach.[22] I am surely not the first person to make these points, and others have made one or the other observation in ways that are both eloquent and trenchant. But I have always considered myself an observer who was the last in the room to resort to legal action and the least likely to resort to the courts, unless all else fails. Therefore, when I see the issues today being conducted in administrative law frameworks or to have become so legalized, especially in conservative religious jihads against the secular state, my first reaction is despair.

Notwithstanding the naysayers and the restrictionists, whose agendas are aimed not at progressive action or equity but largely at preserving white privilege, I think that the country's demography is in not in their favor. When the smoke clears and the adults take over, we will not merely endure but prevail. I believe this even more in the context of comprehensive immigration reform, where nativists and restrictionists are monkey-wrenching modest efforts to incorporate undocumented college students, such as opposing residency requirements and DREAM Act legislation. They have not prevailed in any of their court challenges to these initiatives, even as they lay claim, with extraordinary hubris, to the legacy of the Mexican American Legal Defense and Educational Fund (MALDEF) efforts to resist such nativism.[23] I do not believe that Christianity is in peril in the United States, particularly in our colleges, or that there is a threat to its proper and meaningful role in our secular nation-state, although any observer can see that threats and hateful speech to Muslims are on the rise, sometimes even by other persons of faith. And there is a growing strain of intolerance among conservative Christians who have aligned themselves with political conservatives who act as if only they have the keys to the kingdom.[24] They do not.

The Alliance Defense Fund has armed itself for its own crusade, contending: "We *must* continue the fight for religious freedom and the right of conscience, so that the life-changing message of Jesus Christ can be proclaimed and transform our culture. Each win for the Body of Christ is a loss for the opposition. It's that black and white."[25] The ADF's battleground is an exceedingly narrow view both of religious freedom and of the question of whose culture is at risk. Muslims and Jews are the target of much religious bigotry in the United States and worldwide, and I am not certain if Christian groups have entirely thought through what a win for "the Body of Christ" means when Mormons cannot join the Christian Legal Society, when other groups are excluded from participating on pretextual grounds, or when the BYX fraternity sues after prevailing because the University of Florida had already settled for what BYX terms all the wrong reasons.

The terms "black and white" used in this context also have a disturbing and ironic racial resonance. Exactly who constitutes the "opposition" in such a Manichean worldview, and how is it implemented? Why is it that religious free exercise cases are brought almost exclusively by Christians, who overwhelmingly form the religious majority in the United States? Who anointed them in this plural religious community? Indeed, it is likely that these very demographic trends, which make conservative and predominantly white and Christian groups uneasy, will make it more difficult to preserve their historical advantages when there are simply more qualified people of color, more people of different faiths, and more immigrants. Mark my words: When that day dawns, there will be much more support for pipeline programs and for the cultivation of what will then be considered "minority" talent. Ask Professor Adams, who counts himself the only Christian conservative in his department, who not only sued but also found a ready vehicle for his litigation in a national legal organization trolling for such aggrieved clients. And their organizational roadmap was drawn by minority and progressive plaintiff organizations.

This book project has brought me full circle to the late political scientist Stephen K. Bailey, whose ideas drew me to this evolving field some forty years ago:

> Today, as we perceive this elemental paradox in the tensions between the academy and the state, it is useful to keep in mind its generic quality. For at heart we are dealing, I submit, with a dilemma we cannot rationally wish to resolve. The public interest would not . . . be served if the academy were to enjoy an untroubled im-

munity. Nor could the public interest be served by the academy's being subjected to an intimate surveillance. . . . Whatever our current discomforts, because of a sense that the state is crowding us a bit, the underlying tension is benign. . . . The academy is for the state a benign antibody and the state is the academy's legitimator, benefactor, and protector. Both perspectives are valid. May they remain in tension.[26]

Today's "underlying tension" is largely a script of the struggles over religious accommodation and racial and gender integration. The first is one that earlier higher education scholars did not scan or foresee on the horizon, while the latter has been evident in higher education for over a century. Legal and first amendment scholar Rodney Smolla has perceptively observed that the United States polity, like Caesar's Gaul, "might be divided into three strains of thought, representing three different positions on the 'separation spectrum,' three different judgments as to how much separation of church and state should be required under our constitutional system. The different strains of thought may be labeled 'high separationists,' 'middle separationists,' and 'low separationists.' These labels are intended to be nonjudgmental."[27] His examples along this spectrum or sliding scale strike me as accurate and fair: "Theoretically, an extreme high separationist might not permit religious displays, symbols, or language in any governmental enterprise. Such an individual might wish to banish religious art from public museums, prohibit the study of religions at universities, and ban publicly supported symphonies or choral groups from performing religious music."

> But such extreme separationism is rarely, if ever, seriously advanced, and most high separationists will acknowledge that government may permit the study or performance of religious phenomena for academic, artistic, or musical purposes. The academic study of religions at state universities (such as in religious studies departments), the display of religious art in government museums, or the performance of religious music by government symphonies are thus accepted as undertaken for a secular academic or artistic purpose. A state university symphony and choir performing Handel's Messiah is sharing the music for its musical value, not as an expression of worship.[28]
>
> Middle separationists will tolerate relatively modest invocations of general religious sentiments by government that are not sharply denominational. The middle separationist will not be offended by "In God We Trust" on currency, the inclusion of the phrase "under God" in the Pledge of Allegiance, or the opening of public events and ceremonies with a "nondenominational prayer." Middle separationists are particularly apt to support governmental religious language, symbols or rituals

if the practice has a long historic pedigree. Prayers to begin legislative sessions fall within this category.

Middle separationists are likely to have a number of nuanced positions. Invocations of religion are generally more permissible when directed at the general population than when directed at children or done within the public school setting. It will matter a great deal to middle separationists whether the practice is perceived as an endorsement of religion, particularly of one religion. Most middle separationists will deem such endorsements impermissible, and as jurists they will align with the high separationists to strike such measures down. Similarly, it will matter a great deal to middle separationists whether there is a coercive quality to the expression, and whether there is a "captive audience" that is forced to listen to it, particularly when those captive audience members are children.

Low separationists are likely to find no constitutional fault in government displays of religious language or symbols, or government participation in religious rituals. Short of an official recognition of one established church, or government coercion of professions of faith or belief, low separationists tend to treat such government displays as permissible.[29]

I adopt these guidelines and aggressively stake out a space in the middle separationist camp, particularly with college cases, where students are legally adults and where they can choose from among many sources and influences, in contrast to the more doctrinaire public schooling. I also find myself in the position of noting that a number of the disputes I have chronicled here are not nuanced whatsoever and involve low separationists who have arrogated religious exercise in their favor, but only insofar as the decision would protect their own faith, usually Christianity and, within that universe, usually evangelical Christian free exercise.

It is clear that the struggles will continue in determining the extent to which student organizations can try to have it both ways. In the context of registered student organizations that wish to receive the financial and other material support of a public institution, the U.S. Supreme Court held that an "all-comers" policy requiring all student groups to accept all members may not discriminate on the basis of viewpoint. A college's policy such as this would be "justified without reference to the content [or viewpoint] of the regulated speech.'" The permissible "all-comers requirement draws no distinction between groups based on their message or perspective."[30] But the most active litigants in this field are certainly Christian purposive organizations that continue to want it both ways. On the one hand, they wish to have full support of the state and its largesse and endorsement while wishing at the same time to exclude all who do not share their ascriptive requirements, such as a professed sexuality, a clear religious choice, or a feature that will be nourished by the group.

In my experience, virtually all affiliational student groups draw the believers, or those inclined to believe, to their membership. This is the magnet pull of such groups; while numerical majoritarianism is fine as far as it goes, true growth and development are more likely to flourish in a diverse and plural world, such as the one we live in. Like any other social organism, including families, there will always be core participants and those more comfortable on the periphery. Anyone who wishes only to join groups that align perfectly and steadfastly with what a nineteen-year-old thinks of as his or her orientation is misapprehending the entire point of having such a comprehensive regime of student groups on most public campuses. Could Christians at the University of Florida seriously demand and receive support for forty-eight Christian groups? While I can envision a hostile takeover of a Young Republican Organization by rabid Young Democrats, identification with a political party or partisan agenda will, unremarkably, draw political partisans—an appropriate purposive function and democratic lesson that is envisioned by the whole structure of these groups as small-scale laboratories for student learning and programming. They will survive and likely thrive. Or, if they wished to prevent Young Democrats from infiltrating their ranks, they could be subsidized instead by the national party rather than by the state taxpayers or student fees—and would likely do so without wringing their hands. While I could imagine a Muslim group taken over by Christians, I cannot envision the reverse happening, given the sheer demography and disposition of the likely participants. And if that did happen and the Muslim group wished to expel all nonbelievers, it could do so but would then not be allowed to take state support for its programs and recognition by the public college administration. These issues are being hammered out in *Alpha Delta Chi v. Reed*,[31] a Ninth Circuit case wending its way after *CLS v. Martinez*; as these cases multiply and dominate the federal courts, they, too, will suck all the oxygen out of the room. But the Alliance Defense Fund, taken at its purposive word, will not be happy until its sectarian jihad is accomplished and evangelical Christians—as narrowly trademarked by their singular creed—have full access to all college resources and enjoy full financial and organizational resources from secular institutions, even while denying all apostates and sinners from membership in their many organizations.

I am certain that I have not persuaded many others to my view that these are essentially fools' errands that entangle the state with what have become religious missions disguised as First Amendment protections. I believe that not only should the state resist, especially when purposive groups wish to exclude others from their membership on personal characteristics, but also that the groups would not be helped by prevailing and should not wish to do so. Any truly popular or efficacious group can find the requisite support without having to yield to the state college or without having to render unto Caesar. And this is how they should make their way. Further, they should examine their consciences about what charitable instincts they are developing when they exclude others who would wish to join them in the larger purpose of their fellowship or programs. If there is a rogue group or intermittent leadership, so be it. This, too, shall pass.

In my documentation of the hundreds of cases I considered and reviewed for this book, I could find no more than a small handful of non-Christians who have ever brought a legal action based on free exercise against a college and not a single one that survived to be decided by the U.S. Supreme Court. One such case was undertaken in 1998 by Orthodox Jews who sued Yale College in *Hack v. Yale* for its mandatory residence hall policy, which the students interpreted as violating their belief that coed living arrangements were morally wrong. They lost their claim for want of a nail—one I believe they probably should have won for its operational details and the exceptions already carved out.[32] This is not to say that there have not been other such cases, but the rights being asserted are largely if not exclusively by certain Christians and for certain Christians, even if they are advanced in the name of comprehensive free exercise and universal religious freedom. And it goes without saying that Christians or those claiming that their religious free exercise rights were not accorded them do not win all these cases.

And some cases are close calls. For example, the snarky language employed by some of Axson-Flynn's teachers revealed an intolerance and insensitivity that were very troubling to the Tenth Circuit. A remand with a better fact pattern and less veiled hostility to LDS students might have prevailed even in that case, but I cringed when I saw the remarks directed at her, even if she was too thin-skinned and even if she did choose the elective class. But in the end, it is hard to fully apprehend how a public college in Utah can oppress Mormon students. Apart from such outliers, faculty members must have the autonomy to coordinate their class assignments, and the students should simply have rendered unto Caesar here.

And the opposite type of error has also occurred. Why does Professor Bishop, as noted in the Primer, feel the need to bring his Christian precepts into the exercise physiology class and then offer supplemental instruction where he promises to elaborate upon his religious views? I cannot imagine a Hindu or other minority religion adherent doing the same thing, and I have not found a case resulting from such hubris. While the *Bishop v. Aronov* case predated *Garcetti*, it is clear from its reasoning that Professor Bishop's situation would likely be reached by *Garcetti*, and he would be even more likely to lose than he was in 1991.

> In short, Dr. Bishop and the University disagree about a matter of content in the courses he teaches. The University must have the final say in such a dispute. Though Dr. Bishop's sincerity cannot be doubted, his educational judgment can be questioned and redirected by the University when he is acting under its auspices as a course instructor, but not when he acts as an independent educator or researcher. The University's conclusions about course content must be allowed to hold sway over an individual professor's judgments. By its memo to Dr. Bishop, the University seeks to prevent him from presenting his religious viewpoint during instructional time, even to the extent that it represents his professional opinion about his subject matter. We have simply concluded that the University as an employer and educator can direct Dr. Bishop to refrain from expression of religious viewpoints in the classroom and like settings.[33]

I have been unable to find another case such as this where a non-Christian sought to proselytize in class, although there are a number of cases where Christian professors insisted upon either praying or preaching in class. In a country where pluralism, nourished in particular by immigration and globalization, has such wide and deep roots, this singular purposive focus is unlikely to serve as an integrative force or to be a promoter of the common good. The day that a Mormon, Muslim, Sikh, Wiccan, or a Seventh-day Adventist attempts to do the same will be the day that many persons supportive of evangelical instruction will reconsider the premise that it is fair and necessary and right to share one's religious views with others in a secular class and in a public college.[34]

After the rise of the purposive religious legal organizations focusing on this agenda, and especially after 1981's *Widmar v. Vincent* changed the landscape, the litigation patterns in lower courts and the U.S. Supreme Court have not been the "tensions between the academy and the state," as described by Stephen Bailey, but the cultural wars and tensions over religious accommodation and free exercise and the perennial tensions between a deracinated color-blind country and the real world: one requiring affirmative action for diversity. I hope that they remain in tension and that the next half century will be as fruitful for religious plurality and tolerance.

Annual Reviews of Higher Education Law

Lelia B. Helms and James D. Jorgensen, "Litigation and Postsecondary Education: A Year in Perspective, 2009," 42 *Urban Lawyer* (2010): 713–738.

Lelia Helms and James D. Jorgensen, "Patterns of Litigation and Higher Education: 2008 in Perspective," *West's Education Law Reporter* 245 (2009): 537–550.

James D. Jorgensen and Lelia Helms, "Recent Developments in Public Education Law: Postsecondary Education, 2008," *Urban Lawyer* 41 (2008): 455–487.

Stacy Donoso and Perry A. Zirkel, "The Volume of Higher Education Litigation: An Updated Analysis," *West's Education Law Reporter* 232 (2008): 549–555.

Lelia Helms and James D. Jorgensen, "Litigation and Postsecondary Education: A Year in Perspective, 2007," *West's Education Law Reporter* 236 (2008): 1–26.

Lelia Helms and James D. Jorgensen, "Recent Developments in Public Education Law: Postsecondary Education, 2007," *Urban Lawyer* 40 (2008): 633–665.

James D. Jorgensen and Lelia Helms, "Recent Developments in Public Education Law: Postsecondary Education, 2006," *Urban Lawyer* 39 (2007): 1017–1044.

James D. Jorgensen and Lelia Helms, "Litigation and Postsecondary Education: A Year in Perspective, 2006," *West's Education Law Reporter* 225 (2006): 23–43.

James D. Jorgensen and Lelia Helms, "Recent Developments in Public Education Law: Postsecondary Education, 2005–06," *Urban Lawyer* 38 (2006): 1201–1222.

James D. Jorgensen and Lelia Helms, "Litigation in Postsecondary Education: A Year in Perspective, 2004–05," *West's Education Law Reporter* 206 (2006): 17–35.

James D. Jorgensen and Lelia Helms, "Litigation in Postsecondary Education: A Year in Perspective," *West's Education Law Reporter* 195 (2005): 443–460.

James D. Jorgensen and Lelia Helms, "Recent Developments in Public Education: Postsecondary Education," *Urban Lawyer* 37 (2005): 957–981.

Lelia B. Helms, "Recent Developments in Public Education Law: Postsecondary Education," *Urban Lawyer* 36 (2004): 867–887.

Lelia B. Helms, "Recent Developments in Public Education Law: Postsecondary Education, 2002–03," *Urban Lawyer* 35 (2003): 795–811.

Lelia B. Helms, "Recent Developments in Public Education Law: Postsecondary Education, 2001–02," *Urban Lawyer* 34 (2002): 995–1017.

Lelia B. Helms, "Recent Developments in Public Education Law: Postsecondary Education, 2000–01," *Urban Lawyer* 33 (2001): 1025–1041.

Lelia B. Helms, "Recent Developments in Public Education Law: Postsecondary Education, 1999–2000," *Urban Lawyer* 32 (2000): 913–930.

Perry A. Zirkel, "The Volume of Higher Education Litigation: An Update," *West's Education Law Reporter* 126 (1998): 21–27.

James C. Hanks, Elizabeth A. Grob, and Lelia B. Helms, "Recent Developments in Public Education Law," *Urban Lawyer* 29 (1997): 837–883 [Postsecondary Education: 864–883].

Edgar H. Bittle, Elizabeth A. Grob, and Lelia B. Helms, "Recent Developments in Public Education Law," *Urban Lawyer* 28 (1996): 895–942 [Postsecondary Education: 917–942].

Fernand N. Dutile, "The Law of Higher Education and the Courts: 1992 in Review," *Journal of College and University Law* 20 (1993): 125–224.

Fernand N. Dutile, "The Law of Higher Education and the Courts: 1991 in Review," *Journal of College and University Law* 19 (1992): 73–183.

Fernand N. Dutile, "The Law of Higher Education and the Courts: 1990 in Review," *Journal of College and University Law* 18 (1991): 163–275.

Larry D. Bartlett and Lelia B. Helms, "Report of the Committee on Public Education," *Urban Lawyer* 23 (1991): 879–935 [Postsecondary Education: 914–935].

Lelia B. Helms, "Litigation Patterns: Higher Education and the Courts in 1988," *West's Education Law Reporter* 57 (1990): 1–11.

Lelia B. Helms and Larry D. Bartlett, "Recent Developments in Public Education," *Urban Lawyer* 22 (1990): 833–881 [Postsecondary Education: 857–881].

Fernand N. Dutile, "The Law of Higher Education and the Courts: 1989 in Review," *Journal of College and University Law* 17 (1990): 149–242.

Fernand N. Dutile, "The Law of Higher Education and the Courts: 1988 in Review," *Journal of College and University Law* 16 (1989): 201–285.

Lelia B. Helms and Larry D. Bartlett, "Recent Developments in Public Education Law," *Urban Lawyer* 21: 867–923 [Postsecondary Education: 896–923].

Perry A. Zirkel and Sharon N. Richardson, "The 'Explosion' in Education Litigation," West's Educational Law Reporter 53 (1989): 767–791.

Margaret J. Lam, "Patterns of Litigation at Institutions of Higher Education in Texas, 1878–1988," UHLC/IHELG Monograph 88-9 (1988, www.law.uh.edu/ihelg/monograph/88-9.pdf.

Fernand N. Dutile, "The Law of Higher Education and the Courts: 1987 in Review," *Journal of College and University Law* 15 (1988): 87–148.

Fernand N. Dutile, "The Law of Higher Education and the Courts: 1986 in Review," *Journal of College and University Law* 14 (1997): 303–357.

Harry T. Edwards, "Recent Supreme Court Decisions and Implications for Higher Education," UHLC/IHELG Monograph 87-8 (1987), www.law.uh.edu/ihelg/monograph/87-8.pdf.

Lelia B. Helms, "Patterns of Litigation in Postsecondary Education: A Case Law Study," *Journal of College and University Law* 14 (1987): 99–119.

Perry A. Zirkel, "Research in Education Law," *West's Education Law Reporter* 29 (1986): 475–481.

Michael A. Olivas and Kathleen Denison, "Legalization in the Academy: Higher Education and the Supreme Court," *Journal of College and University Law* 11 (1984): 1–50.

Perry A. Zirkel, "Law and Education: Partnership, Pendulum and Prognosis," Issues in Education 1 (1983): 79–87.

Perry A. Zirkel, "Outcomes Analysis of Court Decisions Concerning Faculty Employment," NOLPE Journal of School Law 10 (1982): 171–183.

United States v. Fordice, 505 U.S. 717 (1992)
Case History

Ayers v. Allain, 674 F.Supp. 1523 (N.D. Miss. 1987)
Reversed by, Remanded by:
    Ayers v. Allain, 893 F.2d 732 (5th Cir. Miss. 1990)
Review or Rehearing granted by, En banc:
    Ayers v. Allain, 898 F.2d 1014 (5th Cir. Miss. 1990)
Affirmed by, En banc:
    Ayers v. Allain, 914 F.2d 676 (5th Cir. Miss. 1990)
Motion granted by, Writ of certiorari granted, in part:
    United States v. Mabus, 499 U.S. 958 (1991)
Motion granted by:
    United States v. Mabus, 501 U.S. 1229 (1991)
Motion granted by, Motion denied by:
    United States v. Mabus, 501 U.S. 1276 (1991)
Motion granted by:
    United States v. Mabus, 501 U.S. 1279 (1991)
Motion granted by:
    United States v. Mabus, 502 U.S. 803 (1991)
Later proceeding at:
    United States v. Mabus, 502 U.S. 904 (1991)
Motion denied by:
    United States v. Mabus, 502 U.S. 936 (1991)
Vacated by, Remanded by:
    United States v. Fordice, 505 U.S. 717 (1992)
Vacated by, En banc:
    Ayers v. Fordice, 970 F.2d 1378 (5th Cir. Miss. 1992)

Subsequent Appellate History:
Findings of fact/conclusions of law at, On remand at:
    Ayers v. Fordice, 879 F.Supp. 1419 (N.D. Miss. 1995)

Stay denied by:

Ayers v. Fordice, 517 U.S. 1153 (1996)

Affirmed without opinion by:

Ayers v. Fordice, 99 F.3d 1136 (5th Cir. Miss. 1996)

Affirmed in part and reversed in part by, Remanded by:

Ayers v. Fordice, 111 F.3d 1183 (5th Cir. Miss. 1997)

Writ of certiorari denied, Motion granted by:

Ayers v. Fordice, 522 U.S. 1084 (1998)

Motion denied by, Injunction granted at:

Ayers v. Fordice, 40 F.Supp.2d 382 (N.D. Miss. 1999)

Vacated by, Motion granted by:

Ayers v. Fordice (N.D. Miss., Nov. 29, 1999)

Later proceeding at:

Ayers v. Fordice (N.D. Miss., July 6, 2000)

Later proceeding at:

Ayers v. Musgrove (N.D. Miss., May 8, 2001)

Later proceeding at:

Ayers v. Musgrove (N.D. Miss., May 8, 2001)

Motions ruled upon by:

Ayers v. Musgrove (N.D. Miss., Nov. 26, 2001)

Subsequent appeal at:

Ayers v. Musgrove, 31 Fed. Appx. 160 (5th Cir. Miss. 2001)

Later proceeding at:

Ayers v. Musgrove, 2002 U.S. Dist. LEXIS 1973 (N.D. Miss. Jan. 2, 2002)

Dismissed by:

Ayers v. Musgrove, 37 Fed. Appx. 87 (5th Cir. Miss. 2002)

Writ of certiorari denied:

Ayers v. Musgrove, 537 U.S. 861 (2002)

Affirmed by:

Ayers v. Thompson, 358 F.3d 356 (5th Cir. Miss. 2004)

Writ of certiorari denied, Motion granted by:

Ayers v. Thompson, 543 U.S. 951 (2004)

Chapter 1 · *A Primer on Higher Education Law in the United States*

1. Browne, *Fire and Rain.*

2. Brubacher, *Courts and Higher Education*, xii.

3. Bailey, "Education and the State."

4. Thomas, *Youngest Science*; Goodman, *Community of Scholars*; Millett, *Academic Community.*

5. Stroup, *Bureaucracy in Higher Education.*

6. Baldridge, *Power and Conflict in the University*; Clark, *Higher Education System*; Kerr, *Uses of the University*; Nelson, *No University Is an Island.*

7. Collins, *Credential Society*; Edwards, *Higher Education*; Horowitz, *Indoctrination U*; Horowitz and Laksin, *One-Party Classroom*; Baez, *Affirmative Action, Hate Speech, and Tenure*; Bousquet, *How the University Works*; Freire, *Education for Critical Consciousness.*

8. Coffee v. Rice University, 408 S.W.2d 269 (1966).

9. Shapiro v. Columbia Union, 576 S.W.2d 310 (1979).

10. U.S. on behalf of U.S. Coast Guard v. Cerio, 831 F.Supp. 530 (E.D. Va. 1993).

11. Fountain Gate Ministries, Inc. v. City of Plano, 654 S.W.2d 841 (Tex. App. 5 Dist. 1983).

12. Philip Crosby Associates, Inc. v. Florida State Board of Independent Colleges, 506 So.2d 490 (Fla. App. 5 Dist. 1987).

13. Hacker v. Hacker, 522 N.Y.S.2d 768 (1987).

14. Beth Rochel v. Bennett, 825 F.2d 478 (D.C. Cir. 1987).

15. City of Morgantown v. West Virginia Board of Regents, 354 S.E.2d 616 (W. Va. 1987).

16. Trustees of Dartmouth v. Woodward, 4 Wheaton (U.S.) 518 (1819).

17. Powe v. Miles, 407 F.2d 73 (1968).

18. Krynicky v. University of Pittsburgh, 742 F.2d 94 (1984).

19. Clark v. Dine College, 9 Am. Tribal Law 359 (Navajo 2010).

20. See, for example, Amar, "Of Sovereignty and Federalism"; Thro, "Eleventh Amendment Revolution"; Davidson, "Cooperative Localism."

21. Alden v. Maine, 527 U.S. 706, 713 (1999) (citations omitted). Three exceptions have been created by the Supreme Court to limit a state's sovereign immunity: waiver, abrogation, and the *Ex Parte Young* exceptions. The first exception to the doctrine of sovereign immunity occurs when a state waives its immunity. A state's waiver of sovereign immunity may subject it to suit in state court, but it is not enough, absent some other indicator of intent, to subject the state to suit in federal court. A state can also waive its Eleventh Amendment immunity against suits in federal court by other clearly stated means, such as successfully moving a federal case to state court. Congress can abrogate a state's sovereign immunity by exercising its powers under Section 5 of the Fourteenth Amendment. Since the 1996 decision in Seminole Tribe of Florida v. Florida, 517 U.S. 44, 54 (1996), the Court has begun to limit Congress's right to abrogate a state's sovereign immunity. Thus, Congress has the power to abrogate a state's sovereign immunity when it is acting pursuant to its Fourteenth Amendment powers under Section 5, but the Court requires the Congress to act clearly and without ambiguity when it does so.

22. For an excellent summary of these complex issues, see Snow and Thro, "Significance of Blackstone's Understanding." Snow and Thro have summarized the *Ex Parte Young* exemption: "This doctrine holds that sovereign immunity does not bar federal court actions against individual state officers . . . seeking (1) declaratory judgment that the state officer is currently violating federal law and (2) an injunction forcing the state officer to conform his current conduct to federal law." At 123, citing DeBauche v. Trani, 191 F.3d 499, 505 (4th Cir. 1999), *cert. denied*, 529 U.S. 1033 (2000).

23. Ibid., 123, citing Seminole Tribe v. Florida, 517 U.S. 44, 71–75 (1996).

24. Ibid., 124, citing Coeur d'Alene Tribe, 521 U.S. 261, 287–288 (1997).

25. Cahn and Cahn v. Antioch University, 482 A.2d 120 (1984).

26. Fenn College v. Nance, 210 N.E.2d 418 (1965).

27. Nasson College v. New England Association of Schools and Colleges, 16 B.C.D. 1299 (1988).

28. Radian Asset Assurance, Inc. v. College of the Christian Bros. of New Mexico, 274 F.R.D. 682 (D. N. M. 2011). This complicated issue arose when the College of Santa Fe declared bankruptcy after many years of mismanagement and closed, and its campus was purchased by the City of Santa Fe, New Mexico. See Sena, "City Panel OKs CSF Bonds, Lease"; Salazar, "Insurer Accuses CSF of Fraud."

29. NCAA v. University of Oklahoma, 488 U.S. 85 (1984).

30. U.S. v. Brown University, 5 F.3d 658 (3d Cir. 1993).

31. Marjorie Webster Junior College v. Middle States Association, 139 U.S. App. D.C. 217, 432 F.2d 650 (1970).

32. Beth Rochel Seminary v. Bennett, 825 F.2d 478 (D.C. Cir. 1987).

33. Helms, "Patterns of Litigation."

34. Lam, *Patterns of Litigation*.

35. Kaplin, *Law of Higher Education*, 4; see also the successor volumes, Kaplin and Lee, *The Law of Higher Education*; as well as LaNoue and Lee, *Academics in Court*; Poskanzer, *Higher Education Law*; Spacks, ed., *Advocacy in the Classroom*.

36. Perry v. Sindermann, 408 U.S. 593 (1972).

37. Board of Regents v. Roth, 408 U.S. 564 (1972).

38. Wellner v. Minnesota State Junior College Board, 487 F.2d 153 (1973); State ex rel. McLendon v. Morton, 249 S.E.2d 919 (1978).

39. Hill v. Talladega College, 502 So.2d 735 (Ala. 1987); Honore v. Douglas, 833 F.2d 565 (5th Cir. 1987); Spuler v. Pickar, 958 F.2d 103 (5th Cir. 1992); Lewis v. Loyola University of Chicago, 500 N.E.2d 47 (Ill. App. 1 Dist. 1996).

40. See generally LaNoue and Lee, *Academics in Court*; Colker, "Whores, Fags, Dumb-Ass Women," 195; Gajda, *Trials of Academe*.

41. Scott v. University of Delaware, 455 F.Supp. 1102 (D. Del. 1978).

42. Faro v. NYU, 502 F.2d 1229 (1974).

43. Clark v. Claremont University Center, 8 Cal. Rptr. 2d 151 (Cal. App. 2 Dist. 1992).

44. Sweeney v. Board of Trustees of Keene State College, 569 F.2d 169 (1978); Kunda v. Muhlenberg College, 463 F.Supp. 294 (E.D. Pa. 1978); Mecklenberg v. Montana State Board of Regents, 13 EPD 11, 438 (1976); Kemp v. Irvin, 651 F.Supp. 495 (N.D. Ga. 1986); Jew v. University of Iowa, 749 F.Supp. 946 (S. D. Iowa 1990).

45. Kemp v. Irvin, 651 F.Supp. 495 (N.D. Ga. 1986). For an excellent study of this interesting case, see Footlick, *Truth and Consequences*, 52–72.

46. Hazelwood School District v. Kuhlmeier, 108 S.Ct. 562 (1988); Bishop v. Aronov, 926 F.2d 1066 (11th Cir. 1991); Scallet v. Rosenblum, 106 F.3d 391 (4th Cir. 1997); Connick v. Myers, 461 U.S. (1983); Waters v. Churchill, 114 S.Ct. 1878 (1994); Jeffries v. Harleston, 828 F.Supp. 1066 (S.D.N.Y. 1993), 21 F.3d 1238 (2d Cir. 1994), *vac. and rem.* 115 S.Ct. 502 (1995) *vac. and rev'd,* 52 F.3d 9 (2d Cir. 1995), *cert den.* 116 S.Ct. 173 (1995).

47. Connick v. Myers, 461 U.S. 138 (1983); Jeffries v. Harleston, id., 115 S.Ct. 502 (1995) citing Waters v. Churchill (1994). For a very critical review of this case, see Glazer, "Levin, Jeffries, and the Fate of Academic Autonomy," 703.

48. Jeffries v. Harleston, 828 F.Supp. 1066 (S.D.N.Y. 1993) 21 F.3d 1238 (2d Cir. 1994), *vac. and rem.* 115 S.Ct. 502 (1995) *vac. and rev'd,* 52 F.3d 9 (2d Cir. 1995), *cert den.* 116 S.Ct. 173 (1995).

49. Garcetti v. Ceballos, 547 U.S. 410 (2006). See Rosenthal, "Emerging First Amendment Law," 33, 93–105. Several examples of the predominance of *Garcetti* in the college setting appear in the final chapter of this book.

50. These data are from Douglas, "Professors on Strike." See also Schmidt, "Part-Time Faculty Are Catching Up"; Schmidt, "Unions Confront the Fault Lines"; Schmidt, "Faculty Unions in Ohio and Wis. Hunker Down."

51. Trustees of Columbia University, 29 LRRM 1098 (1951).

52. Cornell University, 183 NLRB 329 (1970).

53. NLRB v. Yeshiva University, 444 U.S. 672 (1980).

54. See generally, Matthew W. Finkin, "'A Higher Order of Liberty,'" 357; Metchick and Singh, "*Yeshiva* and Faculty Unionization," 45. Kniffin, "Organizing to Organize," 333, about college organizing successes in Wisconsin, will have to be evaluated in light of the 2011 developments that played out in the national press. See also Schmidt, "Faculty Unions in Ohio and Wis. Hunker Down."

55. United Faculty v. University of Pittsburgh, PLRB No. PERA-84-53W (Mar. 11, 1987).

56. NLRB v. Cooper Union, 78 3 F.2d 29 (2d Cir. 1985); NLRB v. Florida Memorial College, 820 F.2d 1182 (11th Cir. 1987).

57. Hayden, "'The University Works Because We Do,'" 1233; Nelson and Watt, *Office Hours*, 139–164; Bousquet and Nelson, *How the University Works*. For the more recent data, see Schmidt, "Part-Time Faculty Are Catching Up"; Schmidt, "Unions Confront the Fault Lines."

58. Bakke v. Regents of University of California, 438 U.S. 265 (1978).

59. Anthony v. Syracuse University, 231 N.Y.S. 435 (1928).

60. Gott v. Berea College, 156 Ky. 376, 161 S.W. 204 (1913).

61. Dixon v. Alabama State Board of Education, 294 F.2d 150 (5th Cir. 1961). This case was one of the several I considered as a deep case study for this project. It was a Legal Defense Fund case litigated by Thurgood Marshall and Derrick A. Bell Jr., a distinguished law professor colleague who discussed much of the litigation backstory with me, including why he and Marshall chose to sue on behalf of students expelled from a public historically black college, Alabama State College. (My notes from 2009 record the following observation by Professor Bell, since deceased: "If they can get screwed by a black college, they can get screwed worse by a white one.")

62. Tarasoff v. Regents of University of California, 551 F.2d 334 (1976); see also Schuck and Givelbar, "Tarasoff v. Regents of the University of California"; Mullins v. Pine Manor College, 449 N.E.2d 331 (Mass. 1983).

63. Johnson v. Lincoln Christian College, 501 N.E.2d 1380 (Ill. App. 4 Dist. 1986); Ross v. Creighton University, 957 F.2d 410 (7th Cir. 1992).

64. Beh, "Student Versus University," 183.

65. Beh, "Downsizing Higher Education," 155. See also Brine v. University of Iowa, 90 F.3d 271 (8th Cir. 1996), upholding elimination of an all-female dental hygiene program.

66. Gonzalez v. North American College of Louisiana, 700 F.Supp. 362 (S.D. Tex. 1988); American Commercial Colleges, Inc. v. Davis, 821 S.W.2d 450 (Tex. App.-Eastland 1991). See Melear, "From *In Loco Parentis* to Consumerism," 124.

67. Gratz v. Bollinger, 123 S.Ct. 2411 (2003).

68. Grutter v. Bollinger, 123 S.Ct. 2325 (2003). As one might expect from such a publicized case, it has prompted a great deal of scholarly literature on admissions and affirmative action. For a representative range of this research, see, for example, Crump, "Narrow Tailoring Issue," 483; George, "*Gratz* and *Grutter*," 1634; Greenhouse, "Supreme Court Overview"; Guinier, "Admissions Rituals as Political Acts," 113; Brown-Nagin, "Elites, Social Movements, and the Law," 1436.

69. Coalition to Defend Affirmation Action, Integration and Immigrant Rights and Fight for Equality by Any Means Necessary (BAMN) et al. v. Regents of the University of Michigan, 652 F.3d 607 (6th Cir. 2011); Lewin, "Michigan Rule on Admission to University Is Overturned."

70. Benjamin-Alvarado, DeSipio, and Montoya-Kirk, "Latino Mobilization in New Immigrant Destinations"; Tang, "Colleges to Start Checking"; Reich and Mendoza, "'Educating Kids' Versus 'Coddling Criminals,'" 177; Olivas, "Political Economy of the DREAM Act," 1757; Facchini and Steinhardt, "What Drives U.S. Immigration Policy?" 734; Olivas, *No Undocumented Child Left Behind*.

71. Things heated up in 2011, as the litigation in Arizona and Alabama advanced and as there were state-level developments in the DREAM Act. See, for example, Davis, "Md. Tuition Law May Be Halted"; Seidman, "Backers of Maryland DREAM Act"; Flores-Yeffal, Vidales, and Plemons, "Latino Cyber Moral Panic Process"; Robertson, "Part of Alabama Immigrant Law Blocked," A13.

72. Lynch v. Indiana State University, 378 N.E.2d 900 (1978).

73. Bishop v. Aronov, 926 F.2d 1066 (11th Cir. 1991).

74. Carley v. Arizona Board of Regents, 153 Ariz. 461, 737 P.2d 1099 (1987). In a variation of this practice, a professor was admonished for requiring his students to bring food to class and then refusing to meet with them when they did not comply; he argued that this practice was intended to create and encourage "team-building" in the psychology class. Jaschik, "Professor Told to Stop Requiring Students to Bring Snacks."

75. Martin v. Parrish, 805 F.2d 583 (5th Cir. 1986). See also Bonnell v. Lorenzo 241 F.3d 800 (6th Cir. 2001).

76. Hayut v. SUNY, 352 F.3d 733 (2d Cir. 2003). See Wirenius, "Actions as Words, Words as Actions," 905, 923–927.

77. Levin v. Harleston, 770 F.Supp. 895 (S.D.N.Y. 1991), *aff'd in relevant part, vac. on other grounds,* 996 F.2d 85 (2d Cir. 1992). See Olivas, "Reflections on Professorial Academic Freedom," 1835, 1854.

78. Silva v. University of New Hampshire, 888 F.Supp. 293 (D. N. H. 1994). A number of students in Silva's writing class complained about the highly sexual language and innuendo he employed. He won the case, in part because the college used an overly broad sexual harassment policy to bring the action against him: "(1) the USNH Sexual Harassment Policy as applied to Silva's classroom speech employs an impermissibly subjective standard that fails to take into account the nation's interest in academic freedom and (2) said policy was erroneously applied in this case, the court finds that under the Connick-Pickering balancing test Silva's First Amendment interest in the speech at issue is overwhelmingly superior to UNH's interest in proscribing said speech." 888 F.Supp. 293, 316. The Center for Individual Rights lists this case as among its "Greatest Courtroom Victories."

79. "General Report of the Committee on Academic Freedom and Academic Tenure."

80. Braxton, Bayer, and Finkelstein, "Teaching Performance Norms in Academia," 533, 535–536.

81. Mincone v. Nassau County Community College, 923 F.Supp. 398 (E.D. N.Y. 1996). See also Gheta v. NCCC, 33 F.Supp.2d 179 (E.D.N.Y. 1999).

82. See, for example, Wirenius, "Actions as Words, Words as Actions," 923–927; Post, "Debating Disciplinarity," 533, 535–536.

83. Cohen v. San Bernardino Valley Community College, 883 F.Supp. 1407 (C.D. Cal. 1995), *rev'd in part,* 92 F.3d 968 (9th Cir. 1996).

84. American Association of University Professors, "AAUP Proposed Statement of Policy for Sexual Harassment," 171.

85. See for example, Baez, *Affirmative Action, Hate Speech, and Tenure*; Gajda, *Trials of Academe*. There has been a rise in the number of classroom-conflict cases, which

almost always involve religion, sexual orientation, race, or a mixture of these features. In reading these cases, one cannot help but be struck by how both students and, worse, faculty behave in stressful situations. And sometimes these become public because the institution, caught between the two sides, itself either overreacts or acts badly. Wilson, "Brandeis Prof in Trouble" (classroom comments); Jaschik, "Teaching or Preaching?" (sample exam questions seen as homophobic); O'Neal v. Falcon, 668 F.Supp.2d 979 (W. D. Tex., 2009); see also Lopez v. Candaele, 630 F.3d 775 (9th Cir. 2010), *cert. denied,* 131 S.Ct. 2456 (2011) (class presentation on religious theme).

86. Sylvester v. Texas Southern University, 957 F.Supp. 944 (S. D. Tex. 1997). For critical commentary on the issues concerning the law of grading, see Post, "Power and the Morality of Grading," 777.

87. Olivas, "Rise of Nonlegal Legal Influences," 258.

Chapter 2 · A Brief History of Higher Education Litigation in the United States Supreme Court

1. Trustees of Dartmouth College v. Woodward, 17 U.S. (4 Wheat.) 518 (1819).
2. Rudolph, *American College and University,* 211.
3. Pickering v. Board of Education, 391 U.S. 563 (1968).
4. Connick v. Myers, 461 U.S. 138 (1983); Garcetti v. Ceballos, 547 U.S. 410 (2006).
5. As one measure of how influential the solicitor general (SG) is in the process of winnowing cases and for an insight into the workload of the Court, consider the effect for SG Elena Kagan in her 2010 appointment to SCOTUS and her recusals in cases in which as solicitor general she had either formally participated or for which she had reviewed for the cert petition recommendations. In the 2010 term, she recused herself from 271 cases, while in 2011, she did so in 66, many of them procedural motions or denials of review. (In 2010, there were over 7,800 petitions or motions.) Of the actual cases argued before the Court in the 2010 term, she recused herself from 27 of the 86 cases. Even so, only two of those cases ended in a 4–4 tie, leaving the lower court rulings to stand. Mauro, "Kagan Bows out of 66 Cases." See also Salokar, "Solicitor General," 835.
6. LaNoue and Lee, *Academics in Court.*
7. "[B]ecause recommendations to deny are the norm, law clerks pay far less attention to those recommendations than to recommendations to grant during the annotation process, increasing the likelihood that an issue of importance will be overlooked." Fletcher, "Factbound and Splitless," 933, 935. See also Stras, "Supreme Court's Gatekeepers," 947, 974; Starr, "Supreme Court and Its Shrinking Docket," 1363, 1377.
8. Fletcher, "Factbound and Splitless," 939–942.
9. Ibid., 980–981, emphasis omitted.
10. Coyle, "Indians Try to Keep Cases Away from High Court."
11. See, for example, Caldeira and Wright, "Discuss List," 807; Caldeira and Wright, "Organized Interests and Agenda Setting," 1109; Cordray and Cordray, "Philosophy of Certiorari," 389; Stras, "Supreme Court's Gatekeepers," 974–976.
12. Baird, *Answering the Call.* See also Caldeira, Wright, and Zorn, "Sophisticated Voting and Gate-Keeping"; Baird and Jacobi, "How the Dissent Becomes the Majority";

Clark and Lauderdale, "Locating Supreme Court Opinions"; Clark and Strauss, "Implications of High Court Docket Control"; Blake and Hacker, "'Brooding Spirit of the Law.'"

13. See, for example, [Spaeth], "Original U.S. Supreme Court Judicial Database"; Sanchez-Urribarri et al., "Explaining Changes to Rights Litigation."

14. Elkins v. Moreno, 435 U.S. 647 (1978); Toll v. Moreno, 441 U.S. 458 (1979) (*per curiam*); Toll v. Moreno, 458 U.S. 1, 3–10 (1982) (complex litigation history at 3–10). See also Olivas, "*Plyler v. Doe, Toll v. Moreno*."

15. Christian Legal Society Chapter of the University of California, Hastings College of the Law v. Martinez 130 S.Ct. 2971, *affirmed and remanded*: "Neither lower court addressed CLS's argument that Hastings selectively enforces its all-comers policy. This Court is not the proper forum to air the issue in the first instance. On remand, the Ninth Circuit may consider this argument if, and to the extent, it is preserved" (at 31–32), 319 Fed. Appx. 645.

16. Christian Legal Society v. Wu, 626 F.3d 483 (9th Cir. 2010). The case may have been decided, but its fallout is just beginning. "On remand, organization sought remand to the district court for consideration of its claim that law school selectively applied its nondiscrimination policy against it. Holding: The Court of Appeals held that organization failed to preserve for appeal its argument that law school selectively applied its nondiscrimination policy. Denied."

The Alliance Defense Fund is actively litigating *CLS* as applied, such as in Alpha Delta Chi-Delta Chapter v. Charles Reed, a case involving RSOs in California State University at Long Beach, where the trial court held for the defendant CSU. Ultimate victory here will not likely be to the fleet but to the persistent. Alpha Delta Chi-Delta Chapter v. Charles Reed, www.ca9.uscourts.gov/datastore/opinions/2011/08/02/09-55299.pdf (accessed Oct. 14, 2011). See also "Christian Legal Society and Montana Law School Settle Dispute." For a study of how difficult it is to discern a completed case, see Bruhl, "When is Finality . . . Final?"

17. LaNoue and Lee, *Academics in Court*, 27.

18. Ibid., 30.

19. Chew and Kelley, "Unwrapping Racial Harassment Law." See also Chew and Kelley, "Myth of the Color-Blind Judge."

20. Chew and Kelley, "Unwrapping Racial Harassment Law."

21. Ibid., 84–85.

22. Ibid., 61–63 (citations and footnotes omitted).

23. Ibid., text accompanying tables 4 and 7.

24. Olivas, "Governing Badly."

Chapter 3 · *Making It to the Supreme Court and the Rise of Purposive Organizations*

1. There is also a little-known and miniscule "Special Docket" reserved for a handful of vexing and contentious cases that do not fit into the regular flow of cases. Crocker, "Not to Decide Is to Decide"; Chin and Lindenbaum, "Reaching Out to Do Justice," 197. In very rare instances, even after the Court has heard a case, it can "DIG" it, or "dismiss it as

improvidently granted," before deciding on the merits of the matter. An example was Robertson v. U.S., which the Court dismissed (or DIG'ged) in a 2010 order. Another form of hybrid process is used to undertake a small number of granting/vacating/remanding (GVR) determinations. Robertson v. United States ex rel. Watson, 560 U.S. ___, 130 S.Ct. 2184, 176 L.Ed.2d 1024 (2010). See also Bruhl, "Supreme Court's Controversial GVRs."

2. Recent data sources on this complex calculation can be found at U.S. Census Statistical Abstract, "U.S. Supreme Court—Cases Filed and Disposition: 1980 to 2010." See also data at Administrative Office, U.S. Courts: www.uscourts.gov/Statistics/Judicial Business.aspx#4; and SCOTUSBlog: www.scotusblog.com/statistics/.

3. Taxman v. Piscataway Township Board of Education, 91 F.3d 1547 (3d Cir. 1996) (en banc), cert. granted, 117 S.Ct. 2506 (1997), *cert. dismissed pursuant to Rule 46.1,* 118 S.Ct. 595 (1997). See Biskupic, "Rights Groups Pay to Settle Bias Case."

4. Sup. Ct. R. 10, www.supremecourt.gov/ctrules/2010RulesoftheCourt.pdf (accessed Jan. 22, 2012). Over time, the various rules have been renumbered; this is now Rule 10.

5. See generally, Farber, "Statutory Interpretation, Legislative Inaction, and Civil Rights," 8–14; Larsen, "Perpetual Dissents"; Heinz et al., "Inner Circles or Hollow Cores?" 356; Paik, Heinz, and Southworth, "Political Lawyers," 892. See also Salokar, "Solicitor General," 835, 836.

6. Linzer, "Meaning of Certiorari Denials," 1304–1305 (citations omitted). To do so, a case must affirmatively be selected by the Chief Justice's Conference List, or by the Discuss List, where the other Justices nominate cases for hearing (1248–1251). See also Caldeira and Wright, "Discuss List," 807; Caldeira and Wright, "Organized Interests and Agenda Setting," 1109; Boucher and Segal, "Supreme Court Justices as Strategic Decision Makers," 824; Cordray and Cordray, "Philosophy of Certiorari," 389; Stras, "Supreme Court's Gatekeepers," 947, 974; http://papers.ssrn.com/sol3/papers.cfm?abstract _id=1958190 and http://papers.ssrn.com/sol3/papers.cfm?abstract_id=1996776.

7. This literature has increased substantially. See, for instance, Stack, "Practice of Dissent"; Jacobson, "Publishing Dissent"; Larsen, "Perpetual Dissents," 447–478; Johnson, Black, and Ringsmuth, "Hear Me Roar," 1560.

8. Kennedy, "Doing What You Can." Another Marshall clerk, Professor Mark Tushnet, later wrote about the internal politicking on the Court, and how Justice Marshall maneuvered within the procedural space (and racial space) available to him. See Tushnet, "Thurgood Marshall and the Brethren."

9. Simmons, "Picking Friends from the Crowd," 233 (citations omitted).

10. See Clark and Lauderdale, "Locating Supreme Court Opinions," 871, 872; Clark and Strauss, "Implications of High Court Docket Control," 247.

11. Huetteman, "Breyer and Scalia Testify."

12. Baird, *Answering the Call of the Court,* 31. See also Perry, *Deciding to Decide;* Smith, "Certiorari and the Supreme Court Agenda," 727; Epstein, Segal, and Victor, "Dynamic Agenda-Setting," 395; Stras, "Supreme Court's Gatekeepers," 947.

13. Tinker v. Des Moines Independent Community School District, 393 U.S. 503 (1969). See also Baird, *Answering the Call of the Court,* 29–30.

14. American Academy of Religion v. Napolitano, 573 F.3d 115 (2d Cir. 2009). See also Schmidt, "2 Muslim Scholars Touch U.S. Ground," A10.

15. Wilson, *Political Organizations*, xii. The Princeton paperback version updated the original 1974 Basic Books edition, elaborating substantially on Wilson's original purposive organizations analysis.

16. Simmons, "Picking Friends From the Crowd," esp. 216 (citations omitted).

17. Brown v. Board of Education of Topeka, 347 U.S. 483 (1954).

18. Center for Equal Opportunity, www.ceousa.org/content/view/533/127/; Center for Individual Rights, www.cir-usa.org/mission_new.html (both accessed Dec. 20, 2011).

19. Preston, "Lawyer Leads an Immigration Fight." Interestingly, when Secretary of State Kobach (R-KS) endorsed Mitt Romney in the Republican presidential race, with great fanfare, it drew much more public play—both positive and negative—in the traditional media and the blogosphere than do most other endorsements. See, for instance, Gibson, "Romney Stirs Immigration Debate"; Fausset, "Immigration Offers an Opening for Romney." After Romney became the presumptive GOP candidate, Kobach was demoted to being "just a supporter," as Romney tried to move to the center. See Downes, "Kobach and Romney."

20. *CIR Annual Report*, 2009 [20th Anniversary]: 7, www.cirusa.org/articles/cir_ar_2009.pdf (accessed Jan. 22, 2012).

21. Hopwood v. Texas, 236 F.3d 256 (5th Cir. 2000) (*Hopwood II*); Regents of the Univ. of Cal. v. Bakke, 438 U.S. 265 (1978); Grutter v. Bollinger, 539 U.S. 306 (2003); Gratz v. Bollinger, 539 U.S. 244 (2003). In 2012, *Fisher v. University of Texas* emerged.

22. Coalition to Defend Affirmation Action, Integration and Immigrant Rights and Fight for Equality by Any Means Necessary (BAMN) et al. v. Regents of the University of Michigan, 652 F.3d 607 (6th Cir. 2011); Lewin, "Michigan Rule on Admission to University Is Overturned."

23. Davis, "Md. Tuition Law May Be Halted"; Seidman, "Backers of Maryland DREAM Act Challenge Referendum Effort."

24. This event generated a great many scholarly articles. Two examples are Chemerinsky, "Impact of the Proposed California Civil Rights Initiative"; Volokh, "California Civil Rights Initiative."

25. Liberty Institute was founded as The Free Market Foundation in 1972 and began its litigation efforts "dedicated to protecting freedoms and strengthening families" through its legal division, formerly known as the Liberty Legal Institute, in 1997. Since 2009, it has been known as the Liberty Institute. Among other conservative cases, it brought *Collegiate Community Outreach (CCO) d/b/a UNT Chi Alpha, and Nathan Wesson v. City of Denton, et al.* in federal court to challenge the right of a religious ministry located in a residential area close to the University of North Texas campus to operate on its property, after being found by the City of Denton, Texas, to have been in violation of its zoning laws. After Liberty brought suit, the city relented and allowed the ministry to continue its operations. See also Martinez v. U.C. Regents, 50 Cal.4th 1277, 241 P.3d 855, 117 Cal. Rptr. 3d 359 (2010).

26. Lee, "Fifty Years of Higher Education Law," 686–689, note 240.

27. Foundation for Individual Rights in Education (FIRE), "FIRE's Lawsuit to Proceed"; Horowitz and Laksin, *One-Party Classroom*; Horowitz, *Reforming Our Universities.*
28. Foundation for Individual Rights in Education (FIRE), "FIRE's Legal Network."
29. CLS Christian Legal Society Chapter of the University of California, Hastings College of the Law v. Martinez, 561 U.S. ____, 130 S.Ct. 2971, 177 L.Ed.2d 838 (2010).
30. Rosenberger v. Rector and Visitors of the University of Virginia, 515 U.S. 819 (1995).
31. See Teles, *Rise of the Conservative Legal Movement.*

Chapter 4 · The Traditional Model of Higher Education in the Litigation Spotlight

1. United States v. Fordice, 505 U.S. 717 (1992). See appendix B for the complete litigation history.
2. See generally, Kluger, *Simple Justice*; Gil Kujovich, "Equal Opportunity in Higher Education," 29; Cottrol, Diamond, and Ware, *Brown v. Board of Education*; Riva, "The Coldest Case of All?"
3. Brown v. Board of Education, 347 U.S. 483 (1954).
4. Brown v. Board of Education (*Brown II*), 49 U.S. 294, 301 (1955), mandating implementation "with all deliberate speed."
5. McLaurin v. Oklahoma State Regents for Higher Education, 339 U.S. 637, 640 (1950).
6. Olivas, *Law and Higher Education*, 895.
7. Adams v. Richardson, 356 F.Supp. 92 (D. D. C. 1973), *modified*, 480 F.2d 1159 (D. C. Cir. 1973).
8. United States v. Fordice, 505 U.S. 717, 731–732 (1992), *remanded to* 970 F.2d 1378 (5th Cir. 1992), *remanded to* 879 F.Supp. 1419 (N.D. Miss. 1995).
9. Ayers v. Fordice, 879 F.Supp. 1419 (N.D. Miss. 1995), *aff'd* 99 F.3d 1136 (5th Cir. 1996) (table), *aff'd in part, rev'd in part* 111 F.3d 1183 (5th Cir. 1997) (*en banc*).
10. Regents of the University of California v. Bakke, 438 U.S. 265 (1978); Grutter v. Bollinger, 539 U.S. 306 (2003); Gratz v. Bollinger, 539 U.S. 244 (2003). In a case that began in 1971, white law applicant Marco DeFunis Jr. applied to the University of Washington Law School and was denied admission. During the trial, he was admitted by mandatory injunction, and after the case had been argued before the Supreme Court on appeal, it was vacated and remanded as moot, inasmuch as he was on the verge of graduation. The DeFunis case was the first college admissions case brought by a white applicant that made it to SCOTUS. DeFunis v. Odegaard, 416 U.S. 312 (1974).
11. Meredith v. Fair, 305 F.2d 343 (1962).
12. Fordice, 505 U.S. 734–735.
13. Ibid., 738.
14. Ibid., 743; Ayers v. Fordice, 879 F.Supp. 1419 (N.D. Miss. 1995), *aff'd*, 99 F.3d 1136 (5th Cir. 1996) (table), *aff'd in part, rev'd in part*, 111 F.3d 1183 (5th Cir. 1997) (*en banc*).
15. Ayers, 1477–1479, 1482.
16. Ayers v. Fordice, 111 F.3d 1183, 1209 (5th Cir. 1997) (*en banc*).

17. Ayers v. Thompson, 358 F.3d 356, 364 (5th Cir. 2004), *cert. denied*, 125 S.Ct. 372 (2004).

18. Id. at 366.

19. Id. at 359.

20. Ayers v. Thompson, 125 S.Ct. 372 (U.S., Oct. 18, 2004) (No. 03-10623); Appellant's Petition for Cert., Ayers v. Thompson, 358 F.3d 356 (5th Cir. 2004) (No. 03-10623) (filed May 20, 2004). Hebel, "Federal Court Upholds Plan."

21. Johnson, "Bid Whist, Tonk, and *United States v. Fordice*," 1401, 1468.

22. Ibid., 1468.

23. 451 U.S. 100 (1981). The case involved a dispute concerning a highway location and racially distinct neighborhoods.

24. The events have been recounted in various news stories, especially in the black press: "Mississippi Lawyer Ousted From Job"; Covington, "Troubles Deepen"; Alvin Chambliss, one of the original civil rights lawyers, joins IU faculty, September 30, 2004, http://newsinfo.iu.edu/news/page/normal/1663.html; Paul Bonner, Alvin Chambliss — 'the last civil rights attorney'; Lawyer associated with 29-year Ayers suit, [Durham, NC] Herald-Sun, Feb. 27, 2006, A1.

25. For recent views of legislative and legal threats to law school clinics, see Kuehn and Joy, " 'Kneecapping' Academic Freedom," 8; Joy, "Government Interference with Law School Clinics."

26. AAUP, Bloomfield Chapter v. Bloomfield College, 322 A.2d 846 (N.J. Super. Ct. 1974), *aff'd* 346 A.2d 615 (App. Div. 1975).

27. NCAA v. Board of Regents, University of Oklahoma, 468 U.S. 85 (1984).

28. See generally, Smith, *Idea Brokers*; Stefancic and Delgado, *No Mercy*; Abelson, *Do Think Tanks Matter?*; Rich, *Think Tanks, Public Policy, and the Politics of Expertise*. A useful summary of the rise of nongovernmental actors appears in Harcleroad and Eaton, "Hidden Hand."

29. Baird, *Answering the Call of the Court*, 51–52.

30. CLS v. Martinez, Brief of Hastings College of the Law Respondents, www.americanbar.org/content/dam/aba/publishing/preview/publiced_preview_briefs_pdfs_09 _10_08_1371_RespondentHastingsLaw.authcheckdam.pdf, 2 (accessed Jan. 22, 2012).

31. CLS v. Martinez, Amicus Brief for the CATO Institute in Support of Petitioner, www.scotusblog.com/case-files/cases/christian-legal-society-v-martinez/, (accessed Jan. 22, 2012). The American Bar Association maintains a very useful and comprehensive listing of all the merit and amicus briefs submitted for SCOTUS cases pending, in searchable and digital format: Christian Legal Society Chapter v. Martinez, Docket No. 08-1371 (Apr. 2010), www.americanbar.org/publications/preview_home/publiced_preview _briefs_april2010.html.

32. Regents of the University of California v. Bakke, 438 U.S. 265 (1978).

33. Sweatt v. Painter, 339 U.S. 629 (1950).

34. Healy v. James, 408 U.S. 169 (1972).

35. Widmar v. Vincent, 454 U.S. 263 (1981); Rosenberger v. Rector and Visitors of University of Virginia, 515 U.S. 819 (1995); CLS v. Martinez, 130 S.Ct. 2971 (2010).

36. For exemplars of the polar opposites in this debate, see, for example, Horowitz, *Reforming Our Universities*; Blum, *I'm Not a Racist, But . . .*

37. CLS v. Walker, 453 F.3d 853 (7th Cir. 2006).

38. Beta Upsilon Chi Upsilon [BYX] Chapter v. Machen, 559 F.Supp.2d 1274 (N.D. Fla. 2008), 586 F.3d 908 (11th Cir. 2009).

39. Ibid.

40. Ibid., 910–911.

41. Ibid., footnote 4. Interestingly, the court in its first opinion included Roman Catholicism in this list of ineligible religions and corrected the record when ADF pointed out the error. 586 F.3d 910 www.leagle.com/xmlResult.aspx?xmldoc=in%20fco %2020091027096.xml&docbase=cslwar3-2007-curr (accessed Nov. 28, 2011). Nonetheless, there are Christian organizations that do not consider traditional Roman Catholics to be mainstream "Christian." There is a growing tension about the extent to which these Christian groups consider each other to be "Christian," largely led by evangelicals. See, for example, Stevens-Arroyo, "Are Catholics Christians?" Some of this tension also plays out in the inconsistent messaging sent by Catholics and other Christians on the legislative issues they single out for condemning: "The Catholic Church, [and by extension, other Christian groups] like any citizen or institution, has every right to take a position on political issues, and to use its influence as vigorously as it can. And no political position is invalid simply because it derives from religious belief. But there's a catch: The church cannot then complain of prejudice against Catholicism or, even more absurd, prejudice against Christianity when other people just as vigorously disagree with it." Kinsley, "Christians Are Being Oppressed?" See also Wuthnow, *Struggle for America's Soul*.

42. Beta Upsilon Chi Upsilon [BYX] Chapter v. Machen, 586 F.3d 908, 910–911, footnote 5 (11th Cir. 2009).

43. Ibid., 915.

44. Ibid., 915, emphasis added.

45. Oppel and Eckholm, "Prominent Pastor Calls Romney's Church a Cult"; Stolberg, "For Romney, a Role of Faith and Authority"; Goodstein, "Mormons' Ad Campaign"; Laurie Goodstein, "Theological Differences"; Oppenheimer, "Faith and Family Values"; Eckholm, "Evangelicals Step Up Efforts"; Gibson, "Hard-Liner Stirs Debate."

46. Chemerinsky, *Conservative Assault on the Constitution*, 269.

47. Ellis, Olivas, and Brittain, "Now Aggies Need to Take the Next Step."

48. Cohen, "Minority Aid at SIU."

49. CLS v. Walker, 453 F.3d 853 (7th Cir. 2006).

50. See, for example, Maddox, "Senseless Surprise."

51. Fisher v. University of Texas, 645 F.Supp.2d 587 (W. D. Tex. 2009), Fisher v. UT-Austin, 5th circ 09-50822-CV0, 2011.

52. Jaschik, "Texas Limits '10%' Admissions." InsideHigherEd.com, June 1, 2009, www.insidehighered.com/news/2009/06/01/texas (accessed Jan. 22, 2012). See Implementation and Results of the Texas Automatic Admissions Law (HB 588) at the University of Texas at Austin (Report 13, Dec. 23, 2010), www.utexas.edu/student/admissions/research/HB588-Report13.pdf (accessed Jan. 22, 2012).

53. Ibid., Report 13, Dec. 23, 2010. See generally, Long and Tienda, "Winners and Losers," 255.

54. See, for example, Kobach, "Immigration Nullification"; Kasarda, "Affirmative Action Gone Haywire"; Graglia, "Birthright Citizenship for Children of Illegal Aliens." In Florida, it was discovered after many years of administering its traditional residency requirements that colleges were misapplying the domicile statute to deny such status to U.S. citizen children whose parents were undocumented. A suit in California, where state officials made the same mistake in administering financial aid programs for citizen residents, was required to end these patently unconstitutional practices. Vasquez, "U.S.-Citizen Children of Immigrants Protest."

55. A 2006 Migration Policy Institute (MPI) study estimated that approximately fifty thousand undocumented college students were enrolled, either full-time and part-time, and would be eligible for permanent status under the DREAM Act. Batalova and Fix, "New Estimates of Unauthorized Youth." These data do not include persons who might be eligible for the Act's military options for legalization. For additional data, see Redden, "Data on the Undocumented"; Passel and Cohn, *Pew Hispanic Center*, 4: "Among unauthorized immigrants ages 18 to 24 who have graduated from high school, half (49%) are in college or have attended college. The comparable figure for U.S.-born residents is 71%"; Konet, *Migration Policy Institute*; Olivas, "Political Economy of the DREAM Act," 1758.

56. Examples of litigation include *Mannschreck v. Clare*: order of dismissal on grounds of standing in NE case, www.law.uh.edu/ihelg/ab540/mannschreck.pdf (accessed Jan. 22, 2012); IRCOT v. Texas, 706 F.Supp.2d 760 (S. D. Tex. 2010) [ongoing in 2012]; Martinez v. UC Regents, 241 P.3d 855 (Cal. 2010). See also Abourezk, "Judge Tosses Suit"; Nienhusser and Dougherty, *Implementation of College In-State Tuition*; Reich and Mendoza, "'Educating Kids' Versus 'Coddling Criminals'"; Tang, "Colleges to Start Checking Legal Residency"; Benjamin-Alvarado, DeSipio, and Montoya-Kirk, "Latino Mobilization in New Immigrant Destinations." Many of the ongoing cases are reviewed in Olivas, *Political Economy of the DREAM Act and the Legislative Process*.

57. In a 2011 interview, a restrictionist lawyer conceded that the legislation in Alabama was enacted to try and get a case to SCOTUS to challenge *Plyler,* and ultimately, birthright citizenship. Robertson, "Critics See 'Chilling Effect' in Alabama Immigration Law"; Sefsaf, "Restrictionist Lawyer Reveals Long-Term Assault on Immigrant Children." For a review of these legislative and litigation efforts, see the websites of the Immigration Reform Law Institute (www.irli.org/about) and the Federation for American Immigration Reform (www.fairus.org) (accessed Jan. 22, 2012).

58. Ziff, "Very Few Illegal Immigrants Use UW Tuition Deal." The 2009 tuition law was rescinded in 2011, after fewer than 200 students invoked it. See Ziff, "UW Would Comply with Rule for Tuition."

59. "Maryland's 'Dream Act' Suspended"; Linskey, "In-State Tuition Opponents"; Davis, "Md. Voters to Decide Immigrant Tuition Law"; Davis, "Md. Tuition Law May Be Halted."

60. Gordon and Savage, "Supreme Court Order on California Immigrant Tuition Rates"; Vara, "California Sets New Course." In early 2012, the ballot drive was not certified, as it failed to attract the requisite number of legitimate signatures. Riccardi, "Dream Act Opponents' Petition Drive Fails."

61. See, for example, Stefancic and Delgado, *No Mercy*; Vogel, *Fluctuating Fortunes*; Miller, *Gift of Freedom*; Messer-Davidow,"Manufacturing the Attack."

62. Barnes, Chemerinsky, and Jones, "Post-Race Equal Protection?" 989–990 (citations omitted). Law professor Chemerinsky has bitingly noted these developments in a book as well: "Over the last few decades, the Court has abandoned the effort at equalizing schools and the result has been separate and unequal education, to the tremendous detriment of African-American and Latino children. Ironically, the focus of the Court has been far more on limiting affirmative action and protecting whites than remedying discrimination and advancing equality for racial minorities. The Court has failed to realize that there is a world of difference between the government using race to subordinate minorities and using race to benefit minorities and advance equality." Chemerinsky, *Conservative Assault on the Constitution*, 268–269.

63. Spann, "Disparate Impact," 1163.

64. Lee, "Fifty Years of Higher Education Law," 686–689 and note 240.

65. See generally, LaNoue and Lee, *Academics in Court*; Finkin and Post, *For the Common Good*.

66. Garcetti v. Ceballos, 547 U.S. 410 (2006). This case has begun to provoke considerable scholarly attention. Among the most careful articles are Nahmod, "Academic Freedom and the Post-*Garcetti* Blues"; Areen, "Government as Educator."

67. Schrecker, "Roots of the Right-Wing Attack on Higher Education," 82.

68. Teles, *Rise of the Conservative Legal Movement*.

Chapter 5 · Hopwood v. Texas

1. Regents of the University of California v. Bakke, 438 U.S. 265 (1978). For a review of the college cases that led to the K–12 Brown v. Board of Education, 347 U.S. 483 (1954), see Olivas, "Brown and the Desegregative Ideal," and chapter 4 of this book, which examines in case study detail United States v. Fordice, 505 U.S. 717 (1992).

2. DeFunis v. Odegaard, 416 U.S. 312, 320 (1974) *per curiam* (Justice Douglas, dissenting).

3. Grutter v. Bollinger, 539 U.S. 306 (2003).

4. City of Richmond v. J. A. Croson Co., 488 U.S. 469 (1989); Metro Broadcasting, Inc. v. Federal Communications Commission, 497 U.S. 547 (1990); Adarand Constructors, Inc. v. Pena, 515 U.S. 200 (1995).

5. Amar and Katyal, "Bakke's Fate," 1745, 1768. Professor Christopher Eisgruber has usefully added to the record of the complex events, noting how Justice Stevens was undergoing a change of heart about these cases during this time. Eisgruber, "Tough Act To Follow"; Eisgruber, "How the Maverick Became a Lion."

6. Ibid., 1769, citing Adarand, 115 S.Ct. 2113.

7. Hopwood v. Texas, 78 F.3d 932, 963 (5th Cir. 1996) (opinion of Weiner, J., specially concurring).

8. Grutter v. Bollinger, 539 U.S. 306 (2003).

9. Gratz v. Bollinger, 539 U.S. 244 (2003).

10. Regents of the University of California v. Bakke, 18 Cal.3d 34, 553 P.2d 1152 (1976)

11. Regents of the University of California v. Bakke, 18 Cal.3d 34, 132 Cal. Rptr. 680, 553 P.2d 1152, 1976 Cal. LEXIS 336 (1976)

12. Justice Powell announced the Court's judgment and filed an opinion expressing his views of the case in Parts I, III-A, and V-C, which Justice White joined; and in Parts I and V-C, which Justices Brennan, Marshall, and Blackmun concurred in the judgment in part and dissented in part. Justices White, Marshall, and Blackmun filed separate opinions. Justice Stevens filed an opinion concurring in the judgment in part and dissenting in part, in which Chief Justice Burger, Justice Stewart, and Justice Rehnquist joined.

13. Bakke, 438 U.S. 265, 270–272.

14. See, for example, Olivas, "Federal Law and Scholarship Policy," 21.

15. Bakke, 438 U.S. 265, 320.

16. Ibid., 317 (Part V-A).

17. Ibid., 374.

18. Amar and Katyal, "Bakke's Fate," 1754.

19. See Olivas, "Federal Law and Scholarship Policy," 21.

20. Adams v. Richardson. 356 F.Supp. 92 (D. D. C. 1973); 480 F.2d 1159 (D. C. Cir. 1973); Adams v. Califano, Civil Action No. 3095-70, Second Supplemental Order (D. D. C. Apr. 1, 1977). See also Marcus, "Adams Case."

21. Hopwood v. Texas, 861 F.Supp. 551 (W.D. Tex. 1994), *aff'd*, 78 F.3d 932 (5th Cir.), *cert. denied*, 116 S.Ct. 2581 (1996).

22. Ibid., 570–571.

23. He awarded one dollar in damages to each plaintiff and ordered that they be allowed to reapply without any charge the following year. Ibid., 580.

24. Hopwood v. Texas, 78 F.3d 932, 945 (5th Cir.).

25. Ibid., 944.

26. Ibid., 944.

27. Ibid., 945–946.

28. Ibid., 948 note 36 (citing Bakke, 438 U.S. at 378). The devil had made them do this, against their will, so they would not "contravene precedent." Or presumably, not disregard the "lonely opinion" of the Supreme Court.

29. Ibid., 962 (Wiener, J., specially concurring).

30. Texas v. Hopwood, 116 S.Ct. 2581, 2582 (1996) (opinion of Ginsburg, J., joined by Souter, J.), *denying cert.* to Hopwood v. Texas, 78 F.3d 932 (5th Cir. 1996).

31. In reaction, Rice University, a private institution, actually reversed several decisions made earlier to admit black students and denied them admission. "Short History," 36, 38. Office for Civil Rights Assistant Secretary Norma Cantu subsequently wrote Texas officials that *Hopwood* was limited to the UTLS setting and that *Bakke* was controlling. Attorney General Dan Morales then wrote Education Secretary Richard Riley that he disagreed with the OCR findings. Cantu was forced to retreat when the Department of Justice determined that *Hopwood* was controlling in the state. See generally Lederman, "Texas Colleges May Consider"; Dickson, "Vital Crucible of the Law," 495. Texas politics watchers were quite surprised when Attorney General John Cornyn rescinded the Morales Letter Opinion—restoring *Bakke* as the *status quo ante* authority on scholarships and the like. Thus, it was a conservative Republican AG who reinstated affirmative action

in this area, following the restrictive advice of the liberal Democrat Morales. Morales, "Letter Opinion LO-97-001"; Cornyn, "Texas Attorney General's Opinion."

32. The attorney general in Georgia indicated that his office would abide by Hopwood, although the state is in the 11th Circuit. See "Georgia Colleges Ordered."

33. Bakke v. Regents of the University of California, 438 U.S. 265, 320 (1978).

34. Ibid., 311–313.

35. Wygant v. Jackson Board of Education, 476 U.S. 267, 286 (1995) (O'Connor, J., concurring in part and concurring in the judgment, citations omitted, quoting *Bakke*).

36. Adarand Constructors, Inc. v. Pena, 115 S.Ct. 2097, 2117 (1995).

37. Hopwood, 78 F.3d at 946.

38. Ibid.

39. See *University of Houston Law Center Alumni Directory*, 1993, on file at UHLC Development Office.

40. There is a small bookshelf available on this topic. See, for example, Texas Higher Education Coordinating Board, "Criteria Identified"; Fallon, "Affirmative Action Based on Economic Disadvantage," 1913; Malamud, "Class-Based Affirmative Action," 1847; Ellis, Olivas, and Brittain, "Now Aggies Need to Take the Next Step." But see also Kahlenberg, *Remedy*; Sander, "Class in American Legal Education," 631.

41. Hopwood, 861 F.Supp. 566.

42. Chen, "Embryonic Thoughts," 1123; Chen notes that he and I have "at least one point of agreement: Bakke lives" (1124).

43. Podberesky v. Kirwan, 956 F.2d 52 (4th Cir. 1992). This case challenged financial aid and programs undertaken by the University of Maryland, under the auspices of the *Adams* consent decree in Maryland, which had been approved by the Office for Civil Rights. It was brought by the Washington Legal Foundation on behalf of a student whose mother was Latina.

44. Hopwood v. Texas, 78 F.3d 932, 946 (5th Cir.), *cert. denied*, 116 S.Ct. 2581 (1996); Bakke, 438 U.S. 265, 404 (1978) (Blackmun, J., concurring in part and dissenting in part).

45. As this panel misread *Bakke*, so the judges misread the admissions process. The panel also did not understand that Cheryl Hopwood wanted some form of affirmative action or special consideration to apply in her case. She was a mother of a child born with cerebral palsy, and the panel found the case one of "unique background," in which Hopwood's "circumstances would bring a different perspective to the law school." But when she applied, the University of Texas law school committee did not have this information. Incredibly, Hopwood provided no letters of recommendation and no personal statement outlining her unique background. Hopwood v. State of Texas, 78 F.3d 946 (5th Cir. 1996). Yet she was certain she was displaced from her rightful place by less-qualified minorities. Another of the plaintiffs had a letter of recommendation from a professor describing the plaintiff's academic performance at his undergraduate institution as "uneven, disappointing, and mediocre." Hopwood v. State of Texas, 861 F.Supp. 551, 566–567 (W. D. Tex. 1994). That such students could score high on an index utilizing only grade point averages and Law School Admission Test (LSAT) scores indicates why law schools look to features other than mere scores. And any law school would be wary of incomplete applica-

tions or those in which letters of recommendation singled out a student for "mediocre" academic achievement.

46. The father of co-plaintiff Kenneth Elliott wrote to the UTLS dean complaining that his son had been denied admission due to "mandatory minority and women quotas which use a large percentage of the openings." Hopwood v. Texas, 861 F.Supp. 551 (W.D. Tex. 1994), *aff'd* 78 F.3d 932 (5th Cir.), *cert. denied*, 116 S.Ct. 2581 (1996).

47. For Southern Methodist University in the same year (1996–1997), the figures were 3.13/157 for the entire class; at University of Houston Law Center, the scores were 3.5/159. A 159 LSAT score in 1992 was at the 82nd percentile.

48. See U.S. v. Fordice, 505 U.S. 717 (1992); see also Knight v. Alabama, 801 F.Supp. 577 (N.D. Ala. 1992).

49. Similarly, the SAT measures less well for math ability and better for verbal ability for females than it does for males. For a review of the psychometrics of standardized admissions examinations, see generally Olivas, "Constitutional Criteria," 1065.

50. Table of Admitted Applicants: whites were 39,570/60,400 (66%); reporting minorities were 22%; Table of Applicants: whites were 52,790/87,900 (60%); reporting minorities were 28%. Law School Admissions Council, *LSAC Volume Summary*.

51. LSATs Administered, www.lsac.org/LSACResources/Data/LSAC-volume-summary .asp (accessed Jan. 23, 2012).

52. I write this at Thanksgiving 2011, even as a number of legal education issues swirl around, suggesting that the overall economy and the architecture of law school attendance have made it a less valuable credential now than it has been previously. For a comprehensive review of these issues, see Matasar, "Viability of the Law Degree." For substantive analyses of college costs, see Ehrenberg, *Tuition Rising*; Archibald and Feldman, *Why Does College Cost So Much?*

53. Christ, "Affirmative Action." Professor Christ made available many of these data from a UC Committee on which she served: http://cio.chance.berkeley.edu/chancellor/ar /001219att.doc (accessed Sept. 29, 2011).

54. Proposition 209 drew a great deal of scholarly attention and well over one hundred articles and book chapters, by my imperfect count. See, for example, Chemerinsky, "Impact of the Proposed California Civil Rights Initiative"; Volokh, "California Civil Rights Initiative."

55. The California college financial situation has worsened to the point of triggering a drumbeat of media stories and analyses. See, for instance, Gordon and Rivera, "Budget Ax Means More Tuition Hikes"; Medina, "California Cuts Weigh Heavily On Its Colleges"; Nagourney, "Californians Asked for $6.9 Billion in New Taxes."

56. See generally, Olivas, "Legal Norms in Law School Admissions," 103; Weber, "Inside the Meritocracy Machine." Weber recounts the story of several Harvard College applicants from one California high school during the Prop. 209 period, noting that more than 2,900 valedictorians applied for the 1,620 places in the class of 2000.

57. LSAC data in October 2011 show that there were 602,300 applications to ABA law schools in 2009–2010, a record high, and 171,500 LSAT exams administered the same year, also a record high. LSATs Administered, www.lsac.org/LSACResources/Data/LSAC -volume-summary.asp (accessed Jan. 23, 2012). While many of these are multiple-school

applications and exams taken more than once by individuals, somewhat inflating the picture, they are still an astounding defiance of all the laws of gravity.

58. See Olivas, "Reflections on Professorial Academic Freedom," 1835. There is a wide-ranging genre, including general analytic monographs, and more detailed state or institution case studies about race in higher education, and how it is decidedly not "post-racial." See, for example, Baez, *Affirmative Action, Hate Speech, and Tenure*; Russell, "'Keep Negroes Out of Most Classes.'"

59. There is a substantial and comprehensive series of studies on the Texas percentage plan. See, for example, Torres, "*Grutter v. Bollinger/Gratz v. Bollinger*," 1596; Alon and Tienda, "Assessing the 'Mismatch' Hypothesis"; Niu, Tienda, and Cortes, "College Selectivity and the Texas Top 10% Law"; Long and Tienda, "Winners and Losers"; University of Texas at Austin Office of Admissions, Implementation and Results of the Texas Automatic Admissions Law (HB 588), Report 13, Dec. 23, 2010, http://www.utexas.edu/student /admissions/research/HB588-Report13.pdf (accessed Jan. 23, 2012).

60. Jaschik, "Texas Limits '10%' Admissions."

61. Fisher v. University of Texas, 631F.3d 213, 234 (5th Cir. 2011), emphasis in original.

62. 631F.3d 213, 242.

63. Olivas, "Don't Mess With College 'Top 10 Percent' Plan."

64. 631F.3d 213, 247 (King, Circuit Judge, specially concurring).

65. Ibid. (Garza, Circuit Judge, specially concurring).

66. I end, not with a civil procedure citation but with compelling evidence from the psychosocial literature. See, for instance, Blum, "*I'm Not a Racist, But . . . ,*" 42–52. Blum analyzes the deep and unexamined investment that whites have in retaining their racial and class privilege in the United States. That thesis is not the major focus of this project, but his conclusions have haunted me, especially as I see the fulminations of those aggrieved whites who resist college affirmative action after the many years of *Bakke* and now *Grutter*, especially the judges who are required to apply the law currently in force but who have engaged in rearguard action and virtually invited the monkeywrenching that has resulted. He is particularly focused on what he calls the "moral asymmetries" or the ways that such purposive elites invoke progressive justifications and pieties but are simply opposed to racial justice and the Supreme Court's modest and sporadic implementation of these principles. See also Lawrence, "Id, the Ego, and Equal Protection"; Harris, "Theorizing Class, Gender, and the Law."

67. Cert granted, Fisher v. Univ. of Texas at Austin, 132 S.Ct. 1536, 182 L. Ed. 2d 160 (Feb. 21, 2012). Justice Kagan recused herself from the case.

Chapter 6 · Abrams v. Baylor College of Medicine

1. Abrams v. Baylor College of Medicine, 581 F.Supp. 1570 (S. D. Tex., 1984).

2. Ibid., 1574.

3. Ibid., 1574–1576. Officials at the University of Colorado and University of Washington refused to keep Jewish doctors out of the program.

4. Ibid., 1579.

5. Abrams v. Baylor College of Medicine, 805 F.2d 528, 533 (5th Cir. 1986) (emphasis in text).

6. Ibid., 533.

7. Judge DeAnda, among his many accomplishments, was a cofounder of the Mexican American Legal Defense and Educational Fund (MALDEF) in 1968. Legal historian Steven H. Wilson interviewed Judge DeAnda, who figures prominently in Wilson's "Brown over 'Other White.' "

8. Shahan, "Determining Whether Title VII"; Schneyer, "Nostalgia in the Fifth Circuit."

9. "Baylor just danced all around this; it never zeroed in on this as a BFOQ." Abrams v. BCOM, 805 F.2d 528, 533 (5th Cir. 1986)

10. Rivenburg, "Baylor University's Decision"; "Stop the Presses!"

11. Connell and Savage, "Role of Collegiality," 833; Heiser, " 'Because the Stakes Are So Small' "; Connell, Melear, and Savage, "Collegiality in Higher Education Employment Decisions."

12. "Defendant's Motion to Dismiss or in the Alternative for Summary Judgment" (which he granted in part and dismissed in part), the "Plaintiffs' Unopposed Motion for Continuance" (which he granted), and the "Motion to Intervene as a Plaintiff" Motion of Marcee Lundeen, a Jewish nurse in the unit (which he denied, for not filing timely). 1983 U.S. Dist. LEXIS 14878; 32 Fair Employment Practice Cases (BNA) 935; 33 Employment Practice Decisions (CCH) P34,020 (S.D. Tex. 1983).

13. Ibid.

14. Ibid.

15. Bulk Oil (ZUG) A.G. v. Sun Co., Inc., 583 F.Supp. 1134, 1138–1139 (D. C. N. Y., 1983) ("Sun argues (1) that no private right of action exists under this statute, and (2) even if one does, the statute was not violated. We agree that no private right of action exists under the Export Administration Act, and grant defendants' motion to dismiss this claim."). See King, "2 Jewish Doctors Sue to Join Saudi Program"; King, "Court Says Baylor is Discriminatory."

16. Fair Empl. Prac. Cas. (BNA) 935; 33 Empl. Prac. Dec. (CCH) P34,020 (S.D. Tex. 1983).

17. There is a distressingly large literature documenting how Jews have been demonized and treated as a people over history. The most useful work I have relied upon for situating anti-Semitism in the United States is Brodkin, *How Jews Became White Folks*. See also Lindemann, *Esau's Tears*; Probst, *Demonizing the Jews*.

18. St. Francis College v. Al-Khazraji, 481 U.S. 604, 609–613 (1987).

19. Shaare Tefila Congregation v. Cobb, 481 U.S. 615 (1987).

20. Abrams, 581 F.Supp. 1570, 1578.

21. Hernandez v. Texas, 347 U.S. 475 (1954). See Olivas, ed., *"Colored Men" and "Hombres Aquí"*; Lopez and Olivas, *"Hernandez v. Texas."* After he left the bench and reentered private practice, I asked Judge DeAnda, who had become a close personal friend, why he had ruled this way on the racialization of Jews. He said he had done so because it was not essential to the case and because of all the bad faith evident in the record. He also said he was afraid that the Fifth Circuit might overturn him if he "reached too far on the issue"

and that he had "enough hooks in them [BCOM]" already. When I asked him about the EAA matter, when no federal court had yet found a private remedy, he said that no judge had ever had a better fact pattern than had been presented to him. He also allowed that he thought the case went to trial because of bad BCOM lawyering at the board governance level and what he thought was a conflict of interest between the board chair's law firm and the board, so that they did not get good advice and cut their losses earlier. He also felt that the medical school appealed to the Circuit to save face and to "pin it down," not because they thought they could win. He also indicated that this was why he thought BCOM did not push it to SCOTUS.

22. The BCOM case was not helped in the press or in court by its own lawyers. A *New York Times* piece noted:

> "Baylor vehemently denies the charge," said William Pakalka, a lawyer for Baylor. He said the two plaintiffs had not maintained that they had been rejected but contended that they had been "chilled" from doing so by their own belief they would be rejected. He also said neither the Saudis nor Baylor had any policy regarding the religious beliefs of participants in the Saudi program. . . . However, he said he did not know if the Saudis would grant a visa to either of the plaintiffs if they had applied for the program and been selected by Baylor to participate. "We don't have any understanding with the Saudis," he said. "We don't know what the Saudis will or will not do." He said he believed the suit was frivolous and was brought to publicize "pro-Jewish or anti-Arab causes." Nancy O'Connor, another lawyer for Baylor, observed that the safety of the doctors themselves could be considered and there could conceivably be "judicial notice of the fact that Saudi patients might not want a Jewish doctor" treating them.

King, "2 Jewish Doctors Sue to Join Saudi Program." Pride goeth before the fall.

23. In addition, the Fifth Circuit hammered the BCOM's legal strategy, commenting: "Worse than that, Baylor's own witnesses went a long way toward destroying the BFOQ defense." 805 F.2d 528, 533. They might have added that the public statements made by the lawyers went a long way to destroying their credibility.

24. 1983 U.S. Dist. LEXIS 14878; 32 Fair Empl. Prac. Cas. (BNA) 935; 33 Empl. Prac. Dec. (CCH) P 34,020 (S.D. Tex. 1983): 3.

25. The "Final Judgment," which set out the various fees and financial matters of the case, was not published, but is reported at 1984 WL 1046 (S. D. Tex.), 35 Fair Empl. Prac. Cas. (BNA) 695; 35 Empl. Prac. Dec. P 34,595.

26. Judge DeAnda simply did not trust or believe the official BCOM version of events that demonized the Jewish plaintiff doctors, and wrote:

> Dr. Abrams eventually became a spokesman for Baylor personnel who were protesting the marked inequities in compensation between faculty members who went on rotations to King Faisal and faculty members who did not. Dr. Storey resented Dr. Abrams' protests and Dr. Abrams was later transferred, over his objections, from Fondren-Brown to Ben Taub Hospital. The Court finds that this trans-

fer resulted from official displeasure with Dr. Abrams' protestations, and that this transfer had a deleterious impact on his research projects.

Dr. Abrams persisted in his desire to participate in the program, even after his transfer to Ben Taub Hospital. As noted above, Dr. Abrams was fully qualified to participate in the King Faisal program. . . . The Court is not persuaded by Baylor's attempts to paint a picture of Dr. Abrams as being noncooperative, difficult to work with, and a person with a volatile ego. These attempts merely reflect an effort to label Abrams as a man who is not a "team player." (Abrams, 581 F.Supp. 1570, 1576).

27. Ackerman, "Baylor, Rice End Their Talks on Merger"; Ackerman, "Baylor Med Paying Off $260 Million of Debt." See also Ackerman, "Rivals Reunite."

Chapter 7 · Axson-Flynn v. Johnson

1. Axson-Flynn v. Johnson, 151 F.Supp.2d 1326, 1328 (D.Utah, 2001).
2. Ibid., 1329.
3. 151 F.Supp.2d 1326, 1342.
4. 356 F.3d 1277, 1285.
5. Ibid., quoting Hazelwood v. Kuhlmeier, 484 U.S. 260, 273 (1988).
6. See, for example, Casarez, "Student Press," 1, 5–6; Dupre, *Speaking Up*, ch. 4.
7. Hazelwood v. Kuhlmeier, 484 U.S. 260, 273 (1988).
8. Casarez, "Student Press," 17–19 (citations omitted).
9. *Axson-Flynn*, 356 F.3d 1277, 1287, note 6.
10. Ibid., 1287–1292, emphasis in original.
11. Ibid., 1292–1293, emphasis in original.
12. Ibid., 1294–1297.
13. Ibid., 1298–1299.
14. Ibid., 1300.
15. Ibid., 1301.
16. See, for instance, Welling, "Thespian May Lose Union Ally in U. Suit." University of Utah professors "refused to allow her to omit profanity from an in-class performance." Welling, "U. Theater Student's Lawyer Wants Trial in 2005." The ownership of the local papers is a matter of public record and politics. See Peters, "Mormon-Owned Paper Stands with Immigrants."
17. University of Utah, Policy 6-100: Instruction and Evaluation, www.regulations .utah.edu/academics/6-100.html (accessed Nov. 25, 2011).
18. Keeton v. Anderson-Wiley, 733 F.Supp.2d 1368 (S. D. Ga., 2010). It was affirmed in 2011, 664 F.2d 865 (11th Cir. 2011), and dismissed in 2012, No. 110-099 (S.D. Ga. June 22, 2012).
19. Ibid., 1381.
20. Julea Ward v. Members of the Board of Control of Eastern Michigan University, 700 F.Supp.2d 803 (E. D. Mich. 2010). The Sixth Circuit reversed the trial court ( ), and the case was scheduled for trial in late Fall 2012.

21. ACA and ASCA Ethics Codes. Additionally, Michigan approves CACREP accreditation standards and required that all professional counselors and school counselors be trained in ethics (M.C.L.A.). Ibid., 7–8.

22. It has been followed by: O'Neal v. Falcon, 668 F.Supp.2d 979 (W.D. Tex. 2009): precluding choice of abortion as paper topic; Ward v. Members of the Bd. of Control of E. Mich. Univ., 700 F.Supp.2d 803 (E.D. Mich. 2010); Head v. Bd. of Trustees of the California State University, 2006 U.S. Dist. LEXIS 60857 (N. D. Cal. Aug. 14, 2006) (Order granting motions to dismiss: student suit on class participation and NCATE standards; Mount St. Scholastica, Inc. v. City of Atchison, 482 F.Supp.2d 1281 (D. Kan. 2007) (concerning college building demolition permit, in federal district court in 10th Circuit).

While not all the cases have cited or, more importantly, followed *Axson-Flynn*'s holding, there are more than a few working their way through the courts, some of them with Alliance Defense Fund involvement. Most notably, they seem to involve a multitude of mixed motives and complex fact patterns. See, for example, Jaschik, "Getting Around the Courts"; Jaschik, "Professor Told to Stop"; Jaschik, "Michigan State Professor Attacked."

23. On Dec. 16, 2011, the 11th Circuit upheld the Keeton trial court. 664 F.3d 865 (11th Cir. 2011), and it was dismissed in 2012. But the Ward case continues in 2012.

24. Jaschik, "New Clash of Rights." Although the decision directly concerns the college classroom, it was premised upon several important elementary and secondary decisions. This ironic citation pattern is also evidence of the religious and conservative wars being waged at the local school board level. See, for example, Berkman and Plutzer, *Ten Thousand Democracies*; Slack, *Battle over the Meaning of Everything*. While none of this work is for the faint of heart, my own observations and reading of these cases over the last dozen or so years have led me to believe that college law cases are Scylla, while K–12 issues are the more dangerous and whirling Charybdis.

25. The fund labels colleges and universities as "A Hostile Environment": www.alliancedefensefund.org/University (accessed Nov. 25, 2011).

Chapter 8 · Location, Location, Location

1. Corson, "Reform of Domicile Law," 327; Olivas, "Administering Intentions"; Williams, "Taking Care of Ourselves"; Ishitani, "Determinants of Out-Migration."

2. This is an area where scholars across disciplines have reconceptualized the Mexico–United States border in its various manifestations, especially its liminal features. See, for instance, Gutiérrez-Jones, *Rethinking the Borderlands*; Menchaca, *Naturalizing Mexican Immigrants*; Campbell, "Road to S.B. 1070"; Hernandez, *Mexican American Colonization*. The sense of place and an enclave from undesirable populations also permeates the research literature on hate movements operating within the United States. See, for example, Perry and Blazak, "Places for Races."

3. To get a sense of the proximity, plug San Antonio, Texas/Nuevo Laredo, Tamaulipas, Mexico, into Google Maps. The convenient service shows that using Interstate I-35 will require 159 miles and will likely take two hours and thirty-eight minutes.

4. Plyler v. Doe, 457 U.S. 202 (1982). See Olivas, *No Undocumented Child Left Behind.*

5. The topic of schooling and Mexican American litigation and resistance efforts in Texas has grown exponentially, both for the salience of this history and for the archival resources available to explore the subject. Some of the more comprehensive include Romo, "Southern California and the Origins," 379; Martinez, "Legal Indeterminacy, Judicial Discretion," 555; Blanton, "From Intellectual Deficiency to Cultural Deficiency"; Blanton, " 'They Cannot Master Abstractions' "; Nissimov, "Unequal Access?"; Kauffman, "Texas School Finance Litigation Saga"; Badillo, *MALDEF and the Evolution of Latino Civil Rights*; Wilson, "*Chicanismo* and the Flexible Fourteenth Amendment."

6. Clements v. LULAC, 800 S.W.2d 948 (1990) (Court of Appeals, 13th Dist., Corpus Christi, *Opinion Certifying Class,* Dec. 6, 1990 and *Rehearing Overruled,* Jan. 10, 1991); Richards v. LULAC, 868 S.W.2d 306 (1993). In online or other searches, readers should not be confused by a similarly named voting rights case: League of United Latin American Citizens (Council # 4434) v. Clements, 999 F.2d 831, 840 (5th Cir. 1993), *cert. denied,* 510 U.S. 1071 (1994).

7. Nissimov, "Unequal Access?"; Valencia, *Chicano Students and the Courts.*

8. Richards v. LULAC, 868 S.W.2d 306, 309 (1993).

9. Of course, Texas is not the only state with substantial numbers of Mexican Americans, but it is the state with the longest shared border with Mexico, and it is the only southern state with a substantial Mexican-origin population. There is a growing literature on the parallel universes inhabited by African Americans and Mexican Americans, coexisting in Texas in the first half of the twentieth century. The growing consensus is that the histories are more linked and interrelated than had been thought. This literature also shows the wariness each group had for the other at the legal and elite professional level. See, for example, San Miguel, *"Let All of Them Take Heed"*; San Miguel, " 'The Community Is Beginning to Rumble,' " 135; Foley, *White Scourge*; Kellar, *Make Haste Slowly*; San Miguel, *Brown, Not White*; Shabazz, *Advancing Democracy*; Olivas, ed., *"Colored Men" and "Hombres Aquí"*; Garcia, *White but Not Equal*; Orozco, *No Mexicans, Women, or Dogs Allowed*; Behnken, "Elusive Unity"; Foley, *Quest for Equality.*

10. Barrera, "Minorities and the University of Texas School of Law (1950–1980)," 99.

11. Richards v. LULAC, 868 S.W.2d 306, 308 (1993).

12. Ibid., 948.

13. Ibid., 309–310.

14. Ibid., 310.

15. Richards v. LULAC, 863 S.W.2d 449 (1993) ("To protect our jurisdiction pending a ruling on the merits of the case, all injunctive relief granted by the trial court in its judgment of January 20, 1992, is stayed pending further order of the Court.").

16. 868 S.W.2d 306, 314 (1993).

17. 868 S.W.2d 306, 314 at n.10 (1993).

18. Gold, "South Texas Universities Make Strides." See also Gold, "College Initiative's Future"; Gold, "Pork Fattens Border Initiative." In 2003, Matt Flores followed up with another look at the initiative a decade after its inception. See Flores, "College Economics

Test"; Flores, "Texas Educators Are on Edge"; Flores, "UTSA's Climb to Top-Tier Status."

19. Garcia v. California State Polytechnic University, San Luis Obispo (CSU-SLO). The pleadings, which set out the detailed admissions policy, are available at www.poverty law.org/poverty-law-library/case/55500/55575/55575a.pdf (at 5–8).

20. Garcia v. California State Polytechnic University, San Luis Obispo Garcia v. Board of Trustees of the Calif. State University, 131 Cal. App. 4th 1283, 32 Cal. Rptr. 3d 724 (2005). Subsequently, in 2006 the request for review was denied, and the court took the additional step of ordering that the opinion not be published. 2005 Cal. LEXIS 12600, 2005 Cal. Daily Op. Service 9812, 2005 D.A.R. 13387 (Cal. Nov. 16, 2005).

21. 32 Cal. Rptr. 3d 724, 725 (2005).

22. See, for example, Henig et al., *Color of School Reform*; Deckman, *School Board Battles*; Berkman and Plutzer, *Ten Thousand Democracies*; Slack, *Battle over the Meaning of Everything*.

23. The overcrowding in California public colleges and the financial straits in the overall finance structure of the state's public institutions have caused a reexamination of the mix of local and out-of-state, nonresident students as well as a failed proposal to charge differential tuition for "gateway" courses. Hoover and Keller, "More Students Migrate"; Medina, "2-Year College, Squeezed"; Medina, "Chancellor Asks California Community College"; Gordon, "Offering Deals on Out-of-State Tuition." And the public high school attendance zones are also contested, especially in the relatively affluent and desirable districts. See, for example, Jennings, "California Briefing."

24. Valencia, *Chicano Students and the Courts*, 267.

25. See, for example, McLendon, Hearn, and Mokher, "Partisans, Professionals, and Power"; Doyle, Delaney, and Naughton, "Public Institutional Aid and State Policy"; McLendon, Mokher, and Doyle, " 'Privileging' Public Research Universities."

26. Weinbaum v. Cuomo, 631 N.Y.S.2d 825, *appeal dismissed* 641 N.Y.S.2d 595 (1996).

27. Weinbaum v. Cuomo, 219 A.D.2d 554, 556–557 (1995).

28. Tennessee was one of the few southern states that was not an *Adams* state. Geier v. Dunn, 337 F.Supp. 573 (M.D. Tenn. 1972), Geier v. Blanton, 427 F.Supp. 644 (M.D. Tenn. 1977).

29. Geier v. Alexander, 801 F.2d 799 (6th Cir. 1986). See also Geier v. Sundquist, 372 F.3d 784 (6th Cir. 2004). This case, like Mississippi's *Fordice* (discussed in chapter 4), just stretched on forever.

Chapter 9 · Clark v. Claremont University Center

1. Bartholet, "Application of Title VII to Jobs in High Places," 945, 949–950.

2. Chew and Kelley, "Unwrapping Racial Harassment Law," 49, 61–63. See also Chew and Kelley, "Myth of the Color-Blind Judge," 117.

3. Ibid., 61–63, text accompanying tables 4 and 7.

4. Ibid., 106–107.

5. Clark v. Claremont University Center and Graduate School, 6 Cal. App. 4th 639, 8 Cal. Rptr. 2d 151 (1992).

6. Connell and Savage, "Role of Collegiality," 833; Heiser, "'Because the Stakes Are So Small,'" 385; Connell, Melear, and Savage, "Collegiality in Higher Education Employment Decisions," 529; Petry, "Top Ten Workplace Issues."

7. Clark v. Claremont, 6 Cal. App. 4th 639, 648–649.

8. Ibid., 648–649.

9. "The jury awarded Clark $1 million in compensatory damages and $16,327 in punitive damages, and the trial court awarded Clark attorney fees of $419,633.13. Defendants appeal from the judgment. In the published portion of the opinion, we hold the verdict is supported by sufficient evidence. We affirm the judgment." Ibid., 643.

10. Ibid., 652–653.

11. Ibid., 667–668.

12. Ibid., 668.

13. McGraw, "Jury Awards Black Professor $1 Million."

14. Clark, 6 Cal. App. 4th 662.

15. Ibid., 670. Because parts of the fee issues were treated in the unpublished part of the opinion, it required persistence, detective work, and suspension of disbelief to apprehend the extent to which CGU's lawyers played legal hardball. Not only did they refuse to hold over or postpone the trial due to the jurors' sickness, but they opposed the attorneys' fees motion (the $419,000) and, on appeal, argued that since the first trial had resulted in a mistrial (due to juror attrition), Clark had not been the prevailing party and therefore should not be awarded any of the fees related to the first trial—which is where the bulk of the actual trial preparation and expenses occurred. This hard line was in addition to the artificial bank account matter that limited the punitive damage award. From the final opinion: "We affirm the judgment and award Clark costs and attorney fees on appeal. We direct the trial court on remand to determine a reasonable amount of attorney fees on appeal." Ibid., 670. Both sides eventually agreed on the fee amounts, and the court accepted the decision.

16. Ibid. Of course, because *Abrams* was not a tenure review matter but a program participation issue over the Saudi rotations, the case would likely not have surfaced in the appellate review of college tenure denial litigation. Likewise, *Jew v. University of Iowa* resulted in her promotion, against all odds, but she had already earned tenure. And, remarkably, *Abrams, Jew,* and *Clark* cases have not gained the prominence or notoriety they richly deserve. I know several of the players in the *Clark* saga, and all seem sorrowful at the notorious and embarrassing turn of events.

17. Brown v. Boston University, 891 F.2d 337 (1st Cir. 1989).

18. Bennun v. Rutgers, 941 F.2d 154 (3d Cir. 1991).

19. Jew v. University of Iowa, 749 F.Supp. 946 (S.D. Iowa 1990). In an eerie foreshadowing of the graffiti in Professor Clark's case, such racial and sexual graffiti occurred in Professor Jew's case as well. Ibid., 951.

20. Chamallas, "Jean Jew's Case," 71, 73.

21. Gajda, *Trials of Academe,* 63.

22. See, for instance, Colker, "Whores, Fags, Dumb-Ass Women, Surly Blacks and Competent Heterosexual White Men: The Sexual and Racial Morality Underlying Anti-Discrimination Doctrine," 195, 203, 220–221. I confess for the record that this is a

wonderful article, but by a long margin, it is also among my favorite article titles, across all genres and journals. During a term I spent at the University of Iowa, I was also privileged to meet Professor Jew, a remarkable, resilient, and heroic woman.

23. Mindiola, "Getting Tenure at the U," 29–50.

Chapter 10 · *The Developing Law of Faculty Discontent*

1. Michael S. Adams v. University of North Carolina–Wilmington, 640 F.3d 550, 553 (4th Cir. 2011)

2. Michael S. Adams v. University of North Carolina–Wilmington, ____ F.Supp.____ (E.D. N.C. 2010) [Adams v. Trustees of the University of North Carolina–Wilmington, No. 7:07-cv-00064-H (S.D.N.C. filed Mar. 15, 2010)].

3. Adams, 640 F.3d 550, 553 (4th Cir. 2011) (*Affirmed in part, reversed in part, and remanded by published opinion*).

4. Alliance Defense Fund website, www.alliancedefensefund.org/ReligiousFreedom (emphasis in the original, accessed Nov. 25, 2011). The website also warns: "So why is religious freedom under attack in America today? For decades, the American Civil Liberties Union (ACLU) and other radical anti-Christian groups have been on a mission to eliminate public expression of our nation's faith and heritage. By influencing the government, filing lawsuits, and spreading the myth of the so-called 'separation of church and state,' the opposition has been successful at forcing its leftist agenda on Americans. Their targeted attacks on religious freedom are more serious and widespread than you may realize. In courtrooms and schoolrooms, offices and shops, public buildings and even churches . . . those who believe in God are increasingly threatened, punished, and silenced."

5. The AAUP *amicus* brief is at: www.aaup.org/NR/rdonlyres/58506EE0-4E81-4AA9 -9616-3768FFA8643A/0/Adamsamicusbrief7210.pdf (accessed Nov. 25, 2011).

6. The Fourth Circuit held that the trial court had used the wrong test. "As we explain below, the district court misread *Garcetti*. The district court's decision rests on several fundamental errors including its holding that protected speech was converted into unprotected speech based on its use after the fact. In addition, the district court applied *Garcetti* without acknowledging, let alone addressing, the clear language in that opinion that casts doubt on whether the *Garcetti* analysis applies in the academic context of a public university." 640 F.3d 561 (citing *Garcetti v. Ceballos*, 547 U.S. 410, 425 (2006)). The *Pickering-Connick* doctrine draws from Pickering v. Board of Education, 391 U.S. 563 (1968) and Connick v. Myers, 461 U.S. 138 (1983). For the application of the doctrine, see Nahmod, "Academic Freedom and the Post-*Garcetti* Blues"; Areen, "Government as Educator," 945.

7. Pickering, 640 F.3d 563–565.

8. Garcetti, 547 U.S. 410, 421–422.

9. Ibid., 547 U.S. 410, 423–424.

10. Ibid., 547 U.S. 410, 421.

11. Ibid., 547 U.S. 410, 421–422. While the issue extends beyond this project, any similar book undertaken in a decade will have to reckon with this Trojan Horse sanctioned by

Justice Kennedy. Given my age (sixty-one as of this book's projected publication date), I am confident that I will not have to chart this disastrous result.

12. Garcetti, 547 U.S. 410, 427, 438 (Justice Souter, with whom Justice Stevens and Justice Ginsburg join, dissenting).

13. 547 U.S. 410, 425 (*Vamos a ver*. "We shall see.").

14. Pickering, 640 F.3d 563–564 (citations omitted).

15. Ibid., 640 F.3d 559 (emphasis in original).

Conclusion

1. Lorde, "Master's Tools Will Never," 110.

2. Olivas, "Constitutional Criteria," 1065, 1114–1116. For other uses and critiques of the pipeline metaphor, see Surowiecki, "Pipeline Problem," 72 (describing problems in drug-approval process in pharmaceutical industry); Evensen and Pratt, *End of the Pipeline*.

3. Kahlenberg, "First Monday in October."

4. Kahlenberg, ed., *Affirmative Action for the Rich*; Kahlenberg, *Remedy*.

5. By 2010 at the UT-Austin campus, first-time freshmen enrolled under the percent plan were 46% white, and all enrolled first-time freshman the same year (including automatic admits and regular admits) were 46% white. UT Office of Admissions Report 13, Dec. 23, 2010, www.utexas.edu/student/admissions/research/HB588-Report13.pdf (accessed Nov. 27, 2011), 8 (Table 1a: First-Time Enrolled Freshmen from Texas High Schools).

6. As I write in late 2011, the country is just starting a presidential campaign, so measured rhetoric and constructive dialogue are at low ebb, while pointing out perfidy and class divisions is at full tide. See, for example, Pear, "Tax Bracket Divided"; Peters, "TV Attack Ads Aim."

7. Bernstein, "Spitzer Grants Illegal Immigrants"; Confessore and Hakim, "Spitzer's Plan on Licenses." After the national restrictionist firestorm erupted, Governor Spitzer conceded that he did not have the requisite support for the proposal, and withdrew it. Chan, "Spitzer."

8. Coleman et al., *College Board*, 9.

9. Coleman, Palmer, and Richards, *College Board*, 32–33. Although this is not the setting for a book review, I found this document to be too wordy throughout and not always convincing. Section 4B.1 on "International Students," for example, lumps in nonimmigrants (such as students on F-1 visas) with permanent resident students, not generally thought of or treated as "international" or "foreign" (32).

10. There is a growing critical literature about the racial and ethnic dimensions of higher education in the states, at an individual state and institutional level. See, for instance, Kujovich, "Equal Opportunity in Higher Education," 29; Delgado, "Why Universities Are Morally Obligated," 1165; Donato, *Other Struggle for Equal Schools*; Delgado and Stefancic, "Home-Grown Racism," 703; Delgado and Stefancic, "California's Racial History and Constitutional Rationales," 1521; Blanton, "From Intellectual Deficiency to Cultural Deficiency"; Shabazz, *Advancing Democracy*; Russell, "'Keep Negroes Out of Most Classes.'" On the issue of state initiatives and their affect upon equity issues, see Johnson, "Handicapped, Not 'Sleeping,' Giant," 1259.

11. Malcom, Chubin, and Jesse, *Standing Our Ground.*

12. I take notice of programs such as the Rice University Summer Institute of Statistics and Cal Tech's Minority Undergraduate Research Fellowship Program. There are others, nearly all of which have at their head a very dedicated and accomplished scholar or program director who has devoted his or her life to his endeavor. For examples of the many such initiatives, see Advancing Science Serving Society, www.aaas.org (accessed Nov. 27, 2011). See also Bennof, "Extent of Federal S&E Funding."

13. Parents Involved in Community Schools v. Seattle School District No. 1 (Parents Involved), 127 S.Ct. 2738 (2007).

14. "The second government interest we have recognized as compelling for purposes of strict scrutiny is the interest in diversity in higher education upheld in *Grutter.* The specific interest found compelling in *Grutter* was student body diversity "in the context of higher education." Ibid., 2738, 2753 (citations omitted).

15. Ibid., 2754.

16. "A number of lower federal courts have similarly recognized that educators' decisions with regard to the content of school-sponsored newspapers, dramatic productions, and other expressive activities are entitled to substantial deference. We need not now decide whether the same degree of deference is appropriate with respect to school-sponsored expressive activities at the college and university level." Hazelwood School District v. Kuhlmeier, 484 U.S. 260, 273 note 7 (1988).

17. Lansdale v. Tyler Junior College, 470 F.2d 659, 663 (5th Cir. 1972).

18. Ibid., 666 (Roney, Circuit Judge, dissenting).

19. Richards v. League of United Latin American Citizens, 868 S.W.2d 306, 315 (1993).

20. Renken v. Gregory, 541 F.3d 769 (7th Cir. 2008). The circuit opinion does not even hesitate to speculate upon whether or not *Garcetti* applies in the postsecondary context. It avoids the *Pickering-Connick* issues by determining that Professor Renkin was not engaging in citizen conduct, so it being a "matter of public concern" was not salient: "Because Renken's speech was made as an employee and not a citizen, we need not address whether his speech addressed a matter of public concern to determine whether it not protected by the First Amendment." Ibid., 775, note 3.

21. Isenalumhe v. McDuffie, 697 F.Supp.2d 367, 381 (2010). The exasperated trial judge accepted the *Garcetti* reasoning notwithstanding: "There may be circumstances in which such struggles implicate the First Amendment, as when it involves what may and may not be taught in a public university. Indeed, the Supreme Court has suggested that the *Garcetti* inquiry may not apply 'in the same manner to a case involving speech related to scholarship or teaching.' Here, however, the speech at issue involves a string of complaints by faculty members unhappy with the administration of their department. While the complaints may well be justified, the First Amendment does not transform a federal court into a battleground for their resolution" (citations omitted).

22. Gorum v. Sessoms, 561 F.3d 179 (3d Cir. 2009). The *Gorum* court spent a great deal of time indicating why *Garcetti* might or might not apply, and then determined it did apply: "But here we apply the official duty test because Gorum's actions so clearly were not 'speech related to scholarship or teaching,' and because we believe that such a determination here does not 'imperil First Amendment protection of academic freedom

in public colleges and universities.'" 561 F.3d 179, 186 (citing Souter dissent, citations omitted).

23. Olivas, "Lawmakers Gone Wild?" 99; Preston, "Lawyer Leads an Immigration Fight." Several of the issues already noted, such as the tuition issue and driver's license debacle as well as the failure to gain progress on comprehensive immigration reform all point to additional anger, scapegoating, and social cleavage in these domains. See, for example, Gordon, "Survey Finds Ethnic Divide"; Chavez, *Latino Threat*; Voss and Bloemraad, eds., *Rallying for Immigrant Rights*; Campbell, "Road to S.B. 1070," 1.

24. While this particular point is beyond the scope of this project, there are scholars who have noted the rise of intolerance among evangelical Christians and how this has coincided with the growth of southern white conservatives, inspired by the late Rev. Jerry Falwell. While the rise of litigation about religious freedom is due to many complex factors, surely one is the rise of conservative Christian politics, increasing national attention to religious issues, and developing deliberate strategies to increase the number of lawyers who labor for the evangelical cause in courts, legislatures, and school boards. One historian of religion addressed this phenomenon: "Religious Right activists such as [Rev. Jerry] Falwell may have once been the small-town, undereducated, southern pastors that some pundits imagined them to be, but by the 1980s their devotion to the politics of corporate interests equaled that of any conservative Republican. The alliance between Christian conservatives and the GOP that Falwell helped to create was thus not merely an exercise in political opportunism, but was instead the result of a shared political ideology that reflected the experiences of a particular region. Falwell's politics, like [President Ronald] Reagan's, were a product of the postwar Sunbelt." Williams, "Jerry Falwell's Sunbelt Politics," 125, 142. In addition, Rev. Falwell founded Liberty University, which has a law school that produces Christian lawyers. Its mission statement notes: "In 1971, Jerry Falwell, Sr. followed the vision God gave to him to build a world-class university founded on academic excellence, athletic achievement and biblical truth—and now that vision is quickly becoming a reality!" and "Founded upon the premise that there is an integral relationship between faith and reason, the objective is to build a law school committed to academic and professional excellence in the context of the Christian intellectual tradition." www.liberty.edu/academics/law/index.cfm?PID=3818 (accessed Jan. 23, 2012). See Williams, *God's Own Party*.

25. www.alliancedefensefund.org/ReligiousFreedom, emphasis in original (accessed Nov. 25, 2011).

26. Bailey, "Education and the State," 5–6.

27. Smolla, *Constitution Goes to College*, 53. As I write this on the Friday morning after Thanksgiving ("Black Friday" to retailers), 2011, Van Morrison is belting out "Did Ye Get Healed?" on my iPod.

28. Ibid., 54.

29. Ibid., 54–55.

30. Christian Legal Society, 130 S.Ct. at 2993–2994. A college's policy such as this would be "justified without reference to the content [or viewpoint] of the regulated speech." Ibid., 2994 (brackets in original). And in Arizona, the state legislature has passed a statute to nullify *CLS v. Martinez*. It is simply not good practice to determine

fundamental institutional policy by the state ballot measure and such ragged attempts to do so undermine the autonomy of colleges and faculty governance. Jaschik, "Getting Around the Courts."

31. Every Nation Campus Ministries at San Diego State Univ. v. Achtenberg, 597 F. Supp.2d 1075 (S. D. Cal., 2009), Alpha Delta Chi-Delta Ch. v. Reed, 648 F.3d 790 (9th Cir. 2011), *application granted to extend time to file for cert.,* www.supremecourt.gov/Search .aspx?FileName=/docketfiles/11a349.htm (accessed Oct. 26, 2011).

32. Hack v. President and Fellows of Yale College, 16 F.Supp.2d 183 (D. Conn. 1998), *aff'd,* 237 F.3d 81 (2d Cir. 2000), *cert. denied,* 534 U.S. 888 (2001). See Glaberson, "Five Orthodox Jews Spur Moral Debate."

33. Bishop v. Aronov, 926 F.2d 1066, 1076–1077 (11th Cir. 1991).

34. There was evidence that Muslim scholars were finding it difficult to enter the United States, even with legitimate offers of faculty employment. See, for example, Schmidt, "2 Muslim Scholars Touch."

Abelson, Donald E. *Do Think Tanks Matter? Assessing the Impact of Public Policy Institutes.* Quebec: McGill-Queen's University Press, 2002.

Abourezk, Kevin. "Judge Tosses Suit on Tuition to Illegal Immigrants; Plaintiffs Likely to Refile Suit." *Lincoln Journal Star,* Dec. 18, 2010, A1.

Ackerman, Todd. "Baylor Med Repaying $260 Million of Debt on Shelved Hospital." *Houston Chronicle,* Aug. 10, 2010. Available at www.chron.com/default/article/Baylor -Med-repaying-260-million-of-debt-on-1698651.php (accessed Nov. 11, 2011).

———. "Baylor, Rice End Their Talks on Merger." *Houston Chronicle,* Jan. 13, 2010, A1.

———. "Rivals Reunite, Change of Heart; Renowned Surgeons Cooley and DeBakey Put Their Decades-Old Feud to Rest at Awards Event." *Houston Chronicle,* Nov. 7, 2007, A1.

Alliance Defense Fund. www.alliancedefensefund.org/ReligiousFreedom (accessed Nov. 25, 2011).

Alon, Sigal, and Marta Tienda. "Assessing the 'Mismatch' Hypothesis: Differences in College Graduation Rates by Institutional Selectivity." *Sociology of Education* 78 (2005): 294–315.

Amar, Akhil Reed. "Of Sovereignty and Federalism." *Yale Law Journal* 96 (1987).

Amar, Akhil Reed, and Neal Katyal. "Bakke's Fate." *UCLA Law Review* 43 (1996): 1745–1780.

American Association of University Professors. "AAUP Proposed Statement of Policy for Sexual Harassment." In *Policy Documents and Reports.* Washington, DC: AAUP, 1995.

Archibald, Robert B., and David H. Feldman. *Why Does College Cost So Much?* New York: Oxford University, 2010.

Areen, Judith C. "Government as Educator: A New Understanding of First Amendment Protection of Academic Freedom and Governance." *Georgetown Law Journal* 97 (2009): 945–1000.

Badillo, David. *MALDEF and the Evolution of Latino Civil Rights.* Research Report. Notre Dame, IN: Institute for Latino Studies/Border and Inter-American Affairs, University of Notre Dame, 2005.

Baez, Benjamin. *Affirmative Action, Hate Speech, and Tenure: Narratives about Race and Law in the Academy.* New York: RoutledgeFalmer, 2002.

Bailey, Stephen K. "Education and the State." *Educational Record* (Winter 1974): 5–12.

Baird, Vanessa A. *Answering the Call of the Court: How Justices and Litigants Set the Supreme Court Agenda.* Charlottesville: University of Virginia Press, 2007.

Baird, Vanessa A., and Tonja Jacobi. "How the Dissent Becomes the Majority: Using Federalism to Transform Coalitions in the U.S. Supreme Court." *Duke Law Journal* 59 (2009): 183–238.

Baldridge, Victor. *Power and Conflict in the University.* New York: John Wiley and Sons, 1971.

Barnes, Mario L., Erwin Chemerinsky, and Trina Jones. "A Post-Race Equal Protection?" *Georgetown Law Journal* 98 (2010): 967–1004.

Barrera, Lisa Lizette. "Minorities and the University of Texas School of Law (1950–1980)." *Texas Hispanic Journal of Law and Policy* 4 (1998): 99–109.

Bartholet, Elizabeth. "Application of Title VII to Jobs in High Places." *Harvard Law Review* 95 (1982): 945–1027.

Batalova, Jeanne, and Michael Fix. "New Estimates of Unauthorized Youth Eligible for Legal Status under the DREAM Act." Oct. 2006. www.migrationpolicy.org/pubs /Backgrounder1_Dream_Act.pdf (accessed Aug. 21, 2011).

Beh, Hazel G. "Downsizing Higher Education and Derailing Student Educational Objectives: When Should Student Claims for Program Closures Succeed?" *Georgia Law Review* 33 (1998): 155–210.

———. "Student Versus University: The University's Implied Obligation of Good Faith and Fair Dealing." *Maryland Law Review* 59 (2000): 183–224.

Behnken, Brian D. "Elusive Unity: African Americans, Mexican Americans, and Civil Rights in Houston." In *Seeking Inalienable Rights: Texans and Their Quests for Justice,* ed. Debra A. Reid, 123–145. College Station: Texas A&M University Press, 2009.

Benjamin-Alvarado, Jonathan, Louis DeSipio, and Christine Montoya-Kirk. "Latino Mobilization in New Immigrant Destinations: The Anti-H.R. 4437 Protest in Nebraska's Cities." *Urban Affairs Review* 44 (2009): 718–735.

Bennof, Richard J. *The Extent of Federal S&E Funding to Minority-Serving Institutions.* Washington, DC: National Science Foundation, 2004.

Berkman, Michael B., and Eric Plutzer. *Ten Thousand Democracies: Politics and Public Opinion in America's School Districts.* Washington, DC: Georgetown University Press, 2005.

Berman, Russell A. "The Real Language Crisis." *Academe,* September–October 2011. www.aaup.org/AAUP/pubsres/academe/2011/SO/Feat/berm.htm (accessed Nov. 11, 2011).

Bernstein, Nina. "Spitzer Grants Illegal Immigrants Easier Access to Driver's Licenses." *New York Times,* Sept. 22, 2007. http://query.nytimes.com/gst/fullpage.html?res=99 0DE4D7103AF931A1575AC0A9619C8B63&pagewanted=all&emc=eta1 (accessed Jan. 20, 2012).

Biskupic, Joan. "Rights Groups Pay to Settle Bias Case." *Washington Post,* Nov. 22, 1997, A1.

Blake, William D., and Hans J. Hacker. "'The Brooding Spirit of the Law': Supreme Court Justices Reading Dissents from the Bench." *Justice System Journal* 31 (2010): 1–25.

Blanton, Carlos K. "The Campus and the Capitol: John B. Connally and the Struggle over Higher Education Policy, 1950–1970." *Southwestern Historical Quarterly* 108 (2005): 469–497.

———. "From Intellectual Deficiency to Cultural Deficiency: Mexican Americans, Testing, and Public School Policy in the American Southwest, 1920–1940." *Pacific Historical Review* 72 (2003): 39–62.

———. "'They Cannot Master Abstractions, But They Can Often Be Made Efficient Workers': Race and Class in the Intelligence Testing of Mexican Americans and African Americans in Texas during the 1920s." *Social Science Quarterly* 81 (2000): 1014–1026.

Blum, Lawrence A. *"I'm Not a Racist, But . . .": The Moral Quandary of Race.* Ithaca, NY: Cornell University Press, 2002.

Bonner, Paul. "Alvin Chambliss, 'The Last Civil Rights Attorney'; Lawyer Associated with 29-year Ayers Suit." *Herald-Sun* (Durham, NC), Feb. 27, 2006, A1.

Boucher, Robert, and Jeffrey Segal. "Supreme Court Justices as Strategic Decision Makers: Offensive Grants and Defensive Denials." *Journal of Politics* 54 (1995): 824–837.

Bousquet, Marc, and Cary Nelson. *How the University Works: Higher Education and the Low-Wage Nation.* New York: New York University Press, 2008.

Braxton, John M., Alan Bayer, and Martin Finkelstein. "Teaching Performance Norms in Academia." *Research in Higher Education* 33 (October 1992): 533–570.

Brodkin, Karen. *How Jews Became White Folks and What That Says about Race in America.* New Brunswick, NJ: Rutgers University Press, 1998.

Brown-Nagin, Tomiko. "Elites, Social Movements, and the Law: The Case of Affirmative Action." *Columbia Law Review* 105 (2005): 1436–1528.

Browne, David. *Fire and Rain: The Beatles, Simon and Garfunkel, James Taylor, CSNY, and the Lost Story of 1970.* Cambridge, MA: Da Capo Press, 2011.

Brubacher, John S. *The Courts and Higher Education.* San Francisco: Jossey-Bass, 1971.

Bruhl, Aaron-Andrew P. "The Supreme Court's Controversial GVRs—and an Alternative." *Michigan Law Review* 107 (2009): 711–756.

———. "When Is Finality . . . Final? Rehearing and Resurrection in the Supreme Court." *Journal of Appellate Practice and Process* 12 (2011): 1–24.

Caldeira, Gregory A., and John R. Wright. "The Discuss List: Agenda Building in the Supreme Court." *Law and Society Review* 24 (1990): 807–836.

———. "Organized Interests and Agenda Setting in the U.S. Supreme Court." *American Political Science Review* 82 (1988): 1109–1127.

Caldeira, Gregory A., John R. Wright, and C. Zorn. "Sophisticated Voting and Gate-Keeping in the Supreme Court." *Journal of Law Economics, and Organization* 15 (1999): 549–572.

Campbell, Kristina M. "The Road to S.B. 1070: How Arizona Became Ground Zero for the Immigrants' Rights Movement and the Continuing Struggle for Latino Civil Rights in America." *Harvard Latino Law Review* 14 (2011): 1–21.

Casarez, Nicole B. "The Student Press, the Public Workplace, and Expanding Notions of Government Speech." *Journal of College and University Law* 35 (2008): 1–74.

Center for Individual Rights. "Greatest Courtroom Victories." www.cir-usa.org/great_cases.html (accessed Nov. 30, 2011).

Chamallas, Martha A. "Jean Jew's Case: Resisting Sexual Harassment in the Academy." *Yale Journal of Law and Feminism* 6 (1994): 71–90.

Chan, Sewell. "Spitzer: 'The Issue Does Not Disappear.'" *New York Times*, Nov. 14, 2007, http://cityroom.blogs.nytimes.com/2007/11/14/spitzer-the-issue-does-not-disappear/ (accessed Jan. 22, 2012).

Chavez, Leo R. *The Latino Threat: Constructing Immigrants, Citizens, and the Nation*. Stanford, CA: Stanford University Press, 2008.

Chemerinsky, Erwin. *The Conservative Assault on the Constitution*. New York: Simon and Schuster, 2010.

———. "The Impact of the Proposed California Civil Rights Initiative." *Hastings Constitutional Law Quarterly* 23 (1996): 999–1018.

Chen, Jim. "Embryonic Thoughts on Racial Identity as New Property." *University of Colorado Law Review* 68 (1997): 1123–1163.

Chew, Pat K., and Robert E. Kelley. "Myth of the Color-Blind Judge: An Empirical Analysis of Racial Harassment Cases." *Washington University Law Review* 86 (2009): 1117–1166.

———. "Unwrapping Racial Harassment Law." *Berkeley Journal of Employment and Labor Law* 27 (2006): 49–70.

Chin, Gabriel J., and Sara Lindenbaum. "Reaching Out to Do Justice: The Rise and Fall of the Special Docket of the U.S. Supreme Court." *Houston Law Review* 48 (2011): 197–264.

Christ, Carol T. "Affirmative Action and Freshman Admissions at Berkeley." Remarks at the Association for the Study of Higher Education Conference, Nov. 2, 1996, San Francisco, California.

Clark, Burton R. *The Higher Education System*. Berkeley: University of California Press, 1983.

Clark, Tom S., and Benjamin Lauderdale. "Locating Supreme Court Opinions in Doctrine Space." *American Journal of Political Science* 54 (2010): 871–890.

Clark, Tom S., and Aaron B. Strauss. "The Implications of High Court Docket Control for Resource Allocation and Legal Efficiency." *Journal of Theoretical Politics* 22 (2010): 247–268.

Cohen, Jodi S. "Minority Aid at SIU Faces Federal Suit: Whites and Males Seen as Excluded." *Chicago Tribune*, Nov. 13, 2005. http://articles.chicagotribune.com/2005-11-13/news/0511130380_1_fellowships-minority-students-graduate-students (accessed Jan. 22, 2012).

Coleman, Arthur L., Scott R. Palmer, and Femi S. Richards. *College Board: Federal Law and Recruitment, Outreach, and Retention: A Framework for Evaluating Diversity-Related Programs*. The College Board, 2005. www.collegeboard.com/prod_downloads/diversitycollaborative/05diversity-fedlaw-framework.pdf (accessed Jan. 23, 2012).

Coleman, Arthur L., Scott R. Palmer, Elizabeth Sanghavi, and Steven Y. Winnick. *College Board: From Federal Law to State Voter Initiatives: Preserving Higher Education's Authority to Achieve the Educational, Economic, Civic, and Security Benefits Associated with a Diverse Student Body.* The College Board, Mar. 2007. www.collegeboard.com/prod_downloads/diversitycollaborative/preserving-higher-education-authority.pdf (accessed Jan. 23, 2012).

Colker, Ruth. "Whores, Fags, Dumb-Ass Women, Surly Blacks, and Competent Heterosexual White Men: The Sexual and Racial Morality Underlying Anti-Discrimination Doctrine." *Yale Journal of Law and Feminism* 7 (1995): 195–227.

Collins, Randall. *The Credential Society.* New York: Academic Press, 1979.

Confessore, Nicholas, and Danny Hakim. "Spitzer's Plan on Licenses for Immigrants Finds Support." *New York Times,* Oct. 9, 2007, B1.

Connell, Mary Ann, Kerry Brian Melear, and Frederick G. Savage. "Collegiality in Higher Education Employment Decisions: The Evolving Law." *Journal of College and University Law* 37 (2011).

Connell, Mary Ann, and Frederick G. Savage. "The Role of Collegiality in Higher Education Tenure, Promotion, and Termination Decisions." *Journal of College and University Law* 27 (2001): 833–858.

Cordray, Margaret Meriwether, and Richard Cordray. "The Philosophy of Certiorari: Jurisprudential Considerations in Supreme Court Case Selection." *Washington University Law Quarterly* 82 (2004): 389–452.

Cornyn, John. "Texas Attorney General's Opinion, JC-0107, re: Texas Attorney General LO-97-001." www.oag.state.tx.us/opinions/opinions/49cornyn/op/1999/htm/jc0107.htm (acccessed Jan. 22, 2012).

Corson, Christopher T. "Reform of Domicile Law for Application to Transients, Temporary Residents and Multi-Based Persons." *Columbia Journal of Law and Social Problems* 16 (1981): 327–364.

Cottrol, Robert J., Raymond T. Diamond, and Leland B. Ware. *Brown v. Board of Education: Caste, Culture, and the Constitution.* Lawrence: University Press of Kansas, 2003.

Covington, Artelia C. "Troubles Deepen for Education Crusader Alvin Chambliss." *New York Beacon,* Oct. 9, 2002, 4.

Coyle, Marcia. "Indians Try to Keep Cases Away from High Court." *National Law Journal,* Mar. 29, 2010. LexisNexis, Doc. ID 1202447045837 (accessed Nov. 13, 201).

Crocker, Phyllis L. "Not to Decide Is to Decide: The U.S. Supreme Court's Thirty-Year Struggle with One Case about Competency to Waive Death Penalty Appeals." *Wayne Law Review* 49 (2004): 885–938.

Crump, David. "The Narrow Tailoring Issue in the Affirmative Action Cases: Reconsidering the Supreme Court's Approval in *Gratz* and *Grutter* of Race-Based Decision-Making by Individualized Discretion." *Florida Law Review* 56 (2004): 483–540.

Davidson, Nestor M. "Cooperative Localism: Federal-Local Collaboration in an Era of State Sovereignty." *Virginia Law Review* 93 (2007): 959–1034.

Davis, Aaron C. "Md. Tuition Law May Be Halted." *Washington Post,* June 29, 2011, B1.

———. "Md. Voters to Decide Immigrant Tuition Law." *Washington Post,* July 8, 2011, A1.

Deckman, Melissa M. *School Board Battles: The Christian Right in Local Politics.* Washington, DC: Georgetown University Press, 2004.

Delgado, Richard. "Why Universities Are Morally Obligated to Strive for Diversity: Restoring the Remedial Rationale for Affirmative Action." *University of Colorado Law Review* 68 (1997): 1165–1172.

Delgado, Richard, and Jean Stefancic. "California's Racial History and Constitutional Rationales for Race-Conscious Decision Making in Higher Education." *UCLA Law Review* 47 (2000): 1521–1614.

———. "Home-Grown Racism: Colorado's Historic Embrace—and Denial—of Equal Opportunity in Higher Education." *University of Colorado Law Review* 70 (1999): 703–811.

Dickson, James G., Jr. "Vital Crucible of the Law: Politics and Procedures of the Advisory Opinion Function of the Texas Attorney General." *Houston Law Review* 9 (1972): 495–529.

Donato, Ruben. *The Other Struggle for Equal Schools: Mexican Americans during the Civil Rights Era.* Albany: State University of New York Press, 1997.

Douglas, Joel. "Professors on Strike: An Analysis of Two Decades of Faculty Work Stoppages, 1960–1985." *Labor Lawyer* 4 (1988): 87–101.

Downes, Lawrence. "Kobach and Romney." *New York Times,* Apr. 19, 2012. http://taking note.blogs.nytimes.com/2012/04/19/Kobach-and-Romney/ (accessed Apr. 22, 2012).

Doyle, William R., Jennifer A. Delaney, and Blake A. Naughton. "Public Institutional Aid and State Policy: Compensation or Compliance?" *Research in Higher Education* 50 (2009): 502–523.

Dupre, Anne Proffitt. *Speaking Up: The Unintended Costs of Free Speech in Public Schools.* Cambridge, MA: Harvard University Press, 2009.

Eaton, Collin. "Jury Verdict in Sex-Assault Case at Sewanee Is Warning to Private Colleges." *Chronicle of Higher Education,* Sept. 2, 2011, http://chronicle.com/article/Jury-Verdict-in-Sex-Assault/128884 (accessed Nov. 11, 2012).

Eckholm, Erik. "Evangelicals Step Up Efforts to Unite on an Alternative to Romney." *New York Times,* Jan. 7, 2012, A15.

Edwards, Harry T. *Higher Education and the Unholy Crusade against Governmental Regulation.* Cambridge, MA: Institute for Educational Management, 1980.

Ehrenberg, Ronald G. *Tuition Rising: Why College Costs So Much.* Cambridge, MA: Harvard University Press, 2000.

Eisgruber, Christopher L. "How the Maverick Became a Lion: Affirmative Action in the Jurisprudence of John Paul Stevens." *Georgetown Law Journal* 99 (2011): 1279–1288.

———. "A Tough Act to Follow," *Los Angeles Times,* Apr. 20, 2010, A11.

Ellis, Rodney, Michael A. Olivas, and John Brittain. "Now Aggies Need to Take the Next Step." *Houston Chronicle,* Jan. 11, 2004, 1C.

Epstein, Lee, Jeffrey A. Segal, and Jennifer Nicoll Victor. "Dynamic Agenda-Setting on the United States Supreme Court: An Empirical Assessment." *Harvard Journal on Legislation* 39 (2002): 395–433.

Evensen, Dorothy H., and Carla D. Pratt. *The End of the Pipeline: A Journey of Recognition for African Americans Entering the Legal Profession.* Durham, NC: Carolina Academic Press, 2012.

Facchini, Giovanni, and Max Friedrich Steinhardt. "What Drives U.S. Immigration Policy? Evidence from Congressional Roll Call Votes." *Journal of Public Economics* 95 (2011): 734–743.

Fain, Paul. "San Jose State University Gets More Selective, Reluctantly." InsideHigherEd .com. Posted Apr. 11, 2012, www.insidehighered.com/news/2012/04/11/san-jose-state -university-gets-more-selective-reluctantly (accessed May 29, 2012).

Fallon, Richard, Jr. "Affirmative Action Based on Economic Disadvantage." *UCLA Law Review* 43 (1996): 1913–1951.

Farber, Daniel A. "Statutory Interpretation, Legislative Inaction, and Civil Rights." *Michigan Law Review* 87 (1988): 2–19.

Fausset, Richard. "Immigration Offers an Opening for Romney." *Los Angeles Times*, Jan. 19, 2012, A13.

Finkin, Matthew W. "'A Higher Order of Liberty in the Workplace': Academic Freedom and Tenure in the Vortex of Employment Practices and Law." *Law and Contemporary Problems* 53 (1990): 357–379.

Finkin, Matthew W., and Robert C. Post. *For the Common Good: Principles of American Academic Freedom.* New Haven, CT: Yale University Press, 2009.

Fletcher, Matthew L. M. "Factbound and Splitless: The Certiorari Process as Barrier to Justice for Indian Tribes." *Arizona Law Review* 51 (2009): 933–981.

———. "Rebooting Indian Law in the Supreme Court." *South Dakota Law Review* 55 (2010): 510–527.

Flores, Matt. "College Economics Test." *San Antonio Express-News*, Feb. 23, 2003, 1A.

———. "Texas Educators Are on Edge at the Top: Most Feel State Budget Cuts Will Target Higher Education Significantly." *San Antonio Express-News*, Feb. 25, 2003, 1A.

———. "UTSA's Climb to Top-Tier Status Is Getting Tougher: State's Shaky Financial Picture Could Frustrate Local University's Ambitions." *San Antonio Express-News*, Feb. 24, 2003, 1A.

Flores-Yeffal, Nadia Yamel, Guadalupe Vidales, and April Plemons. "The Latino Cyber Moral Panic Process in the United States." *Information, Communication, and Society* 14 (2011): 568–589.

Foley, Neil. *Quest for Equality: The Failed Promise of Black-Brown Solidarity.* Cambridge, MA: Harvard University Press, 2010.

———. *The White Scourge: Mexicans, Blacks, and Poor Whites in Texas Cotton Culture.* Berkeley: University of California Press, 1997.

Footlick, Jerrold K. *Truth and Consequences: How Colleges and Universities Meet Public Crises.* Phoenix, AZ: American Council on Education/Oryx Press, 1997, 52–72.

Foundation for Individual Rights in Education (FIRE). "FIRE's Lawsuit to Proceed." Sept. 5, 2003. http://thefire.org/article/27.html (accessed Sept. 23, 2012).

———. "FIRE's Legal Network." http://thefire.org/takeaction/lawyers (accessed Nov. 1, 2011).

Freire, Paolo. *Education for Critical Consciousness.* New York: Seabury Press, 1973.

Gajda, Amy. *The Trials of Academe: The New Era of Campus Litigation.* Cambridge, MA: Harvard University Press, 2009.

Garcia, Ignacio M. *White but Not Equal: Mexican Americans, Jury Discrimination, and the Supreme Court.* Tucson: University of Arizona Press, 2008.

"General Report of the Committee on Academic Freedom and Academic Tenure." *AAUP Bulletin* 17 (1915): 1. Rpt. *Law and Contemporary Problems* 53 (1990): 393–406 and appendix A.

George, Robert P. "*Gratz* and *Grutter*: Some Hard Questions." *Columbia Law Review* 103 (2003): 1634–1639.

"Georgia Colleges Ordered to Drop Racial Preferences." *Washington Post*, Apr. 10, 1996, A20.

Gibson, William E. "Hard-Liner Stirs Debate for Romney." *Sun-Sentinel* (South Florida), Jan. 17, 2012, 1A.

———. "Romney Stirs Immigration Debate as He's Endorsed by Hard-liner Kobach." *Sun-Sentinel* (South Florida), Jan. 16, 2012. http://articles.sun-sentinel.com/2012-01 -16/news/fl-immigration-romney-kobach-20120116_1_illegal-immigrants-mitt-romney -immigration-debate (accessed Feb. 16, 2012).

Glaberson, William. "Five Orthodox Jews Spur Moral Debate over Housing Rules at Yale." *New York Times*, Sept. 7, 1997, A45.

Glazer, Nathan. "Levin, Jeffries, and the Fate of Academic Autonomy." *William and Mary Law Review* 36 (1995): 703–732.

Gold, Russell. "College Initiative's Future Will Find Funding Tougher?" *San Antonio Express-News*, Nov. 25, 1997, 1A.

———. "Pork Fattens Border Initiative." *San Antonio Express-News*, Nov. 24, 1997, 1A.

———. "South Texas Universities Make Strides, Still Lag." *San Antonio Express-News*, Nov. 23, 1997, 1A.

Goodman, Paul. *The Community of Scholars*. New York: Free Press, 1962.

Goodstein, Laurie. "Mormons' Ad Campaign May Play Out on the '12 Campaign Trail." *New York Times*, Nov. 18, 2011, A1.

———. "The Theological Differences behind Evangelical Unease with Romney." *New York Times*, Jan. 15, 2012, A17.

Gordon, Larry. "Offering Deals on Out-of-State Tuition; a Program Makes It Cheaper to Attend Public Colleges That Aren't Overcrowded." *Los Angeles Times*, Apr. 23, 2012, A1.

———. "Survey Finds Ethnic Divide among Voters on DREAM Act." *Los Angeles Times*, Nov. 19, 2011. www.latimes.com/news/local/la-me-poll-higher-ed-20111119,0,4108035 .story (accessed Jan. 23, 2012).

Gordon, Larry, and Carla Rivera. "Budget Ax Means More Tuition Hikes; Education Funding Cuts Could Prompt an Increase of at Least 10% at UC, Cal State." *Los Angeles Times*, June 30, 2011, AA1.

Gordon, Larry, and David Savage. "Supreme Court Order on California Immigrant Tuition Rates Could Affect Other States' Policies." *Los Angeles Times*, June 7, 2011, A1.

Graglia, Lino A. "Birthright Citizenship for Children of Illegal Aliens: An Irrational Public Policy." *Texas Review of Law and Politics* 14 (2009): 1–14.

Greenhouse, Linda. "Supreme Court Overview: In a Momentous Term, Justices Remake the Law, and the Court." *New York Times*, July 1, 2003, A1.

Guinier, Lani. "Admissions Rituals as Political Acts: Guardians at the Gates of Our Democratic Ideals." *Harvard Law Review* 117 (2003): 113–224.

Gutiérrez-Jones, Carl. *Rethinking the Borderlands: Between Chicano Culture and Legal Discourse.* Berkeley: University of California Press, 1995.

Harcleroad, Fred R., and Judith S. Eaton. "The Hidden Hand: External Constituencies and Their Impact." In *American Higher Education in the Twenty-First Century: Social, Political, and Economic Challenges,* ed. Philip G. Altbach, Patricia J. Gumport, and Robert O. Berdahl, 253–283. 2nd ed. Baltimore: Johns Hopkins University Press, 2005.

Harris, Angela P. "Theorizing Class, Gender, and the Law: Three Approaches." *Law and Contemporary Problems* 72 (2009): 37–56.

Hayden, Grant M. " 'The University Works Because We Do': Collective Bargaining Rights for Graduate Assistants." *Fordham Law Review* 69 (2001): 1233–1264.

Hebel, Sara. "Federal Court Upholds Plan to Settle Mississippi Desegregation Case." *Chronicle of Higher Education,* Feb. 6, 2004, A22.

Heinz, John P., Edward O. Laumann, Robert H. Salisbury, and Robert L. Nelson. "Inner Circles or Hollow Cores? Elite Networks in National Policy Systems." *Journal of Politics* 52 (1990): 356–390.

Heiser, Gregory M. " 'Because the Stakes Are So Small': Collegiality, Polemic, and Professionalism in Academic Employment Decisions." *Kansas Law Review* 52 (2004): 385–428.

Helms, Lelia. "Patterns of Litigation in Postsecondary Education: A Caselaw Study." *Journal of College and University Law* 14 (1987): 99–110.

Henig, Jeffrey R., Richard C. Hula, Marion Orr, and Desiree S. Pedescleaux. *The Color of School Reform: Race, Politics, and the Challenge of Urban Education.* Princeton, NJ: Princeton University Press, 1999.

Hernandez, Jose Angel. *Mexican American Colonization during the Nineteenth Century: A History of the U.S.-Mexico Borderlands.* New York: Cambridge University Press, 2012.

Holley-Walker, Danielle. "Searching for Equality: Equal Protection Clause Challenges to Bans on the Admission of Undocumented Immigrant Students to Public Universities." *Michigan State Law Review* (2011): 357–364.

Hoover, Eric, and Josh Keller. "More Students Migrate Away from Home, Public Universities Expand Recruitment Efforts in Quest for Out-of-State Money." *Chronicle of Higher Education,* Nov. 4, 2011, A1.

Horowitz, David. *Indoctrination U: The Left's War Against Academic Freedom.* New York: Encounter Books, 2007.

———. *Reforming Our Universities: The Campaign for an Academic Bill of Rights.* Washington, DC: Regnery Publishing, 2010.

Horowitz, David, and Jacob Laksin. *One-Party Classroom: How Radical Professors at America's Top Colleges Indoctrinate Students and Undermine Our Democracy.* New York: Crown Forum, 2009.

Huetteman, Emmarie. "Breyer and Scalia Testify at Senate Judiciary Hearing." *New York Times,* Oct. 6, 2011, A21.

Ishitani, Terry T. "The Determinants of Out-Migration among In-State College Students in the United States." *Research in Higher Education* 52 (2011): 107–122.

Jacobson, Arthur J. "Publishing Dissent." *Washington and Lee Law Review* 62 (2005): 1607–1636.

Jaschik, Scott. "Appeals Court Revives Suit on Dismissal of Anti-Gay Psychology Student." InsideHigherEd.com. Posted Jan. 30, 2012. www.insidehighered.com/news/2012/01/30/appeals-court-revives-suit-dismissal-anti-gay-psychology-student (accessed May 29, 2012).

———. "Getting Around the Courts." InsideHigherEd.com, May 4, 2011. www.insidehighered.com/news/2011/05/04/arizona_law_seeks_new_balance_on_anti_bias_rules_of_public_colleges_and_some_degree_programs (accessed Jan. 24, 2012).

———. "Michigan State Professor Attacked over Sexually Charged Photos." InsideHigherEd.com, Nov. 28, 2011. www.insidehighered.com/news/2011/11/28/michigan-state-professor-attacked-over-sexually-charged-photos (accessed June 5, 2012).

———. "The New Clash of Rights." InsideHigherEd.com, July 28, 2010. www.insidehighered.com/news/2010/07/28/counseling (accessed Nov. 11, 2011).

———. "Professor Told to Stop Requiring Students to Bring Snacks." InsideHigherEd.com, Nov. 28, 2011. www.insidehighered.com/news/2011/11/28/professor-told-stop-requiring-students-bring-snacks (accessed June 5, 2012).

———. "Teaching or Preaching?" InsideHigherEd.com, July 15, 2010. www.insidehighered.com/news/2010/07/15/illinois (accessed Oct. 15, 2011).

———. "Texas Limits '10%' Admissions." InsideHigherEd.com, June 1, 2009. www.insidehighered.com/news/2009/06/01/texas (accessed Jan. 22, 2012).

Jennings, Angel. "California Briefing. Beverly Hills: Schools Limit Non-Residents." *Los Angeles Times*, Apr. 26, 2012, AA3.

Johnson, Alex M., Jr. "Bid Whist, Tonk, and *United States v. Fordice*: Why Integrationism Fails African-Americans Again." *California Law Review* 81 (1993): 1401–1470.

Johnson, Kevin R. "A Handicapped, Not 'Sleeping,' Giant: The Devastating Impact of the Initiative Process on Latina/o and Immigrant Communities." *California Law Review* 96 (2008): 1259–1297.

Johnson, Timothy R., Ryan C. Black, and Eve M. Ringsmuth. "Hear Me Roar: What Provokes Supreme Court Justices to Dissent from the Bench?" *Minnesota Law Review* 93 (2009): 1560–1581.

Joy, Peter. "Government Interference with Law School Clinics and Access to Justice: When Is There a Legal Remedy?" *Case Western Reserve Law Review* 61 (2011): 1087–1107.

Kahlenberg, Richard D., ed. *Affirmative Action for the Rich: Legacy Preferences in College Admissions*. Washington, DC: Brookings Institution Press, 2010.

———. "The First Monday in October." *Chronicle of Higher Education*, Oct. 3, 2011. http://chronicle.com/blogs/innovations/the-first-monday-in-october/30483 (accessed Jan. 23, 2012).

———. *The Remedy: Class, Race, and Affirmative Action*. New York: Basic Books, 1997.

———. "Waiting on Fisher v. Texas." *Chronicle of Higher Education*, Feb. 10, 2012. http://chronicle.com/blogs/innovations/waiting-on-fisher-v-texas/31576 (accessed Nov. 11, 2011).

Kaplin, William A. *The Law of Higher Education: Legal Implications of Administrative Decision Making*. San Francisco: Jossey-Bass, 1983.

Kaplin, William A., and Barbara A. Lee, *The Law of Higher Education: Legal Implications of Administrative Decision Making*. 4th ed. 2 vols. San Francisco: Jossey-Bass/John Wiley and Sons, 2006.

Kasarda, Ralph W. "Affirmative Action Gone Haywire: Why State Laws Granting College Tuition Preferences to Illegal Aliens Are Preempted by Federal Law." *BYU Education and Law Journal* (2009): 197–244.

Kauffman, Albert H. "The Texas School Finance Litigation Saga: Great Progress, Then Near Death by a Thousand Cuts." *St. Mary's Law Journal* 40 (2008): 512–579.

Kellar, William Henry. *Make Haste Slowly: Moderates, Conservatives and School Desegregation in Houston*. College Station: Texas A&M University Press, 1999.

Kennedy, Randall L. "Doing What You Can with What You Have: The Greatness of Justice Marshall." *Georgetown Law Journal* 80 (1992): 2081–2091.

Kerr, Clark. *The Uses of the University*. 3d ed. Cambridge, MA: Harvard University Press, 1982.

King, Wayne. "Court Says Baylor Is Discriminatory." *New York Times*, Mar. 8, 1984. www.nytimes.com/1984/03/08/us/court-says-baylor-is-discriminatory.html (accessed Jan. 24, 2012).

Kinsley, Michael. "Christians Are Being Oppressed in the U.S.? Hardly." *Los Angeles Times*, Nov. 18, 2011. www.latimes.com/news/opinion/commentary/la-oe-kinsley-catholics-20111118,0,259917.column (accessed Jan. 22, 2012).

Kluger, Richard. *Simple Justice: The History of Brown v. Board of Education and Black America's Struggle for Equality*. New York: Alfred A. Knopf, 1975.

Kniffin, Kevin M. "Organizing to Organize: The Case of a Successful Long-Haul Campaign for Collective Bargaining Rights." *Labor Studies Journal* 36 (2011): 333–362.

Kobach, Kris W. "Immigration Nullification: In-State Tuition and Lawmakers Who Disregard the Law Immigration Reform: Balancing Enforcement and Integration." *New York University Journal of Legislation and Public Policy* 10 (2007): 473–523.

Konet, Dawn. *Migration Policy Institute, Unauthorized Youths, and Higher Education: The Ongoing Debate*. Migration Information Source, Sept. 2007. www.migrationinformation.org/Feature/display.cfm?id=642 (accessed Aug. 21, 2011).

Kuehn, Robert R., and Peter A. Joy. "'Kneecapping' Academic Freedom." *Academe* 96 (November–December 2010): 8–15.

Kujovich, Gil. "Equal Opportunity in Higher Education and the Black Public College: The Era of Separate But Equal." *Minnesota Law Review* 72 (1987): 29–172.

Lam, Margaret. *Patterns of Litigation at Institutions of Higher Education in Texas, 1878–1978*. Houston, TX: Institute for Higher Education Law and Governance, 1988.

LaNoue, George R., and Barbara A. Lee. *Academics in Court: The Consequences of Faculty Discrimination Litigation*. Ann Arbor: University of Michigan Press, 1987.

Larsen, Allison Orr. "Perpetual Dissents." *George Mason Law Review* 15 (2008): 447–478.

Law School Admissions Council. *LSAC Volume Summary*. Sept. 2011. www.lsac.org/LSACResources/Data/LSAC-volume-summary.asp (accessed Jan. 23, 2012).

Lawrence, Charles R., III. "The Id, the Ego, and Equal Protection: Reckoning with Unconscious Racism." *Stanford Law Review* 39 (1987): 317–388.

Lee, Barbara A. "Fifty Years of Higher Education Law: Turning the Kaleidoscope." *Journal of College and University Law* 36 (2010): 649–690.

Lederman, Douglas. "Texas Colleges May Consider Race in Admissions, Education Department Official Says." *Chronicle of Higher Education,* Mar. 28, 1997, A4.

Lewin, Tamar. "Michigan Rule on Admission to University Is Overturned." *New York Times,* July 2, 2011, A10.

Lindemann, Albert S. *Esau's Tears: Modern Anti-Semitism and the Rise of the Jews.* Cambridge, U.K.: Cambridge University Press, 1996.

Linskey, Annie. "In-State Tuition Opponents Have the Signatures for Referendum." *Baltimore Sun,* July 8, 2011, A1.

Linzer, Peter. "The Meaning of Certiorari Denials." *Columbia Law Review* 79 (1979): 1227–1305.

Long, Mark C., and Marta Tienda. "Winners and Losers: Changes in Texas University Admissions Post-Hopwood." *Educational Evaluation and Policy Analysis* 30 (2008): 255–280.

Lopez, Ian Haney, and Michael A. Olivas. "*Hernandez v. Texas*: Jim Crow, Mexican Americans, and the Anti-Subordination Constitution." In *Race and Law Stories,* ed. Rachel Moran and Devon Carbado, 269–306. New York: Foundation Press, 2008.

Lorde, Audre. "The Master's Tools Will Never Dismantle the Master's House," In *Sister Outsider, Essays and Speeches by Audre Lorde,* 110–113. Berkeley: Crossing Press, 1984.

Maddox, Matthew. "A Senseless Surprise: Top 20 Plan Will Not Solve Problem of Diversity." *Battalion* (Texas A&M), Jan. 16, 2002. www.thebatt.com/2.8482/a-senseless -surprise-1.1214122 (accessed Jan. 24, 2012).

Malamud, Deborah. "Class-Based Affirmative Action: Lessons and Caveats." *Texas Law Review* 74 (1996): 1847–1900.

Malcom, Shirley M., Daryl E. Chubin, and Jolene K. Jesse. *Standing Our Ground: A Guidebook for STEM Educators in the Post Michigan Era.* Washington, DC: American Association for the Advancement of Science, 2004.

Marcus, Laurence R. "The Adams Case: A Hollow Victory?" *Peabody Journal of Education* 51 (1981): 37–42.

Martinez, George A. "Legal Indeterminacy, Judicial Discretion, and Mexican-American Litigation Experience: 1930–80." *U.C. Davis Law Review* 27 (1994): 555–618.

"Maryland's 'Dream Act' Suspended amid Petition Drive for Referendum." FoxNews. com, July 1, 2011. www.foxnews.com/politics/2011/07/01/marylands-dream-act-suspen ded-amid-petition-drive-for-referendum (accessed Jan. 22, 2012).

Matasar, Richard A. "The Viability of the Law Degree: Cost, Value, and Intrinsic Worth." *Iowa Law Review* 96 (2011): 1579–1628.

Mauro, Tony. "Kagan Bows Out of 66 Cases in New Term: Recusals Stem from Tenure at SG." *National Law Journal,* Oct. 17, 2011, 19.

McGraw, Carol. "Jury Awards Black Professor $1 Million in Bias Suit against College; Courts: He Claimed Claremont Graduate School Denied Him Tenure Because of His Race; The Decision Will Be Appealed." *Los Angeles Times,* Mar. 29, 1990, B3.

McLendon, Michael K., James C. Hearn, and Christine G. Mokher. "Partisans, Professionals, and Power: The Role of Political Factors in State Higher Education Funding." *Journal of Higher Education* 80 (2009): 686–713.

McLendon, Michael K., Christine G. Mokher, and William R. Doyle. "'Privileging' Public Research Universities: An Empirical Analysis of the Distribution of State Appropriations across Research and Non-Research Universities." *Journal of Education Finance* 34 (2009): 372–401.

Medina, Jennifer. "2-Year College, Squeezed, Sets 2-Tier Tuition." *New York Times*, Mar. 30, 2012, A1.

———. "California Cuts Weigh Heavily on Its Colleges." *New York Times*, July 9, 2011, A12.

———. "Chancellor Asks California Community College to Hold Off on 2-Tier Tuition Plan." *New York Times*, Apr. 6, 2012, A1.

Melear, K. B. "From *In Loco Parentis* to Consumerism: A Legal Analysis of the Contractual Relationship between Institution and Student." *Journal of Student Affairs Research and Practice* 40 (2003): 656–680.

Menchaca, Martha. *Naturalizing Mexican Immigrants: A Texas History*. Austin: University of Texas Press, 2011.

Messer-Davidow, Ellen. "Manufacturing the Attack on Liberalized Higher Education." *Social Text* 36 (Autumn 1993): 40–80.

Metchick, Robert H., and Parbudyal Singh. "*Yeshiva* and Faculty Unionization in Higher Education." *Labor Studies Journal* 28 (2004): 45–65.

Miller, John J. *A Gift of Freedom: How the John M. Olin Foundation Changed America*. San Francisco: Encounter Books, 2006.

Millett, John. *The Academic Community: An Essay on Organization*. New York: McGraw Hill, 1962.

Mindiola, Tatcho, Jr. "Getting Tenure at the U." In *The Leaning Ivory Tower: Latino Professors in American Universities*, ed. Raymond V. Padilla and Rudolfo Chavez Chavez, 29–50. Albany: State University of New York Press, 1995.

"Mississippi Lawyer Ousted from Job after Winning Education Court Case." *Jet*, Jan. 15, 1996, 18.

Morales, Dan. "Letter: Opinion LO-97-001." Feb. 5, 1997. www.oag.state.tx.us/opinions /opinions/48morales/lo/1997/htm/lo1997001.htm (accessed Sept. 3, 1999).

Nagourney, Adam. "Californians Asked for $6.9 Billion in New Taxes." *New York Times*, Jan. 6, 2012, A14.

Nahmod, Sheldon. "Academic Freedom and the Post-*Garcetti* Blues." *First Amendment Law Review* 7 (2008): 54–74.

Nelson, Cary. *No University Is an Island: Saving Academic Freedom*. New York: New York University Press, 2010.

Nelson, Cary, and Stephen Watt. *Office Hours: Activism and Change in the Academy*. New York: Routledge, 2004.

Nienhusser, H. Kenny, and Kevin J. Dougherty. *Implementation of College In-State Tuition for Undocumented Immigrants in New York*. Albany: State University of New York Press, 2010.

Nissimov, Ron. "Unequal Access? Anti-Segregation Measures Restrict Some College Programs." *Houston Chronicle*, Feb. 19, 2001, A1.

Niu, Sunny X., Marta Tienda, and Kalena E. Cortes. "College Selectivity and the Texas Top 10% Law." *Economics of Education Review* 25 (2006): 259–272.

Olivas, Michael A. "Administering Intentions: Law, Theory, and Practice of Postsecondary Residency Requirements." *Journal of Higher Education* 59 (May-June, 1988): 263–290.

———. "Brown and the Desegregative Ideal: Higher Education, Location, and Racial College Identity." *Cornell Law Review* 90 (2005): 101–127.

———, ed. *"Colored Men" and "Hombres Aquí"*: Hernandez v. Texas *and the Emergence of Mexican-American Lawyering*. Houston: Arte Publico Press, 2006.

———. "Constitutional Criteria: The Social Science and Common Law of College Admissions in Higher Education." *Colorado Law Review* 68 (1997): 1065–1121.

———. "Don't Mess with College 'Top 10 Percent' Plan." *Houston Chronicle*, Apr. 29, 2007, E1.

———. "Federal Law and Scholarship Policy: An Essay on the Office for Civil Rights, Title VI, and Racial Restrictions." *Journal of College and University Law* 18 (1991): 21–28.

———. "Governing Badly: Theory and Practice of Bad Ideas in College Decision Making." *Indiana Law Journal* 87 (2012): 951–977.

———. *The Law and Higher Education: Cases and Materials on Colleges in Court*, 3d ed. Durham, NC: Carolina Academic Press, 2006.

———. "Lawmakers Gone Wild? College Residency and the Response to Professor Kobach." *SMU Law Review* 61 (2008): 99–132.

———. "Legal Norms in Law School Admissions: An Essay on Parallel Universes." *Journal of Legal Education* 42 (1992): 103–117.

———. *No Undocumented Child Left Behind: Plyler v. Doe and the Education of Undocumented Children*. New York: New York University Press, 2012.

———. *"Plyler v. Doe, Toll v. Moreno*, and Postsecondary Education: Undocumented Adults and 'Enduring Disability.'" *Journal of Law and Education* 15 (1986): 19–55.

———. "The Political Economy of the DREAM Act and the Legislative Process." *Wayne Law Review* 55 (2009): 1757–1810.

———. "Reflections on Professorial Academic Freedom: Second Thoughts on the Third 'Essential Freedom.'" *Stanford Law Review* 45 (1993): 1835–1858.

———. "The Rise of Nonlegal Legal Influences." In *Governing Academia*, ed. Ronald G. Ehrenberg, 258–275. Ithaca, NY: Cornell University Press, 2004.

———. "Who Gets to Guard the Gates of Eden?" InsideHigherEd.com, June 29, 2010. www.insidehighered.com/views/2010/06/29/olivas (accessed Nov. 11, 2011).

Olivas, Michael A., and Ronna Greff Schneider, eds. *Education Law Stories*. New York: Foundation Press, 2009.

Oppel, Richard A., Jr., and Erik Eckholm. "Prominent Pastor Calls Romney's Church a Cult." *New York Times*, Oct. 8, 2011, A10.

Oppenheimer, Mark. "A Counselor's Convictions Put Her Profession on Trial." *New York Times*, Feb. 4, 2012, A18.

Orozco, Cynthia. *No Mexicans, Women, or Dogs Allowed: The Rise of the Mexican American Civil Rights Movement.* Austin: University of Texas Press, 2009.

Paik, Anthony, John P. Heinz, and Ann Southworth. "Political Lawyers: The Structure of a National Network." *Law and Social Inquiry* 36 (2011): 892–918.

Passel, Jeffrey S., and D'Vera Cohn. *Pew Hispanic Center: A Portrait of Unauthorized Immigrants in the United States.* Pew Hispanic Center, Apr. 14, 2009. http://pewhispanic .org/files/reports/107.pdf (accessed Aug. 21, 2011).

Pear, Robert. "A Tax Bracket Divided over a Plan to Pay More." *New York Times,* Oct. 31, 2011, A15.

Perry, Barbara, and Randy Blazak. "Places for Races: The White Supremacist Movement Imagines U.S. Geography." *Journal of Hate Studies* 8 (2009): 29–51.

Perry, H. W., Jr. *Deciding to Decide: Agenda Setting in the United States Supreme Court.* Cambridge, MA: Harvard University Press, 1991.

Peters, Jeremy W. "Mormon-Owned Paper Stands with Immigrants." *New York Times,* Sept. 20, 2010, A1.

———. "TV Attack Ads Aim at Obama Early and Often." *New York Times,* Nov. 27, 2011, A1.

Petry, Greta. "Top Ten Workplace Issues for Faculty Members and Higher Education Professionals." *Academe* 98 (July–August 2011): 39–41.

Poskanazer, Steven G. *Higher Education Law: The Faculty.* Baltimore: Johns Hopkins University Press, 2002.

Post, Deborah W. "Power and the Morality of Grading: A Case Study and a Few Critical Thoughts on Grade Normalization." *University of Missouri–Kansas City Law Review* 65 (1997), 777–817.

Post, Robert. "Debating Disciplinarity." *Critical Inquiry* 35 (2009): 749–770.

Preston, Julia. "Lawyer Leads an Immigration Fight." *New York Times,* July 21, 2009, A10.

Probst, Christopher J. *Demonizing the Jews: Luther and the Protestant Church in Nazi Germany.* Bloomington: Indiana University Press, 2012.

Redden, Elizabeth. "Data on the Undocumented." InsideHigherEd.com, Mar. 17, 2009. www.insidehighered.com/news/2009/03/17/undocumented (accessed Jan. 22, 2012).

Reich, Gary, and Alvar Ayala Mendoza. "'Educating Kids' Versus 'Coddling Criminals': Framing the Debate over In-State Tuition for Undocumented Students in Kansas." *State Politics and Policy Quarterly* 8, no. 2 (2008): 177–197.

Rhor, Monica. "Former TSU Law Students Take Grade Dispute to Court." *Houston Chronicle,* Feb. 8, 2012, B1.

Riccardi, Nicholas. "Dream Act Opponents' Petition Drive Fails." *Los Angeles Times,* Jan. 7, 2012, AA5.

Rich, Andrew. *Think Tanks, Public Policy, and the Politics of Expertise.* Cambridge, U.K.: Cambridge University Press, 2004.

Riva, Sarah. "The Coldest Case of All? Lloyd Gaines and the African American Struggle for Higher Education in Missouri." *Western Legal History* 23 (2010): 21–45.

Rivenburg, Roy. "Baylor University's Decision to End Its Ban on Dancing Has the Faithful Wondering Whether They Can Prevent Church-Affiliated Schools from . . . : Losing Their Religion." *Los Angeles Times,* Mar. 13, 1996, E1.

Robertson, Campbell. "Critics See 'Chilling Effect' in Alabama Immigration Law." *New York Times*, Oct. 28, 2011, A1.

———. "Part of Alabama Immigrant Law Blocked." *New York Times,* Oct. 15, 2011, A13.

Romo, Ricardo. "Southern California and the Origins of Latino Civil-Rights Activism." *Western Legal History* 3 (1990): 379–406.

Rosenthal, Lawrence. "The Emerging First Amendment Law of Managerial Prerogative." *Fordham Law Review* 77 (2008): 33–113.

Rudolph, Frederick. *The American College and University: A History.* New York: Vintage, 1962.

Russell, Thomas. " 'Keep Negroes Out of Most Classes Where There Are a Large Number of Girls': The Unseen Power of the Ku Klux Klan and Standardized Testing at the University of Texas, 1899–1999." University Denver Legal Studies Research Paper No. 10–14, Mar. 22, 2010. http://ssrn.com/abstract=1583606 (accessed Mar. 23, 2012).

Salazar, Martin. "Insurer Accuses CSF of Fraud." *Albuquerque Journal,* Feb. 15, 2009, 1.

Salokar, Rebecca Mae. "The Solicitor General: The Politics of Law." In *Inside the Supreme Court: The Institution and Its Procedures,* ed. Susan Low Bloch et al., 835–861. 2d ed. St. Paul, MN: West, 2008.

San Miguel, Guadalupe, Jr. *Brown, Not White: School Integration and the Chicano Movement in Houston.* College Station: Texas A&M University Press, 2001.

———. *"Let All of Them Take Heed": Mexican Americans and the Campaign for Educational Equality in Texas, 1910–1981.* Austin: University of Texas Press, 1987.

Sanchez-Urribarri, Raul, Susanne Schorpp, Kirk A. Randazzo, and Donald R. Songer. "Explaining Changes to Rights Litigation: Testing a Multivariate Model in a Comparative Framework." *Journal of Politics* 73 (2010): 391–405.

Sander, Richard H. "Class in American Legal Education." *Denver University Law Review* 88 (2011): 631–682.

Schmidt, Peter. "2 Muslim Scholars Touch U.S. Ground after Long Ban, and Touch Off Debate." *Chronicle of Higher Education,* Apr. 23, 2010, A10–A11.

———. "Christian Legal Society and Montana Law School Settle Dispute." *Chronicle of Higher Education,* Aug. 11, 2011. http://chronicle.com/blogs/ticker/christian-legal-society-and-montana-law-school-settle-dispute/35285 (accessed Oct. 11, 2011).

———. "Faculty Unions in Ohio and Wis. Hunker Down." *Chronicle of Higher Education,* Oct. 14, 2011, A1.

———. "Part-Time Faculty Are Catching Up to Full-Timers in Union Representation." *Chronicle of Higher Education,* Nov. 18, 2011. http://chronicle.com/article/Part-Time-Faculty-Are-Catching/129819/ (accessed Jan. 21, 2012).

———. "Unions Confront the Fault Lines between Adjuncts and Full-Timers; Some Look Beyond the Big Unions for Real Improvement in Working Conditions." *Chronicle of Higher Education,* Nov. 21, 2011. http://chronicle.com/article/Unions-Confront-Fault-Lines/129836/ (accessed Jan. 21, 2012).

Schneyer, Ted. "Nostalgia in the Fifth Circuit: Holding the Line on Litigation Conflicts through Federal Common Law." *Review of Litigation* 16 (1997): 537–566.

Schrecker, Ellen. "The Roots of the Right-Wing Attack on Higher Education." *Thought and Action* (2010): 71–82.

Schuck, Peter H., and Daniel J. Givelbar. "*Tarasoff v. Regents of the University of California*: The Therapist's Dilemma." In *Torts Stories*, ed. Robert L. Rabin and Stephen D. Sugarman, 99–128. New York: Foundation Press, 2003.

Science Careers Minority Science Network. "Diversity Issues." http://sciencecareers. sciencemag.org/career_development/miscinet (accessed Nov. 27, 2011).

Sefsaf, Wendy. "Restrictionist Lawyer Reveals Long-Term Assault on Immigrant Children." immigrationimpact.com, Oct. 28, 2011. http://immigrationimpact.com/2011/10 /28/restrictionist-lawyer-reveals-long-term-assault-on-immigrant-children/ (accessed Jan. 22, 2012).

Seidman, Andrew. "Backers of Maryland DREAM Act Challenge Referendum Effort." *Los Angeles Times*, Aug. 3, 2011. latimes.com/news/politics/la-pn-maryland-dream -act-20110803,0,6211017.story (accessed Aug. 11, 2011).

Sena, John. "City Panel OKs CSF Bonds, Lease." *Santa Fe New Mexican*, July 21, 2009, 1.

Shabazz, Amilcar. *Advancing Democracy: African Americans and the Struggle for Access and Equity in Higher Education in Texas*. Chapel Hill: University of North Carolina Press, 2004.

Shahan, Amy. "Determining Whether Title VII Provides a Cause of Action for Same-Sex Sexual Harassment." *Baylor Law Review* 48 (1996): 507–527.

"The Short History of Race-Based Affirmative Action at Rice University." *Journal of Blacks in Higher Education* 13 (Autumn 1996): 36–38. Also available at www.jstor.org/stable /2963155.

Simmons, Omari Scott. "Picking Friends from the Crowd: Amicus Participation as Political Symbolism." *Connecticut Law Review* 42 (2009) 187–233.

Slack, Gordy. *The Battle over the Meaning of Everything: Evolution, Intelligent Design, and a School Board in Dover, PA*. San Francisco: Wiley, 2007.

Smith, James Allen. *The Idea Brokers: Think Tanks and the Rise of the New Policy Elite*. New York: Simon and Schuster, 1993.

Smith, Kevin H. "Certiorari and the Supreme Court Agenda: An Empirical Analysis." *Oklahoma Law Review* 54 (2001): 727–773.

Smolla, Rodney A. *The Constitution Goes to College: Five Constitutional Ideas That Have Shaped the American University*. New York: New York University Press, 2011.

Snow, Brian, and William E. Thro. "The Significance of Blackstone's Understanding of Sovereign Immunity for America's Public Institutions of Higher Education." *Journal of College and University Law* 28 (2002): 97–128.

Spacks, Patricia, ed. *Advocacy in the Classroom*. New York: St. Martin's, 1996.

[Spaeth, H. J.] "The Original U.S. Supreme Court Judicial Database: The Judicial Research Initiative." 2008. http://supremecourtdatabase.org/ (accessed Oct. 26, 2012).

Spann, Girardeau A. "Disparate Impact." *Georgetown Law Journal* 98 (2010): 1133–1163.

Stack, Kevin M. "The Practice of Dissent in the Supreme Court." *Yale Law Journal* 105 (1996): 2235–2259.

Starr, Kenneth W. "The Supreme Court and Its Shrinking Docket: The Ghost of William Howard Taft." *Minnesota Law Review* 90 (2006): 1363–1385.

Stefancic, Jean, and Richard Delgado. *No Mercy: How Conservative Think Tanks and Foundations Changed America's Social Agenda*. Philadelphia: Temple University Press, 1996.

Stevens-Arroyo, Anthony. "Are Catholics Christians?" *Washington Post,* Sept. 26, 2008. http://newsweek.washingtonpost.com/onfaith/catholicamerica/2008/09/are _catholics_christians.html (accessed Apr. 22, 2010).

Stolberg, Sheryl Gay. "For Romney, a Role of Faith and Authority." *New York Times,* Oct. 16, 2011, A1.

"Stop the Presses! Dance Fever to Hit Baylor April 18." Baylor University, Apr. 4, 1996. www.baylor.edu/pr/news.php?action=story&story=1052 (accessed Nov. 17, 2011).

Stras, David R. "The Supreme Court's Gatekeepers: The Role of Law Clerks in the Certiorari Process." *Texas Law Review* 85 (2007): 947–997.

Stroup, Herbert. *Bureaucracy in Higher Education.* New York: Free Press, 1966.

Surowiecki, James. "The Pipeline Problem." *New Yorker,* Feb. 16 and 23, 2004. www .newyorker.com/archive/2004/02/16/040216ta_talk_surowiecki (accessed Oct. 1, 2012).

Tang, Didi. "Colleges to Start Checking Legal Residency; New Law Requires the Verification to Keep Illegal Immigrants Out." *News-Leader* (Springfield, MO), Nov. 3, 2008, 1A.

Teles, Steven M. *The Rise of the Conservative Legal Movement: The Battle for Control of the Law.* Princeton, NJ: Princeton University Press, 2008.

Texas Higher Education Coordinating Board. "Criteria Identified to Promote Diversity in Texas Higher Education." October–December 1996, 1–3.

Thomas, Lewis. *The Youngest Science: Notes of a Medicine Watcher.* New York: Viking, 1983.

Thro, William E. "The Eleventh Amendment Revolution in the Lower Federal Courts." *Journal of College and University Law* 25 (1999): 501–526.

———. "The Significance of Blackstone's Understanding of Sovereign Immunity for America's Public Institutions of Higher Education." *Journal of College and University Law* 28 (2002): 97–128.

Torres, Gerald. "*Grutter v. Bollinger/Gratz v. Bollinger*: View from a Limestone Ledge." *Columbia Law Review* 103 (2003): 1596–1609.

Tushnet, Mark. "Thurgood Marshall and the Brethren." *Georgetown Law Journal* 80 (1992): 2109–2130.

U.S. Census Statistical Abstract. "U.S. Supreme Court—Cases Filed and Disposition: 1980 to 2010." Table 331. www.census.gov/compendia/statab/2012/tables/12s0331.pdf (accessed Oct. 13, 2011).

University of Texas at Austin. "Implementation and Results of the Texas Automatic Admissions Law (HB 588) at the University of Texas at Austin." Office of Admissions, University of Texas at Austin, Dec. 23, 2010. www.utexas.edu/student/admissions /research/HB588-Report13.pdf (accessed Mar. 3, 2012).

University of Utah. "Policy 6-100: Instruction and Evaluation." www.regulations.utah. edu/academics/6-100.html (accessed Nov. 25, 2011).

Valencia, Richard R. *Chicano Students and the Courts: The Mexican American Legal Struggle for Educational Equality.* New York: New York University Press, 2008, 251–267.

Vara, Vauhini. "California Sets New Course in Immigrant-Student Law." *Wall Street Journal,* Oct. 10, 2011, A4.

Vasquez, Michael R. "U.S.-Citizen Children of Immigrants Protest Higher Tuition Rates." *Miami Herald,* Oct. 24, 2011, B1.

Vogel, David. *Fluctuating Fortunes: The Political Power of Business in America.* New York: Basic Books, 1989.

Volokh, Eugene. "The California Civil Rights Initiative: An Interpretive Guide." *UCLA Law Review* 44 (1997): 1335–1404.

Voss, Kim, and Irene Bloemraad, eds. *Rallying for Immigrant Rights: The Fight for Inclusion in 21st Century America.* Berkeley: University of California Press, 2011.

Weber, Bruce. "Inside the Meritocracy Machine." *New York Times Magazine,* Apr. 28, 1996, 44.

Welling, Angie. "Thespian May Lose Union Ally in U. Suit." *Deseret News,* Mar. 3, 2002, B1.

———. "U. Theater Student's Lawyer Wants Trial in 2005." *Deseret News,* Apr. 23, 2004, B6.

Williams, Daniel K. *God's Own Party: The Making of the Christian Right.* New York: Oxford University Press, 2010.

———. "Jerry Falwell's Sunbelt Politics: The Regional Origins of the Moral Majority." *Journal of Policy History* 22 (2010): 125–147.

Williams, Norman R. "Taking Care of Ourselves: State Citizenship, the Market, and the State." *Ohio State Law Journal* 69 (2008): 469–524.

Wilson, James Q. *Political Organizations.* Rev. ed. Princeton, NJ: Princeton University Press, 1995.

Wilson, Robin. "Brandeis Prof in Trouble for Classroom Comments Gets Faculty Panel's Support." *Chronicle of Higher Education,* Nov. 30, 2007. http://chronicle.com/daily/2007/11/849n.htm (accessed Jan. 23, 2012).

Wilson, Steven H. "Brown over 'Other White': Mexican Americans' Legal Arguments and Litigation Strategy in School Desegregation Lawsuits." *Law and History Review* 21 (2003): 145–194.

———. "*Chicanismo* and the Flexible Fourteenth Amendment: 1960s Agitation and Litigation by Mexican American Youth in Texas." In *Seeking Inalienable Rights: Texans and Their Quests for Justice,* ed. Debra A. Reid, 147–168. College Station: Texas A&M University Press, 2009.

Wirenius, John F. "Actions as Words, Words as Actions: Sexual Harassment Law, the First Amendment and Verbal Acts." *Whittier Law Review* 28 (2007): 905–980.

Wuthnow, Robert. *The Struggle for America's Soul: Evangelicals, Liberals, and Secularism.* Grand Rapids, MI: William B. Eerdmans, 1989.

Ziff, Deborah. "UW Would Comply with Rule for Tuition." *Wisconsin State Journal,* June 11, 2011, A3.

———. "Very Few Illegal Immigrants Use UW Tuition Deal." *Wisconsin State Journal,* Oct. 24, 2009. http://host.madison.com/wsj/news/local/education/university/article_50619500-c117-11de-afe5-001cc4c002e0.html (accessed Jan. 22, 2012).